T0339784

25 Doctrines of Law

25 Doctrines of Law
You Should Know

Philip Chase Tobin

Algora Publishing
New York

ISBN-13: 978-0-87586-536-2 (trade paper)
ISBN-13: 978-0-87586-537-9 (hard cover)
ISBN-13: 978-0-87586-538-6 (ebook)

Library of Congress Cataloging-in-Publication Data —

Tobin, Philip Chase.
  25 doctrines of law you should know / Philip Chase Tobin.
     p. cm.
Includes index.
   ISBN 978-0-87586-536-2 (soft: alk. paper) — ISBN 978-0-87586-537-9 (hard: alk.
paper) — ISBN 978-0-87586-538-6 (ebook) 1. Jurisprudence—United States—Cases.
2. Law—United States—Cases. 3. Actions and defenses—United States 4. Law—
Philosophy. I. Title.

KF380.C48 2007
349.73—dc22
                         2006036900

Front Cover: Man Holding Scales And Book ©Corbis

Printed in the United States

To Phillip A. Schuman, J.D.

GLOSSARY

ACTIONABLE: [An issue that] provides a basis for legal action

AD HOC: Concerned with a particular end or purpose, e.g. an ad hoc investigating committee.

AFFIRMATIVE DEFENSE: An explanation to an allegation that, if supported by evidence and proven, disposes of the allegation.

APPELLANT: He who has lost a lower-court decision and is now appealing to a higher court.

APPELLEE: He who has won a lower-court decision and is now resisting appeal.

CHATTEL: An item of property apart from real estate.

COMPARATIVE NEGLIGENCE: The relative percentage of negligence between parties.

COURT OF COMPETENT JURISDICTION: A court recognized by law as having the right to decide a particular issue.

DECLARANT: A person who makes a formal declaration.

DELICT: An offence, criminal or tortious.

DE NOVO: Anew, afresh, a second time.

ENJOIN: To prohibit a party from performing an act.

ESTOPPELL: A principle that provides that a person is barred from denying or alleging a given fact or state facts that previous utterances, acts or allegations contradict.

EXCULPATORY: An act or fact that shows that a person is not guilty of wrongdoing.

EXECUTORY CONTRACT: A contract the terms of which have not been fully performed. An executory contract is a contract where some future act of performance is yet to be done, i.e., a contract the terms of agreement of which have not yet been fully performed. For Example, you agree to pay X so much for a cord of wood. X delivers the wood executing his part of the contract. The contract is executory until you pay X the agreed price whereupon the contract becomes executed.

EX PARTE: Performed in the interest of one party to the exclusion of the of the other.

IMPEACH: To debase a claim or standing.

INTER ALIA: Among other things.

INURE: To take effect or result.

JUDGMENT ON THE MERITS: A judgment rendered after investigation and argument determining which party is right.

JUSTICIABLE: Capable of being tried in a court of law.

MOVANT: He who initiates a motion before a court.

PAROL: Oral or verbal.

PER CURIAM: A unanimous decision by a court.

PLENARY: Full, entire, complete.

PRIMA FACIE: At first glance or sight. On the face of things.

PRIVIES: Those who are involved in an action or thing, or are interrelated to one another in an action.

PROBATIVE: That which affords proof or admissible evidence.

QUASI CONTRACTS: A quasi-contract imposes a duty, not as a result of any agreement, whether express or implied, but in spite of the absence of an agreement when one party receives unjust enrichment at the expense of another. In determining if the doctrine applies, a court focuses not on the intention of the parties, but rather on whether the defendant was unjustly enriched.

REPORTERS: Reporters are regional case-law recorders that record case-law decisions of state and federal courts. The Reporters are Atlantic, North Eastern, North Western, Pacific, South Eastern, South Western and Southern. A typical reporter citation would be 801 NW 2d. 444: volume 801 of the second North Western Reporter at page 444.

STRICT LIABILITY: Liability without fault.

SUB JUDICE: Before a judge or court.

SUMMARY JUDGMENT: A procedural device administered by a court dismissing an action or element thereof when there is no dispute of supportable fact.

UNCONSCIONABILITY: The basic test for unconscionability is whether, in the light of the general commercial background and the commercial needs of the particular trade or case, the clauses involved are so one-sided as to be unconscionable under the circumstances existing at the time of the making of a contract.

UNJUST ENRICHMENT: The general principle that one should not be permitted to enrich himself at the expense of another. The elements of unjust enrichment are benefits conferred on a defendant by a plaintiff, appreciation of such benefits by defendant, and acceptance and retention of such benefits under such circumstances that it would be inequitable for the defendant to retain the benefit without payment of value.

Table of Cases

TABLE OF CONTENTS

A Short Preface

I have often heard it said that we in the US are a litigious society. I have often heard it said that this is because we have more personal freedom than other societies. I believe both statements to be true. My purpose in bringing forth this book is to show the average person that he or she can be an informed citizen and, if not exhaustively informed, at least well enough informed to arrive at an intelligent decision about when to consult an attorney and what to believe when the attorney gives an assessment of a controversy.

Every year thousands of citizens are victimized by their ignorance of the law. They would not have been so afflicted had they known enough basic law to have consulted an attorney in good time. Had these individuals been lay-familiar with the doctrines of law contained in this book, they very well could have avoided their loss: countless thousands of individuals who should have consulted a lawyer and didn't because they lacked a fundamental understanding of the most rudimentary law as manifested by the contents of the doctrines contained herein.

To my knowledge, no work has ever been published that treats the doctrines of law as a subject area of law. In the short term, I believe this is a good read; in the long term, and upon reflection, the reader will have developed a sense for the legal arena.

There are over three hundred doctrines of law. Most are very narrow in their application. The Doctrine of Riparian Rights has to do with water rights; the Pullman-Abstention Doctrine has to do with avoiding the possibility of federal courts unnecessarily deciding Constitutional questions. The Lis-Pendens Doctrine binds a purchaser or encumbrancer of property to the results of any pending lawsuit which may effect title. By contrast the doctrines I have selected and discussed are, I feel, relevant to the average person in the broad sweep of his every day activity.

The case material is interesting stuff cut from the day-to-day tourney of legal Americana. The initial case presented under a given doctrine is abstracted from an actual case, followed by a derived rendition of a specific public-record case.

Any writing that attempts to treat the subject of doctrines of law must, in the very beginning, attempt to define the term it seeks to explain. In his address, "The Path of the Law," given at the dedication of the New Hall of the Boston University School of Law on January 8, 1897, the later-to-be Supreme Court Justice Oliver Wendell Holmes stated that "It is not the nature of the crime, but the dangerousness of the criminal that constitutes the only reasonable legal criterion to guide the inevitable social reaction against the criminal."

I suspect that if this was true to such a legal clairvoyant as Oliver Wendell Holmes in 1897, it was also true to those nameless great Anglo-Saxon legal minds that came before him, and it was in an effort to encapsulate and solemnize the social reaction against perceived criminal and civil miscreants that the doctrines of law came into being. Doctrines of law are, then, judge-made legal clichés that describe social reactions to legal conundrums that result from errant criminal and civil behavior.

Let us begin with *Res Ipsa Loquitur*!

Philip Chase Tobin
Ellsworth, Maine

CHAPTER 1. RES IPSA LOQUITUR

The fact of the Latin name for this doctrine of law (pronounced "race ipsah lo-quit-tur") bespeaks its ancient origin. *Res* is the feminine nominative singular of the Latin noun *Res, Rei*, meaning the thing or the matter. *Ipsa* is the feminine nominative singular of the Latin pronoun *ipsus, ipsa, ipsum*, meaning "itself," and *loquitur* is the third person singular active voice of the Latin deponent verb *loquor, loqui, locutus sum*, meaning "to speak." So, The Matter Speaks for Itself.

Under the doctrine of *res ipsa loquitur*, a matter is deemed to speak for itself when an injury to another happens such that the cause of that injury was exclusively under the control of the accused. Or, as Black's Law Dictionary puts it, "When the instrumentality causing an accident was in the defendant's exclusive control, the accident being one that does not usually happen in the absence of negligence."

In one case, a lady went into the hospital for an abdominal operation. After the operation, she was returned to her room to begin convalescence. Things did not go well, however, and she was in the hospital for a month before being moved to an outside care facility. Even then her progress was fitful until, finally, she was returned to the hospital for exploratory surgery. On reopening the wound, a 4"x 4" surgical sponge was discovered. Once the sponge was removed, she experienced a speedy recovery; the surgical mistake had nearly resulted in her death due to infection.

Once she was herself again, the lady brought a malpractice suit against the hospital and the doctor who had performed her operation, claiming gross negligence. Before going to trial the doctor's malpractice insurer settled for $250,000. Once the lady's case against the hospital was underway, the hospital filed for summary judgment on the basis that the lady could not place facts before the court supporting the elements of the claim she intended to prove. Summary judgment was granted as a matter of law. The case was dismissed. She appealed.

On appeal, the reviewing court ruled that under the doctrine of *res ipsa loquitur* the presence of the sponge in the surgical wound spoke for itself. Hospital employees are supposed to count their sponges. Had this team counted its sponges, the missing item would have been discovered and removed from the surgical cavity before the wound was closed, thus avoiding the life-threatening consequences that developed. The appeals court ruled that the lady was not required to prove which individual missed the sponge or to provide expert testimony to substantiate that the presence of the sponge was the responsible cause for the infection that developed.

The appeals court sent the case back to the trial court. A trial was held in which the lady prevailed and received a substantial damage award for negligence.

CHRISTINE BASSETT V. KMART CORPORATION
SUPREME COURT OF ALABAMA
769 SO. 2D 282; 2000
APRIL 21, 2000, RELEASED

LEGAL CONSIDERATIONS

Proof of Negligence / Res Ipsa Loquitur

The *res-ipsa-loquitur doctrine* allows an inference of negligence where there is no direct evidence of negligence. For the doctrine to apply, a plaintiff must show that: (1) the defendant had full management and control of the instrumentality which caused the injury; (2) the circumstances are such that according to common knowledge and the experience of mankind the accident could not have happened if those having control of the instrumentality had not been negligent; and (3) the plaintiff's injury resulted from the accident. However, if one can reasonably conclude that the accident could have happened without any negligence on the part of the defendant, then the *res ipsa loquitur* presumption does not apply.

Negligence / Res Ipsa Loquitur

Mechanical devices get out of working order and sometimes become dangerous and cause injury without negligence on the part of anyone.

Res Ipsa Loquitur

The doctrine of *res ipsa loquitur* can be applied if expert testimony is presented.

Judicial Notice

A court may take judicial notice of certain facts that are within the common knowledge. Whether a fact is a matter of common knowledge is an issue to be determined by the court.

Inferences & Presumptions

An inference cannot be derived from another inference. An inference must be based on a known or proven fact.

PRIOR HISTORY: Appeal from Montgomery Circuit Court
DISPOSITION: REVERSED AND REMANDED.
PROCEDURAL POSTURE: Defendant property owner appealed the judgment of the Montgomery Circuit Court (Alabama) entered in plaintiff's favor, awarding her damages for injuries she sustained in a fall on defendant's property.
OVERVIEW: Plaintiff sued defendant seeking damages for injuries she sustained when the automatic doors of defendant's store prematurely closed, causing her to fall and break her hip. The trial-court jury entered a verdict in plaintiff's favor. The Appeals Court reversed holding that the trial court erred in denying defendant's post-verdict motion for a judgment as a matter of law because plaintiff did not show that the defendant failed to use reasonable care in maintaining its automatic doors in a safe condition, or that the defendant's failure caused the doors to malfunction. The Court found that defendant's failure to contract for a preventative maintenance program and its policy to wait until a door needed repair or maintenance before calling for repairs was neither a breach of duty nor evidence of negligence. The Appeals Court maintained that the doctrine of res ipsa loquitur did not apply because it was not common knowledge that automatic doors could malfunction when a defendant was negligent in maintaining them.
OUTCOME: The Appeals Court reversed the judgment of the trial court because the plaintiff failed to show that defendant breached its duty to her by failing to contract for a preventative maintenance program for its automatic doors and by waiting until a door needed repairs before requesting maintenance.
OPINION: On Application for Rehearing, the trial-court opinion was withdrawn, and the following opinion was substituted.

Christine Bassett sued Kmart Corporation ("Kmart"), seeking damages for personal injuries she sustained when the automatic entry doors at a Kmart store prematurely closed on her, causing her to fall and break her hip. After the first trial of her claims ended in a mistrial, the jury in a second trial awarded her $ 289,000 in damages. Because it was held that the trial court erred in denying Kmart's post verdict motion for a judgment as a matter of law, the trial court's decision was reversed and remanded.

I

In January 1995, Christine Bassett, an 83-year-old woman who walked with the aid of a cane, went to a Kmart store in Montgomery, Alabama. Bassett stepped on a rubber mat outside the store to open the automatic doors. The doors swung open but closed prematurely, and one of the doors struck her left hip and caused her to fall. As a result, Bassett suffered a broken hip. After the accident, the store manager examined the doors. The doors worked properly and did not need to be repaired.

In January 1996, Bassett sued Kmart, claiming negligent or wanton maintenance or repair. The jury returned a verdict in favor of Kmart. On a technicality, however, the trial court granted Bassett a new trial. After the retrial, the court submitted to the jury only Bassett's claims alleging negligent maintenance or negligent repair, and the jury returned a verdict in favor of Bassett, awarding her $289,000 in damages. Kmart moved for a judgment as a matter of law or, alternatively, for a new trial or a remittitur (a reduction in damages). The motion was denied and Kmart appealed.

II

When reviewing a trial court's denial of a motion for a judgment as a matter of law ("JML"), the Court applies the same standard used by the trial court in granting or denying the motion. The denial of a defendant's motion for a JML is proper only when the plaintiff has presented substantial evidence to support each element of the plaintiff's claim. "Substantial evidence" is evidence of such weight and quality that fair-minded persons in the exercise of impartial judgment can reasonably infer the existence of the fact sought to be proved. In determining whether the nonmoving party presented substantial evidence, the Supreme Court, like the trial court, must view all evidence in the light most favorable to the nonmoving party.

In order to prove a claim of negligence, a plaintiff must establish that a defendant breached a duty owed by the defendant to the plaintiff and that the breach was the cause of injury or damage to the plaintiff. The owner of a business owes a duty to business invitees to use reasonable care and diligence to keep the premises in a safe condition, or, at the very least, to give sufficient warning if the premises are unsafe so that harm can be avoided. This duty does not, however, convert a premises owner into an insurer of its patrons' safety. That is to say that a premises owner is liable in negligence only if it fails to use reasonable care in maintaining its premises in a reasonably safe manner.

Thus, in order to defeat Kmart's motion for a judgment as a matter of law on her negligence claim, Bassett had to present substantial evidence indicating that Kmart had failed to use reasonable care to maintain its automatic doors in a reasonably safe condition, and that Kmart's failure to do so caused the doors to malfunction in such a way as to injure her. At trial, however, Bassett did not produce any evidence to indicate what caused the automatic doors to malfunction as she entered the store.

Kmart argued that Bassett was unable to prove a case of negligence because she could not produce convincing evidence that Kmart breached its duty of care.

Bassett argued that it was the policy of Kmart not to service its doors until they malfunctioned as evidenced by the fact that Kmart maintained no service contract on its doors with the company that installed the doors.

Bassett argued, then, that she produced evidence that, under the doctrine of res ipsa loquitur, permitted the jury to infer that Kmart had negligently maintained the automatic doors. Specifically, she argued that evidence that the automatic doors closed while she was still standing on the inside mat was sufficient to allow the jury to infer that Kmart was negligent. The trial court agreed with Bassett; it denied Kmart's motions for a judgment as a matter of law and instructed the jury on the doctrine of res ipsa loquitur, the matter speaks for itself. Kmart argued that the trial court erred in submitting Bassett's case to the jury under the res-ipsa-loquitur doctrine because Bassett did not satisfy the requirements for applying the doctrine. Specifically, Kmart argued that Bassett failed to satisfy the second requirement for applying that doctrine, i.e., that she did not eliminate the possibility that the company that installed the door was negligent, or another company that sometimes serviced the door was negligent, or that the safety mat itself was inherently defective, or that the alleged malfunction could have occurred even in the absence of any negligence.

The *res-ipsa-loquitur* doctrine allows an inference of negligence where there is no direct evidence of negligence. For the doctrine to apply, a plaintiff must show that: "(1) the defendant had full management and control of the instrumentality which caused the injury; (2) the circumstances are such that, according to common knowledge and the experience of mankind, the accident could not have happened if those having control of the instrumentality had not been negligent; and (3) the plaintiff's injury resulted from the accident. However, "if one can reasonably conclude that the accident could have happened without any negligence on the part of the defendant, then the res ipsa loquitur presumption does not apply."

Bassett argued that it was common knowledge and the experience of the community that the malfunctioning of an automatic door is "unusual." A New Jersey court has held that evidence indicating that an automatic door malfunctioned is sufficient to allow the trier of fact to infer, under the doctrine of res ipsa loquitur, that the premises owner was negligent. The New Jersey court reasoned that because what happened to the plaintiff was unusual, negligence was suggested.

In support of its conclusion that the doctrine of *res ipsa loquitur* applied, that court cited a similar New Jersey slip-and-fall case in which the doctrine of *res ipsa loquitur* had been held to apply. In contrast, the Alabama Appeals Court held that, under Alabama law, the doctrine of *res ipsa loquitur* is not applicable in slip-and-fall cases. See, e.g., Ex parte Mountain Top Indoor Flea Market, Inc., 699 So. 2d 158 (Ala. 1997).

The Alabama Appeals Court found the New Jersey court's reasoning unpersuasive. The New Jersey court inferred negligence on the part of the premises owner from the inference of the door's malfunction. Such reasoning violated Alabama's rule against deriving an inference from another inference. "An inference cannot be derived from another inference. An inference must be based on a known or proven fact." Even if the doors' malfunction were proved by direct evidence (and, thus, was not an inference), a mere malfunction would be insufficient to invoke the doctrine of *res ipsa loquitur* under Alabama law, because "one can reasonably conclude that such a one-time accident could have happened without any negligence on the part of the defendant."

For example, the malfunction could have occurred because the doors were defective or because the company that serviced the doors had been negligent. Also, mechanical devices, such as automatic doors, get out of working order and sometimes become dangerous and cause injury without negligence on the part of anyone. A Georgia court has held that the doctrine of *res ipsa loquitur* does not apply to allow, from the fact that automatic elevator doors closed on an invitee, the inference that the building owner was negligent. Therefore, the Appeals Court did not consider it to be common knowledge that automatic doors cannot malfunction unless the premises owner is negligent in maintaining the doors.

The doctrine of *res ipsa loquitur* can still be applied if expert testimony is presented. As has been stated in Prosser and Keeton in the Law of Torts, "Expert testimony may provide a sufficient foundation for inference of negligence even where the basis of common knowledge is lacking." Therefore, the court had to consider whether Bassett produced sufficient expert testimony that indicated Kmart's automatic doors could not have malfunctioned unless Kmart had failed to use reasonable care to keep its automatic doors in a safe condition.

Bassett engaged Jack Cherry as an expert witness, and Cherry testified that, "without preventive maintenance, eventually automatic doors are going to malfunction or stop working properly." That testimony in itself is insufficient to show that automatic doors cannot malfunction unless the premises owner fails to use reasonable care to keep them in a safe condition. Bassett did not satisfy, then, the second requirement for applying the doctrine of *res ipsa loquitur* because she did not show that, according to common knowledge and the experience of mankind (or according to expert testimony), the accident could not have happened absent Kmart's failure to use reasonable care in maintaining its premises in a reasonably safe manner.

It can also be said that the conclusion that the doctrine of *res ipsa loquitur* did not apply in this case is in accord with the holdings of the Supreme Court of New Mexico and the Court of Appeals of Georgia in similar automatic-door cases. See *Hisey v. Cashway Supermarkets, Inc.*, 426 P.2d 784 (N.M. 1967); and *Johnston v. Grand Union Co*, 375 S.E.2d 249 (Georgia 1988). In *Hisey*, the Supreme Court of New Mexico held that the doctrine of *res ipsa loquitur* did not apply to permit the trier of fact to infer negligence on the part of a supermarket operator from the fact that its automatic doors malfunctioned by suddenly closing and striking a store patron. The *Hisey* court reasoned that "the absence of any evidence that an accident is the kind which ordinarily does not occur in the absence of negligence defeats the application of the doctrine of *res ipsa loquitur*." Furthermore, the fact that the door had been operating properly before the accident and that it thereafter operated normally without any repairs being required clearly fails to sustain an inference that the isolated malfunction would not have occurred but for the defendant's negligence. The facts in Bassett are quite similar to those in *Hisey* and *Johnston*. In both of those cases, automatic doors malfunctioned by closing prematurely. In both of those cases, the doors worked properly after the isolated malfunction and did not need to be repaired. In neither case did the plaintiff produce evidence indicating that the defendant had breached its duty of care to the store patron, the invitee.

III

The Supreme Court concluded that the doctrine of *res ipsa loquitur* did not apply to the facts in Bassett. Because Bassett did not produce substantial evidence indicating that Kmart breached its duty of care to her, the trial court erred in denying Kmart's motion for a judgment as a matter of law.

The case was reversed and remanded.

Chapter 2. The Doctrine of Promissory Estoppel

The *Doctrine of Promissory Estoppel* comes down to us through the centuries and is intended to stop parties from breaking their promises to each other where those promises have not been memorialized in written contract. Situations do develop between individuals where a party requesting a contract of another party is sometimes seen to be lacking in trust. In such situations the doctrine of *promissory estoppel* can prevent the trusting party from suffering from the lack of a contract when that party can show that (1) there was a clear and definite promise made with (2) the expectation that the party to whom the promise was made would rely on that promise, and, as a result, (3) the party did reasonably rely on the promise and (4) suffered a meaningful loss as a consequence.

Because Ms. X found out that her boss, Mr. Y, was having an affair, or so her boss, a real estate developer, suspected, she was pushed out of the company so that Mr. Y could carry on his shenanigans without fear of his wife finding out what a womanizer he was. It seems that Ms. X and Mrs. Y were long-standing friends, and the boss apparently reasoned that it was just a matter of time before Ms. X spilled the beans, if she hadn't already. So he fired Ms. X and thought he was home free.

Well, not so fast, Mr. Bossman! Ms. X had gone to work for Mr. Y on the promise that if she worked dutifully and helped sell the thirty remaining condos in his completed development, she would have a part in selling another development he had that was nearing completion. The first twenty-five condos in the old development sold briskly and Ms. X profited handsomely the first couple of years. The last five condos sold slowly, however, with the result that Ms. X's income during the third year was much depressed; but she stayed on in the belief that once the new development opened, she would be back on top financially.

When the Bossman fired Ms. X she got a lawyer and brought a lawsuit for wrongful discharge, citing *promissory estoppel*. Well, don't you know, Mr. Y's law-yer motioned for summary judgment and the court denied the motion. The case went to trial and Ms. X received a hefty damage award. In reaching its verdict the jury found, based on the testimony, that (1) a clear and definite promise had been made; otherwise Ms. X would not have come to work for Mr. Y and stayed on despite the downturn; that (2) in making his promise, Mr. Y fully expected that Ms. X would come to work for him, which she did; and that (3) Ms. X did rely on Y's promise, to her (4) detriment, i.e., her loss of income in her third year of employment.

The following case expands on the doctrine of *promissory estoppel*.

POP'S CONES, INC., PLAINTIFF-APPELLANT,
v. RESORTS INTERNATIONAL HOTEL, INC., DEFENDANT-RESPONDENT.
SUPERIOR COURT OF NEW JERSEY, APPELLATE DIVISION
704 A.2D 1321(1998 N.J.)
JANUARY 23, 1998, DECIDED

LEGAL CONSIDERATIONS

Promissory Estoppel / Detrimental Reliance

A *promissory estoppel* claim will be justified if the plaintiff satisfies its burden of demonstrating the existence of, or for purposes of summary judgment, a dispute as to a material fact with regard to four separate elements which include: (1) a clear and definite promise by the promisor; (2) the promise must be made with the expectation that the promisee will rely thereon; (3) the promisee must in fact reasonably rely on the promise, and (4) detriment of a definite and substantial nature must be incurred in reliance on the promise. The essential justification for the *promissory-estoppel* doctrine is to avoid the substantial hardship or injustice which would result if such promises were not enforced.

Promissory Estoppel / Detrimental Reliance

The promisor is affected only by the reliance which he does or should foresee, and enforcement of the promise must be necessary to avoid injustice. Satisfaction of the latter requirement may depend on the reasonableness of the promisee's reliance, on (1) its definite and substantial character in relation to the remedy sought, on (2) the formality with which the promise was made, on (3) the ex-tent to which evidentiary, cautionary, deterrent and channeling functions of form were met by the commercial setting or otherwise, and on (4) the extent to which such other policies as the enforcement of bargains and the prevention of unjust enrichment were relevant.

PRIOR HISTORY: On appeal from the Superior Court of New Jersey, Law Division, Atlantic County.

DISPOSITION: Reversed and remanded for further appropriate proceedings.

PROCEDURAL POSTURE: Plaintiff shop appealed the order of the Superior Court of New Jersey, which granted defendant casino's motion for summary judgment and dismissed plaintiff's complaint that sought damages predicated on a theory of *promissory estoppel.*

OVERVIEW: The trial court granted defendant casino's motion for summary judgment in plaintiff's claim of *promissory estoppel.* Plaintiff appealed and the Superior Court reversed the grant of summary judgment because plaintiff relied to its detriment on the promises of defendant casino that plaintiff would be permitted to relocate its operation to defendant's location. The Court found that plaintiff was not claiming breach of contract, but that plaintiff sought damages that resulted from its reasonable reliance on defendant's promises. Plaintiff suffered the loss of its prior location and its ability to earn profits during a summer season, out-of-pocket expenses including attorney fees, and expenses in finding an alternate location. Affording plaintiff all favorable inferences, the Court found that the plaintiff's claim raised a jury question, and defendant's motion for summary judgment should not have been granted.

OUTCOME: The Supreme Court reversed the grant of defendant casino's motion for summary judgment because plaintiff shop raised genuine issues of material fact of its reasonable reliance on defendant's promises that plaintiff could relocate its shop to defendant's location. Plaintiff lost its prior location and ability to earn a profit during a summer season as well as out-of-pocket expenses in finding an alternate location.

OPINION: Plaintiff, Pop's Cones, Inc., t/a TCBY Yogurt, ("Pop's"), appealed from an order of the Law Division granting defendant, Resorts International, Inc. ("Resorts"), summary judgment and dismissing its complaint seeking damages predicated on the doctrine of promissory estoppel. Affording all favorable inferences to plaintiff's contentions, the Court concluded that Pop's presented a prima facie claim sufficient to withstand summary dismissal of its complaint. (A prima facie claim is a claim that in all appearances is adequate to support the action of the lawsuit.) In reversing summary judgment, the court relied on principles of promissory estoppel enunciated in Section 90 of the Restatement (Second) of Contracts, and recent cases which, in order to avoid injustice, seemingly relax the strict requirement of "a clear and definite promise" in making a prima facie case of promissory estoppel.

I

Pop's was an authorized franchisee of TCBY Systems, Inc. ("TCBY"), a national franchisor of frozen yogurt products. Resorts is a casino hotel in Atlantic City that leases retail space along "prime Boardwalk frontage." From June of 1991 to September 1994, Pop's operated a TCBY franchise in Margate, New Jersey. In May or June 1994, Brenda Taube ("Taube"), President of Pop's, had "a number of discussions" with Marlon Phoenix ("Phoenix") about the possible relocation of Pop's business to space owned by Resorts. Phoenix was the Executive Director of Business Development and Sales for Resorts.

According to Taube, she and Phoenix specifically discussed a boardwalk property occupied at that time by another business. The discussions included Taube's concerns with rental fees. Phoenix indicated that Resorts' management was "very anxious to have Pop's as a tenant" and that financial issues could easily be resolved on the bases of a percentage of gross revenue. In order to show the potential for profitably, Phoenix offered to permit Pop's to operate a vending cart free of charge within Resorts during the summer of 1994 so as to "test the traffic flow." This offer was considered and approved by Paul Ryan, Vice President for Hotel Operations at Resorts.

Based on Pop's marketing assessment of the Resorts' location, Taube drafted a written proposal dated August 18, 1994, addressing the leasing of Resorts' Players Club location and hand-delivered it to Phoenix. Taube's proposal offered Resorts "7% of net monthly sales (gross less sales tax) for the duration of the Player's Club lease asking in return a 6 year lease, and a renewable option for another 6 years.

In mid-September 1994, Taube spoke with Phoenix about the status of Pop's lease proposal and "pressed him to advise her of Resorts' position. Taube specifically advised Phoenix that Pop's had an option to renew the lease for its Margate location and needed to give notice to its landlord as to whether Pop's would be staying at that location later than October 1, 1994." Another conversation on this subject occurred in late September when Taube asked Phoenix if Pop's proposal was in the ballpark of what Resorts was looking for. Phoenix responded that Pop's offer was within the range of acceptability and that "we are 95% there, we just need Belisle's signature on the deal." (This reference to Belisle was to John Belisle, then Chief Operating Officer of Resorts.)

Taube admitted to having been advised that Belisle had "ultimate responsibility for signing off on the deal," saying that Phoenix assured her that Mr. Belisle would follow his recommendation, which was to approve the deal, and that he, Phoenix, did not anticipate any difficulties. Mr. Phoenix assured Taube that there would be little difficulty in concluding an agreement and advised Taube to give notice that Pop's would not be extending its Margate lease and to "pack up the Margate store and plan on moving."

Relying on Phoenix's "advice and assurances," Taube notified Pop's landlord in late-September 1994 that it would not be renewing the lease for the Margate location. In early October, Pop's moved its equipment out of the Margate location and placed it in temporary storage. Taube then commenced a number of new site preparations including: (1) sending designs for the new store to its franchisor, TCBY, in October 1994; and (2) retaining an attorney to represent Pop's in finalizing the terms of the lease with Resorts.

By letter dated November 1, 1994, General Counsel for Resorts forwarded a proposed form of the lease for The Players Club location to Pop's attorney. In a letter dated December 1, 1994, General Counsel for Resorts forwarded to Pop's attorney a written offer of the terms upon which Resorts was proposing to lease the Players Club space to Pop's. The terms provided that: Resorts was willing to offer the space for an initial three (3) year term with a rent calculated at the greater of 7% of gross revenues or: $50,000 in year one; $60,000 in year two; and $ 70,000 in year three with a three (3) year option to renew after the initial term.

The letter also addressed a "boilerplate lease agreement" provision and a proposed addition to the form lease. The letter concluded by stating: "This letter is not intended to be binding upon Resorts. It is intended to set forth the basic terms and conditions upon which Resorts would be willing to negotiate a lease and is subject to those negotiations and the execution of a definitive agreement. We think TCBY will be successful at the Boardwalk location based upon the terms we propose. We look forward to having your client as part of the Resorts family of customer-service providers and believe TCBY will benefit greatly. We would be pleased to discuss this proposal in greater detail."

In early-December 1994, Taube and her attorney met with William Murtha, General Counsel of Resorts, and Paul Ryan to finalize the proposed lease. After a number of discussions about the lease, Murtha and Ryan informed Taube that they desired to reschedule the meeting to finalize the lease until after the holidays. Ryan again assured Taube that rent for the Players Club space was not an issue and that the lease terms would be worked out. He also assured Taube that Resorts wanted TCBY on the boardwalk the following season.

Taube made several attempts in January 1995 to contact Resorts' representatives and confirm that matters were proceeding. On January 30, 1995, Taube's attorney received a letter from Resorts stating: "This letter is to confirm our conversation of this date wherein I advised that Resorts is withdrawing its December 1, 1994 offer to lease space to your client, TCBY." Apparently, in late January 1995, Resorts spoke with another TCBY franchise, Host Marriott, regarding the Players Club's space. Those discussions eventually led to an agreement to have Host Marriott operate a TCBY franchise at the Players Club location. That lease was executed in late May 1995, and TCBY Marriott opened shortly thereafter.

According to Taube's certification, "As soon as Pop's heard that Resorts was withdrawing its offer, we undertook extensive efforts to reopen the franchise at a different location. Because the Margate location had been re-let, it was not available." Ultimately, Pop's found a suitable location but did not reopen for business until July 5, 1996, the loss of a year's operation.

On July 17, 1995, Pop's filed a complaint against Resorts seeking damages. The complaint alleged that Pop's "reasonably relied to its detriment on the promises and assurances of Resorts that it would be permitted to relocate its operation to Resorts' Boardwalk location." After substantial pre-trial discovery, defendant moved for summary judgment. After oral argument, the motion judge, the trial court judge, rendered a detailed oral opinion in which he concluded, in part: "The primary argument of the defendant is that the plaintiff is unable to meet the requirements for a claim of Promissory Estoppel as there was no clear and definite promise ever made to plaintiff; and, therefore, any reliance on the part of plaintiff upon the statements of the Resorts agent were not reasonable.

> I think that even if a jury would find that a lease was promised, there was lack of specificity in its terms so as to not rise to the level of what is necessary to meet the first element for Promissory Estoppel, namely, that there was no specificity as to the term of this lease. There was no specificity as to the starting date of the lease. There was no specificity as to the rent although it was represented that rent would not be a problem. Rent had not been agreed upon, and it is not certified that it had been agreed upon. When they left that meeting, according to plaintiff's own facts, they didn't have a lease; they would still have to work out the terms of the lease. There was no lease in existence at the time. Neither side, neither the defendant nor the plaintiff, can attest to the terms of the lease and the terms of the lease were still not agreed upon at the time the December 1994 meeting was over.

The trial-court judge concluded that the evidence was so one-sided that the defendant was entitled to prevail as a matter of law: It was quite apparent to the Court that the trial-court judge viewed plaintiff's complaint as seeking enforcement of a lease which had not yet been fully negotiated. If that were plaintiff's intended remedy, the Appeals Court stated it would have agreed with the judge's conclusion. However, plaintiff's complaint, after reciting the facts from the inception of Taube's initial contact with defendant until January 30, 1995, stated: "As a result of its reasonable reliance on the promises and assurances made to it by Resorts International, Pop's has suffered significant damages, including the following: a) the loss of its Margate location and its ability to earn profits during the 1995 summer season; b) out-of-pocket expenses, including attorney's fees; and c) out-of-pocket expenses in attempting to locate an alternate location. Wherefore, Pop's demands judgment of damages, costs of suit and other legal and equitable relief as the Court may deem just and proper.

"It seems quite clear from plaintiff's complaint," the Court held, "that plaintiff was not seeking damages relating to a lease of the boardwalk property, but rather was seeking damages flowing from its detrimental reliance upon promises made to it prior to October 1, 1994, when it failed to renew its lease for its Margate location. Thus, plaintiff's claim was predicated upon the concept of *promissory estoppel* and was not a traditional breach of contract claim."

The Supreme Court held that the doctrine of promissory estoppel was well-established in New Jersey, and that the doctrine of promissory estoppel would be enforced saying: "A promissory estoppel claim is justified if the plaintiff satisfies its burden of demonstrating the existence of a dispute as to a material fact with regard to a defendant's adverse motion for summary judgment. There are four separate elements required to support a theory of promissory estoppel. They are: (1) a clear and definite promise by the promisor; (2) the promise must be made with the expectation that the promisee will rely thereon; (3) the promisee must in fact reasonably rely on the promise, and (4) detriment of a definite and substantial nature must be incurred in reliance on the promise. The essential justification for the promissory-estoppel doctrine is to avoid the substantial hardship or injustice which result when such promises are not enforced."

The facts as they were presented by the plaintiff in its pleadings and certifications filed by Taube, which were not refuted or contradicted by defendant before the motion judge or on appeal, clearly showed that when Taube informed Phoenix that Pop's option to renew its lease at its Margate location had to be exercised by October 1, 1994, Phoenix instructed Taube to give notice that Pop's would not be extending its lease. According to Phoenix, virtually nothing remained to be resolved between the parties. Phoenix indicated that the parties were "95% there" and that all that was required for completion of the deal was the signature of John Belisle. Phoenix assured Taube that he had recommended the deal to Belisle, and that Belisle would follow his recommendation. Phoenix also advised Pop's to "pack up the Margate store and plan on moving."

It was also uncontradicted that based upon those representations Pop's, in fact, did not renew its lease. It vacated its Margate location, placed its equipment into temporary storage, retained the services of an attorney to finalize the lease with defendant, and engaged in planning the relocation to defendant's property. Ultimately, it incurred the expense of relocating to its present location. That plaintiff relied to its detriment on defendant's assurances seems unquestionable; the facts clearly raised a jury question. Additionally, whether plaintiff's reliance upon defendant's assurances was reasonable was also a question for the jury.

A jury could conclude that Phoenix, as promisor, should reasonably have expected to induce action on the part of plaintiff by his precise instruction "not to renew the lease" and to "pack up the Margate store and plan on moving." In discussing the "character of reliance," the Court said that the promisor is affected only by reliance which he does or should foresee, and enforcement must be necessary to avoid injustice. Satisfaction of the latter requirement may depend on the reasonableness of the promisee's reliance, and on the definite and substantial character of the promise, i.e., on the formality with which the promise was made.

The Court held that plaintiff's complaint neither sought enforcement of the lease nor speculative lost profits which it might have earned had the lease been fully and successfully negotiated. Plaintiff merely sought to recoup damages it incurred, including the loss of its Margate leasehold, in reasonably relying to its detriment upon the defendant's promise. Affording plaintiff all favorable inferences, its equitable claim raised a jury question, and plaintiff's complaint, therefore, should not have been summarily dismissed.

The court reversed and remanded for further appropriate proceedings.

CHAPTER 3. RESPONDEAT SUPERIOR

Respondeat is the third person singular, subjunctive mood (the hortatory subjunctive) of the Latin verb *repondeo, respondere, responsi, responsus,* meaning "let him respond." *Superior* is the nominative masculine singular of the comparative Latin adjective *superus* and means "more superior," or, in this case, the boss. So the phrase *respondeat superior* ("ray-spon-day-at soo-peer-ee-or") means, let the boss answer, or, the superior is responsible. That is to say that the superior is responsible for the actions of those under him, when, acting within the scope of their employment, those under the superior hurt or injure another person or persons. The boss (or the employer) can be held liable (vicarious liability) for the injurious (tortious) consequences of an employee's actions, collectively or individually.

In some states now, the employer can be held responsible even when the tort feasor (the employee who does the damage) is acting beyond the scope of his employment. Take for example the case where the boys in a bar one slow night got to horsing around for want of other action. When all the good jokes had been told and the boys had determined the arm-wrestling champion for the evening, and it seemed things were on the verge of winding down, the bartender, man of many attributes that he was, pulled out a jackknife and started showing the guys some of his knife tricks. In performing one of his tricks something went awry and the knife hit one of the patrons in the eye, resulting in the eventual loss of the eye. Well, no one likes losing an eye and the injured party brought a lawsuit. As fate would have it, bartenders do not carry large liability insurance policies, but drinking establishments do. The injured patron's lawyer decided right off that to sue the bartender would at best result in little more than a moral victory; whereas suing the establishment could result in a hefty, big-bucks tort-liability award.

The catch was that the tavern owner had not been the one who threw the knife. "No matter," I'm sure the patron's lawyer thought, "RESPONDEAT SUPERIOR!"

The case got to trial and the jury awarded significant damages to the guy with the eye patch. In doing so, the jury decided that the tavern owner was indeed the responsible party because, in failing to train his bartender not to throw knives at patrons, the tavern owner had not trained his employee well and was, therefore, by omission, ultimately responsible for the change in the status of the unfortunate patron's binocular vision.

Thornburg gives a little different twist to the concept:

KEITH THORNBURG, APPELLANT,
V. FEDERAL EXPRESS CORPORATION ET AL., JOE HARDIN, TREVOR TALLEY, RESPONDENTS.
COURT OF APPEALS OF MISSOURI, WESTERN DISTRICT
62 S.W.3D 421
JULY 31, 2001

LEGAL CONSIDERATIONS

Torts / Respondeat Superior

The doctrine of *respondeat superior* holds an employer liable for the torts committed by its employees while they are acting within the scope of their employment.

Civil Procedure / Failure to State a Cause of Action

In reviewing the trial court's dismissal of a petition for failure to state a claim upon which relief can be granted, the appellate court is required to determine whether the facts pleaded and the inferences reasonably drawn therefrom state any ground for relief.

Torts / Intentional Infliction of Emotional Distress

In order to state a claim for intentional infliction of emotional distress, a plaintiff must plead that 1) the defendants' conduct was extreme and outrageous, 2) the conduct was intentional or done recklessly, and 3) the conduct caused severe emotional distress that resulted in bodily harm.

Civil Procedure / Intentional Infliction of Emotional Distress

It is for the court to determine, in the first instance, whether the defendant's conduct may reasonably be regarded as so extreme and outrageous as to permit recovery.

Torts / Negligent Infliction of Emotional Distress

The tort of negligent infliction of emotional distress is a negligence action. The general elements of a negligence action are 1) a legal duty of the defendant to protect the plaintiff from injury, 2) breach of the duty, 3) responsible cause, and 4) injury to the plaintiff.

Torts / Negligent Infliction of Emotional Distress

Claims seeking recovery of damages for the negligent infliction of emotional distress require proof of two additional elements: 1) that the defendant should have realized that his conduct involved an unreasonable risk of causing distress, and 2) that the emotional distress or mental injury must be medically diagnosable and must be of sufficient severity so as to be medically significant.

PRIOR HISTORY: APPEAL FROM THE CIRCUIT COURT OF COLE COUNTY.

DISPOSITION: Affirmed.

PROCEDURAL POSTURE: The Cole County Circuit Court, Missouri, dismissed appellant husband's suit for failure to state a claim upon which relief could be granted. The husband appealed from that order.

OVERVIEW: Husband sued appellee employer of wife for alienation of affections, intentional infliction of emotional distress and negligent infliction of emotional distress, alleging employer's actions forced his wife to leave him. The Appeals Court agreed that dismissal was proper because the husband failed to prove allegations supporting the elements that his wife's employer engaged in wrongful conduct and that that conduct caused his wife to leave him. Furthermore, only acts having a natural and probable consequence of alienating the affections of a spouse were wrongful by law, and the case did not present those acts. While the wife's job relocation may have been a natural consequence of her employer's assistance, her leaving her husband was not. The husband's negligence claim was properly defeated because he failed to show a duty owed to him by his wife's employer and without such a duty no liability can accrue. The intentional negligence claim was also properly denied because the acts of the wife's employer were not outrageous and did not shock the conscience. Finally, there could be no *respondeat-superior* liability because no employees were held liable to the husband, and an employer's liability could be no greater than its employees.

OUTCOME: The order of the circuit court was affirmed.

OPINION: Keith Thornburg appealed the trial court's judgment granting the motion to dismiss for failure to state a cause of action filed by Federal Express's Trevor Tally, and Joe Hardin (the defendants) On appeal, Mr. Thornburg argued that he sufficiently stated his claims for alienation of affections, intentional infliction of emotional distress and negligent infliction of emotional distress, and the trial court, therefore, erred in dismissing his petition. The Appeals Court affirmed the judgment of the trial court.

I. Facts

Keith and Roberta Thornburg were married on November 8, 1986. Two children were born of the marriage. The marriage was dissolved on October 6, 1998. During the marriage, Ms. Thornburg was an employee of Federal Express. Wade Hunt was a manager for Federal Express and Ms. Thornburg's supervisor. Ms. Thornburg and Mr. Hunt began an extra-marital affair in September 1997. At about the time the affair began, Ms. Thornburg was promoted to a full-time position with a desirable work schedule.

When Mr. Thornburg learned of the affair, he confronted Mr. Hunt. As a result of the confrontation, Mr. Hunt ended the affair. The Thornburgs then reconciled their marriage in early 1998. Around this same time, one or more employees of Federal Express filed grievances concerning Mr. Hunt's alleged sexual misconduct in the workplace and alleged unlawful discrimination in the workplace as a result of this conduct, and Federal Express conducted an investigation. The investigation and resultant workplace disclosure of the affair between Ms. Thornburg and Mr. Hunt caused distress to Ms. Thornburg. Because of the stress generated by the investigation that affected Ms. Thornburg, she was placed on light-duty assignments.

Federal Express encouraged Ms. Thornburg to find other employment outside Federal Express and provided her with assistance to do so, but this attempt to find alternative employment was unsuccessful. Around April 1998, Federal Express offered Ms. Thornburg a lateral transfer to Savannah, Georgia. Hoping that Mr. Thornburg would agree to relocate his family to Georgia, Ms. Thornburg discussed this job offer with him. Mr. Thornburg decided he did not want to relocate himself or his family. Mr. Thornburg told Ms. Thornburg that her accepting the transfer would be her choice to abandon the marriage. Ms. Thornburg ultimately accepted the job transfer and moved with her children to Savannah, Georgia, on May 6, 1998, without Mr. Thornburg's knowledge. The physical move took place while Mr. Thornburg was out of town on a business trip. Federal Express provided Ms. Thornburg assistance to facilitate the move.

Upon returning from his business trip and discovering that Ms. Thornburg had moved out of the family home, Mr. Thornburg visited the Federal Express offices where Ms. Thornburg had previously been working and demanded to be told the new address and phone number of Ms. Thornburg in Savannah, Georgia. Federal Express refused to provide Mr. Thornburg with any information regarding Ms. Thornburg's whereabouts. Mr. Thornburg thereafter filed a petition in the Circuit Court of Cole County alleging three separate counts against the defendants including: 1) alienation of affections, 2) negligent infliction of emotional distress, and 3) intentional infliction of emotional distress. The defendants filed a motion to dismiss Mr. Thornburg's claims. The trial court sustained the defendants' motion and dismissed each count in Mr. Thornburg's petition for failing to state a claim. This appeal followed.

II. Standard of Review

In reviewing the trial court's dismissal of a petition for failure to state a claim upon which relief may be granted, an appellate court is required to determine whether the facts pleaded and the inferences reasonably drawn therefrom state any ground for relief. *Veling v. City of Kansas City,* 901 S.W.2d 119, 121 (Mo. App. W.D. 1995). In making such determination, no attempt is made to weigh any facts alleged to conclude whether they are credible or persuasive. Instead, the facts and their reasonable inferences are viewed in the light most favorable to the plaintiff in determining if the facts alleged meet the elements of a recognized cause of action.

III. Points on Appeal

Mr. Thornburg raised a total of seven points on appeal, each stating separate arguments averring reasons why the trial court's dismissal of Mr. Thornburg's petition for failing to state a claim was erroneous. The first four points relate to the trial court's dismissal of Mr. Thornburg's claim against the defendants for alienation of affection. Mr. Thornburg's fifth point argues that he sufficiently stated a claim against the defendants for negligent infliction of emotional distress. Similarly, Mr. Thornburg contends in his sixth point on appeal that his petition adequately stated a claim against the defendants for intentional infliction of emotional distress. Finally, in his last point on appeal, Mr. Thornburg contended that the trial court erred in dismissing the petition on the basis that an employer cannot be held liable under the doctrine of respondeat superior for the adulterous affairs of its employees.

A. Alienation of Affection

An action for alienation of affection is based on inherently wrongful acts of the defendant intentionally done, which have the natural and probable consequence of alienating the affections of the spouse of a plaintiff, and which in the particular case had that result. To sufficiently state a claim for the intentional tort of alienation of affections, a plaintiff must allege that 1) the defendant engaged in wrongful conduct, 2) the plaintiff lost the affections or consortium of his or her spouse, and 3) there was a causal connection between the defendant's conduct and the plaintiff's loss. To withstand a motion to dismiss for failure to state a claim for alienation of affection, the petition must contain allegations of fact in support of each of these essential elements of the tort. Where a petition fails to make allegations in support of any element of this cause of action, a motion to dismiss is properly granted.

The trial court found that Mr. Thornburg failed to state a claim for alienation of affection because he failed to make allegations of fact supporting the elements that 1) the defendants engaged in wrongful conduct and 2) a causal connection between the defendants' conduct and Mr. Thornburg's loss existed. The trial court also found that based on Missouri's narrow interpretation of the tort and the Missouri Supreme Court's abolition of the related tort of criminal conversation, the tort of alienation of affection does not encompass liability for co-workers and employers.

In his first point on appeal, Mr. Thornburg argued that he did not need to allege the wrongfulness of defendants' conduct because the intentional acts and conduct of a third party that interfere in a marriage are deemed wrongful by law. This premise is not absolute, however, only acts that have the natural and probable consequence of alienating the affections of a plaintiff's spouse are deemed wrongful by law.

The natural and probable consequence of the defendants' alleged actions in this case was not to alienate the affections of Ms. Thornburg toward her husband but rather to assist and support Ms. Thornburg in dealing with the resultant stress incurred by her consensual affair with a Fed Ex employee. The defendants provided Ms. Thornburg with an opportunity to relocate to a different work environment to avoid problems she was experiencing. While Ms. Thornburg's job relocation may have been the natural and probable consequence of her employer's assistance, Ms. Thornburg's leaving Mr. Thornburg was not. Mr. Thornburg's petition contains no allegations that the relocation opportunity provided by Ms. Thornburg's employer was contingent upon Ms. Thornburg leaving Mr. Thornburg. Mr. Thornburg could have transferred with Ms. Thornburg. Ms. Thornburg could have chosen to exercise the option for increased job benefits to relocate to Georgia and Mr. Thornburg could have elected to stay in Jefferson City, thereby maintaining a long distance relationship.

Because the natural and probable consequence of the defendants' actions was not to alienate Ms. Thornburg's affections, the defendants' conduct is not deemed wrongful by law. Absent any specific allegations that the defendants' conduct was wrongful, Mr. Thornburg's petition is insufficient to assert an alienation of affection claim. The trial court, therefore, properly dismissed the petition for failing to state a claim upon which relief could be granted. Because this point is dispositive of the alienation of affection claim, Mr. Thornburg's other three points relating to this claim need not be addressed. The judgment as it relates to Mr. Thornburg's alienation of affection claim is affirmed.

B. Negligent Infliction of Emotional Distress

The trial court found that Mr. Thornburg failed to state a claim for negligent infliction of emotional distress because he failed to make allegations of fact supporting the necessary elements of a negligent infliction of emotional distress cause of action. To prove a claim of negligent infliction of emotional distress, a plaintiff must prove that the defendant had a 1) legal duty to protect the plaintiff from injury, 2) that the defendant breached that duty, 3) that the breach was a responsible cause, 4) resulting in injury to the plaintiff. Claims seeking recovery of damages for the negligent infliction of emotional distress require proof of two additional elements: 1) that the defendant should have realized that his conduct involved an unreasonable risk of causing distress, and 2) that the emotional distress or mental injury must be medically diagnosable and must be of sufficient severity so as to be medically significant. Mr. Thornburg's petition must contain allegations of fact in support of the two elements required to recover damages for emotional distress in addition to the even more basic elements of any claim for negligence.

Mr. Thornburg's petition made no allegation that the defendants owed Mr. Thornburg any legally recognized duty. Mr. Thornburg's brief, likewise, failed to cite any Missouri case imposing a legal duty on coworkers or employers to their employees' spouses. Instead, in his brief, Mr. Thornburg argued that the duty in this case was established by the foreseeable likelihood that the defendants' acts would result in harm to him. The asserted facts and reasonable inferences attributable to Mr. Thornburg's petition did not support the necessary conclusion that the defendants' conduct caused Mr. Thornburg to suffer severe emotional distress. Accordingly, the petition failed to allege Mr. Thornburg was owed any legally recognized duty by the defendants, and thus, he failed to state a claim for negligent infliction of emotional distress. The trial court's judgment dismissing Mr. Thornburg's claim for negligent infliction of emotional distress was justifiably affirmed.

C. Intentional Infliction of Emotional Distress

In order to state a claim for intentional infliction of emotional distress, Mr. Thornburg had to plead that 1) the defendants' conduct was extreme and outrageous, 2) that the conduct was intentional or done recklessly, and 3) that the conduct caused severe emotional distress that resulted in bodily harm. Missouri case law recognizes the difficulty in defining acts that are "extreme and outrageous," and thus, each case must turn on its individual facts. The defendant's conduct had to be more than simply malicious or intentional; the conduct had to have been "so outrageous in character, and so extreme in degree, as to go beyond all possible bounds of decency, and to be regarded as atrocious, and utterly intolerable in a civilized community." The conduct had to be also "intended only to cause extreme emotional distress to the victim."

It was for the court to determine, in the first instance, whether the defendant's conduct might have been reasonably regarded so extreme and outrageous as to permit recovery. In making such a determination, the court had to decide whether an average member of the community upon learning of the facts alleged by the plaintiff would exclaim "outrageous!"

The trial court dismissed Mr. Thornburg's claim for intentional infliction of emotional distress finding that he failed to allege the defendants' conduct was extreme and outrageous. Mr. Thornburg argued that this finding by the trial court was erroneous.

In his petition, Mr. Thornburg alleged that: 1) Federal Express offered Ms. Thornburg a transfer to Savannah, Georgia; 2) defendants offered Ms. Thornburg the transfer to remedy the current hostile work environment and to preserve and protect the careers and positions of its managers; 3) the transfer opportunity provided Ms. Thornburg with a lucrative full-time schedule that would allow her to support herself and her children; 4) the transfer opportunity provided Ms. Thornburg with a fresh start in a non-hostile workplace environment; 5) defendants provided Ms. Thornburg with relocation assistance; 6) the relocation occurred while Mr. Thornburg was out of town on a business trip; 7) defendants did not announce the transfer or resulting vacancy at Federal Express until after Ms. Thornburg had already relocated; 8) the defendants provided packing materials and physical assistance to Ms. Thornburg to help her remove property from the Thornburg's home; 9) Federal Express made money in Ms. Thornburg's retirement account available to her; 10) defendants served as an employment reference for Ms. Thornburg; 11) the original transfer opportunity offer was altered from a Tuesday through Saturday to a Monday through Friday work schedule; and 12) after the relocation the defendants refused to provide Mr. Thornburg with Ms. Thornburg's location and address. Mr. Thornburg complains that this conduct by the defendants, and Ms. Thornburg's resulting transfer, caused him to suffer severe emotional distress. In making his allegations, Mr. Thornburg admitted that

1) the defendants did not desire to terminate Ms. Thornburg's employment with Federal Express; and 2) upon learning of Ms. Thornburg's transfer opportunity, he informed Ms. Thornburg that he did not wish to relocate and that if she accepted the transfer it, was her choice to abandon their marriage.

While the defendants' conduct may have been self-serving as argued by Mr. Thornburg, his petition failed to allege conduct so outrageous and extreme as to be utterly intolerable in a civilized society. Accordingly, Mr. Thornburg's petition failed to state a claim for intentional infliction of emotional distress. The trial court's judgment dismissing Mr. Thornburg's intentional infliction of emotional distress claim was affirmed.

D. Respondeat Superior

In his final point on appeal, Mr. Thornburg alleged that the trial court dismissed his *respondeat- superior* claims against Federal Express based on a rule of law that is not applicable to the facts alleged nor the claims raised in Mr. Thornburg's petition. Mr. Thornburg argued that the trial court dismissed his *respondeat-superior* claims against Federal Express based on its finding that an employer cannot be held liable under the doctrine of *respondeat superior* for the adulterous affairs of it employees. Mr. Thornburg, however, contends that his petition did not seek to hold Federal Express liable for the damages that resulted from the affair between Ms. Thornburg and Mr. Hunt but sought recovery for the damages resulting from the conduct of Federal Express and its employees relating to Ms. Thornburg's relocation.

The trial court dismissed Mr. Thornburg's claims against Federal Express under the doctrine of *respondeat superior* based on two different theories. First, the trial court found that Mr. Thornburg had failed to allege any actionable tort by any employee of Federal Express, and, thus, if an employee is not liable to the plaintiff, then neither is the employer. And second, the trial court found that Federal Express cannot be held liable under the doctrine of *respondeat superior* for a consensual affair of one of its employees because participation in such an affair is not within the scope of the participant's employment. It was this second finding that Mr. Thornburg argued was erroneous because it was not based on the facts alleged or claims pleaded in his petition.

Accordingly, because no cause of action was stated against the employees of Federal Express, no cause of action under the doctrine of *respondeat superior* lies against Federal Express. The trial court was, therefore, correct in dismissing Mr. Thornburg's petition on this ground. Thus, the trial court's dismissal of Mr. Thornburg's respondeat-superior claims on the grounds that Federal Express could not be held liable under the doctrine of respondeat superior for a consensual affair between two of its employees was harmless error, if error at all. Only prejudicial error is reversible error.

IV. Conclusion

Mr. Thornburg failed to sufficiently state claims for alienation of affection and negligent and intentional infliction of emotional distress against defendants. Likewise, Mr. Thornburg failed to state a claim for relief against Federal Express under the doctrine of respondeat superior. The Appeals Court held that the trial court was, therefore, correct in dismissing Mr. Thornburg's petition for failure to state a cause of action.

The judgment of the trial court was affirmed.

CHAPTER 4. THE SUDDEN EMERGENCY DOCTRINE

When a person is suddenly confronted with a hazardous situation not of his own making or want of care, he is legally entitled to take action, which, had he had more time for assessment, prudence would not have condoned. Under the *sudden emergency doctrine*, a party placed in a situation of *sudden emergency* or peril other than by his own negligence is not held to the same degree of care as one who has time for thought and reflection.

Let's say that a young man and his girlfriend go off to the cinema one evening. When they get to where they're going, they find all the parking spaces taken. The boyfriend sees that a car is about to back out of a parking space ahead of him, and he pulls up to take the space when the car backs out. He stops his car behind a parked car and his girlfriend gets out to get into the ticket line. A couple of seconds after she gets out, a car he is partially blocking begins to back out of its parking space, and the boyfriend quickly shifts into reverse and backs up to avoid being run into. When he backs up, he hits his girlfriend and breaks her leg. His girlfriend sues him for negligence, or, rather, she sues his insurance company for his negligence.

At trial, boyfriend's insurance company asks that the court give the jury an instruction on the *sudden emergency doctrine*. The judge gives the requested instruction, which would probably have read something to the following effect:

Emergency Situations Instruction

The issue of negligence is considered differently if you find that an emergency situation occurred. A person confronted by an emergency he did not cause is

> not to be held to the same degree of care as an ordinary person with time to con-
> sider his actions. The test which you must apply is whether or not the person
> confronted by an emergency he did not cause acted as a reasonably prudent per-
> son would have acted when confronted by the same or similar circumstances.

After deliberation, the jury returns a verdict for the defendant boyfriend ab-
solving him of all liability in the case. The girlfriend's attorney filed an appeal.

The appeals court denies the girlfriends appeal saying: The *sudden-emergency
doctrine* applies if there is an emergency that is sudden or unanticipated. More
specifically, there must have been a confrontation by a sudden peril requiring
instinctive reaction where the defendant did not have time to consider various
options. Here the defendant did not actually state that he was placed in sudden
peril requiring an instinctive reaction. Rather, the defendant simply stated that
he had to move his vehicle in order to avoid being hit.

JONIE WHITAKER
v. COCA-COLA COMPANY USA, A DIVISION OF THE COCA-
COLA COMPANY, AND CLIFTON E. EDWARDS
COURT OF CIVIL APPEALS OF ALABAMA
812 SO. 2D 1252 (2001 ALA.)
SEPTEMBER 7, 2001.

LEGAL CONSIDERATIONS

Negligence / Standards of Care / Sudden-Emergency Doctrine

The *sudden-emergency doctrine* is available to explain why in certain situations a
person is not held to the strict standard of care required of a reasonably prudent
person acting under ordinary circumstances. Under that doctrine, a person faced
with a *sudden emergency* calling for quick action is not held to the same correctness
of judgment and action that would apply if he had the time and opportunity to
consider fully and choose the best means of escaping peril or preventing injury.
For the *sudden-emergency doctrine* to be applicable, there must be a *sudden emergency*
and the *sudden emergency* must not be the fault of the one seeking to invoke the
doctrine.

Civil Procedure / Summary Judgment / Sudden-Emergency Doctrine

Alabama law requires that a trial court give a *sudden-emergency doctrine* instruction if the jury has heard evidence from which it could conclude that there was
a *sudden emergency*, and it is a question for the finder of fact as to whether the
doctrine is properly applicable. Logically, then, if there is substantial evidence
of disputed material facts upon which a fact-finder could base a determination
that a *sudden emergency* existed, a grant of summary judgment on the issue would
be inappropriate.

CASE SUMMARY: The lower court awarded summary judgment dismissing Whitaker's case.

PROCEDURAL POSTURE: Appellant truck driver, Whitaker, sued appellees, employee and employer, in the Marion Circuit Court (Alabama) for injuries suffered in a traffic accident.

OVERVIEW: A truck driver (Whitaker) alleged that an employee, driving an employer's truck, caused him to run into a bridge as a result of the employee negligently losing control of his vehicle in a sudden rain and jackknifing. The employee and employer alleged that Whitaker was contributorily negligent. There was substantial evidence of disputed material facts from which the fact-finder could determine that the *sudden-emergency doctrine* applied to Whitaker. Under that doctrine, the driver Whitaker would not have been held to the strict standard of care required of a reasonably prudent person acting under ordinary circumstances because he was faced with a *sudden emergency* calling for quick action and did not have the time and opportunity to consider fully and choose the best means of escaping peril or preventing injury. Whitaker maintained that whether the *sudden-emergency doctrine* applied was for a jury not a judge to determine, thus making summary judgment inappropriate.

OUTCOME: The trial court's summary judgment as to the Whitaker's negligence claim was reversed, and the matter was remanded for trial.

OPINION: On July 2, 1991, Jonie Whitaker, a tractor-trailer driver, was driving his "double-trailer rig" westbound on U.S. Highway 78, near Winfield, Alabama. As he approached the old Mallard Creek Bridge, Whitaker noticed another tractor-trailer, driven by Clifton E. Edwards, in the eastbound lane. As Whitaker approached the bridge, it started raining and became very windy. Edwards's truck appeared to Whitaker to be moving erratically, and Whitaker anticipated that it might jackknife. In anticipation of the probable jack-knife, Whitaker decided to stop his truck to avoid a collision with Edwards's truck. He applied his brakes when he was approximately 150 to 200 feet from the eastern end of the bridge. According to Whitaker, braking suddenly on the rain-slick roadway caused his truck to collide with the bridge. Edwards's truck, meanwhile, had jackknifed and had come to rest at some point before reaching the western end of the bridge. The two trucks did not collide.

Whitaker sued Coca-Cola Company USA, a division of The Coca-Cola Company ("Coca-Cola"), and Edwards, alleging that they had negligently, willfully, and/or wantonly caused the accident and his resulting injuries. Coca-Cola and Edwards filed a joint motion for summary judgment. The trial court entered a summary judgment in their favor. Whitaker appealed to the Alabama Supreme Court, which transferred the case to the appellate court.

Whitaker contended that he presented substantial evidence indicating that negligence on the part of Edwards caused the accident. Coca-Cola and Edwards argued that undisputed evidence showed that it was negligence on the part of Whitaker himself that had caused his accident, that is, that Whitaker was contributorily negligent and is precluded from recovery. After reviewing the extensive record, including the affidavits and deposition testimony of two experts proffered by Coca-Cola and Edwards, as well as the testimony of both drivers and a witness to the accident, the Appeals Court concluded that the summary judgment, insofar as it related to the negligence claim, was entered in error. Because Whitaker raised no argument concerning the summary judgment as it related to the willfulness or wantonness claims, the summary judgment, insofar as it related to those claims, was affirmed. See *Bettis v. Thornton,* 662 So. 2d 256, (Ala. 1995) (stating that when an appellant fails to argue the propriety of an aspect of the judgment, the issue is not before the appellate court).

Whitaker alleged in his complaint that negligence on the part of Edwards caused Edwards's truck to jackknife and that the jackknifing of Edwards's truck caused Whitaker, in an effort to avoid a collision with Edwards, to collide with the bridge. Edwards and Coca-Cola argued in their joint motion for summary judgment that Whitaker himself was negligent in failing to maintain control over his truck while executing a controlled stop, and that his negligence was the true cause of his accident. Whitaker argued in response to the summary-judgment motion that Edwards's jackknifing caused a "sudden emergency" and that, under the sudden-emergency doctrine, Whitaker's response to that emergency was reasonably prudent under the circumstances.

An appeals court reviews a summary judgment de novo: applying the same standard as the trial court. A motion for a summary judgment is granted when no genuine issue of material fact exists and the moving party is entitled to a judgment as a matter of law. A party moving for summary judgment must make a prima facie showing that there is no genuine issue as to any material fact and that the party is entitled to a judgment as a matter of law. If the moving party meets this burden, the burden then shifts to the non moving party to rebut the movant's prima facie showing by substantial evidence. Substantial evidence is evidence of such weight and quality that fair-minded persons in the exercise of impartial judgment can reasonably infer the existence of the fact sought to be proved.

The Supreme Court of Alabama has long held that summary judgments are rarely appropriate in negligence actions and that summary judgments in such cases will be reviewed cautiously. Alabama law of summary judgment requires a court to leave for the jury the question of contributory negligence when there is an issue of material fact on a question upon which reasonable persons could disagree.

Recently, the Supreme Court explained that the burden on the party moving for a summary judgment depends on whether that party has the burden of proof at trial. Because at trial Edwards and Coca-Cola would have had the burden of establishing the defense of contributory negligence, they were required to "'support their motion with credible evidence, using any of the materials specified in Rule 56(c) of the Alabama Rules of Civil Procedure, i.e., pleadings, depositions, answers to interrogatories, and admissions on file, along with affidavits if any. The moving party's proof must be such that it would be entitled to judgment as a matter of law if that evidence was not controverted at trial. The defendant Coca-Cola presented affidavits of two experts, Thomas Talbott, an accident reconstructionist, and Jon Cook, a safety consultant; the depositions of both drivers,

Edwards and Whitaker; the deposition of Mary Tucker, an eyewitness to the accident; the deposition of Clyde Reaves, an Alabama state trooper who responded to the accident to direct traffic; and portions of the deposition of Clyde Welch, a witness who lived near the accident scene and who testified concerning the distance from the bridge to the point at which Edwards's truck came to rest. These submissions, they contended, demonstrated that there was no genuine issue of material fact on the question of whether negligence on the part of Whitaker was the actual cause of his accident.

Although Edwards and Coca-Cola indicated that they disputed the contention that Edwards was negligent in the first instance, that argument was not fully developed in their summary-judgment motion or on appeal. In addition, at least one of their experts opined that Edwards was negligent in failing to maintain control of his truck. Therefore, the court assumed that Edwards and Coca-Cola were conceding that the question of Edwards's negligence was for a jury to determine.

According to Whitaker, the following events transpired before the accident: He was driving west on Highway 78 at a speed of 45 miles per hour (mph). Although it had been raining earlier that day as Whitaker drove near Birmingham, it had been partly cloudy on his drive toward Winfield. As he approached the bridge, it began raining again. He crested a hill before seeing the bridge, which was located down an incline. As he surveyed the roadway ahead, Whitaker noticed the Coca-Cola truck driven by Edwards approaching in the opposite lane. Edwards was heading east. Whitaker noticed that Edwards's truck was "bouncing up and down." From that observation, Whitaker concluded that Edwards might be losing control of his truck and that it might jackknife. He looked in his mirrors to observe the traffic around him and quickly returned his gaze to the road ahead, where Edwards had, as Whitaker had anticipated, jackknifed his truck. According to Whitaker, at the time he saw Edwards's truck "bouncing," he was 150 to 200 feet from the eastern end of the bridge; Edwards was, according to Whitaker's estimate, 250 to 300 feet from the western end of the bridge. Whitaker estimated that Edwards's truck, when it jackknifed, was 100 to 125 feet from the western end of the bridge. Whitaker described the road as rough and commented that his truck must have "shot into the bridge" because, he said, "it had just started raining and the road is always slicker right after it starts raining." He had started slowing down when he first suspected that Edwards was about to jackknife, so he explained that he was not going 45 mph when he hit the bridge.

When questioned about the accident report completed by the state trooper who responded to the accident, Whitaker stated that he disagreed with several aspects of the report. He specifically contradicted the stated speed of 55 mph and the statement that his accident had been caused by strong winds that blew his truck into the bridge. He stated, in response to further questioning, that the wind had not caused his accident.

Edwards testified as follows: He said he was driving east on Highway 78, headed to Eldridge. His trailer was empty, and his partner was sleeping in the overhead sleeping compartment. He, too, described the road as rough and bumpy, said he was aware of construction in the area, and testified that he was likely traveling 35 to 40 mph. He said he had encountered some light rain a few miles before reaching the bridge, but that when he was approximately 600 to 700 feet before the bridge, the weather conditions changed suddenly. He described the rain as a sudden deluge and stated that it had become very windy. The wind was "whipping and shaking his trailer," so Edwards checked his mirror to see how the trailer was faring. He noticed the back wheels leaving the roadway, and he felt the "traction" on the trailer break; the trailer came around the side of the tractor damaging the fuel tank and putting the trailer into a skid. He estimated that he was approximately 175 yards from the bridge when the trailer jackknifed and that the truck came to rest, across both lanes, about 75-100 yards away from the bridge. Edwards testified that he had not seen Whitaker's accident. Because he was blocking both lanes of traffic, Edwards moved his truck and parked it along the shoulder of the westbound lane. He, too, disputed the accident report, which stated he was traveling at 55 mph. He also said the state trooper did not complete the accident report at the scene.

Mary Tucker was an eyewitness to the accident. She testified that she saw both trucks as they approached the bridge. She described the weather as rainy and windy and said the road was very slick. She testified that Whitaker's truck was traveling at a reduced speed; she remembers thinking that he must be a safe driver. She recalled seeing Edwards's truck in the middle of the road; it was there, she assumed, because he might be avoiding a pothole. She testified that she thought Edwards was traveling too fast. She said that Edwards's truck jack-knifed and took up both lanes as it slid toward the bridge. She believed that the trucks might collide on the bridge. She said that Edwards's truck stopped approximately 50 to 75 feet from the bridge. After Edwards stopped, Tucker ran to assist Whitaker, who had hit the bridge. She said Edwards moved his truck from the roadway before the state troopers arrived at the scene.

Thomas Talbott and Jon Cook, experts presented by Edwards and Coca-Cola, suggested in their respective affidavits that Whitaker could have stopped his truck well within the distance between his truck and Edwards's truck without colliding with the bridge. They both concluded that Whitaker was negligent and that his own negligence, in failing to maintain control of his truck, caused his accident.

Talbott bases his conclusion on his experience as an accident reconstructionist, the speed at which each truck was traveling, and the distances between Whitaker's truck and Edwards's truck from the time Whitaker first noticed Edwards to the time both trucks came to rest. In his deposition, he also discussed friction ratios, the estimated "slickness" of the road, and how those elements affect braking distances. He states that he believes Whitaker could have stopped his truck without hitting the bridge, but he does say "unless the wind or something affected it."

Cook, who had in the past driven a tractor-trailer for a living, based his conclusion in large part on his experience as a driver as well as variables like speed and distance. According to his deposition testimony, he agreed that Whitaker would not have known where Edwards's truck might have stopped and that Whitaker's decision to stop his truck was appropriate. However, Cook found fault in Whitaker's loss of control over his own truck while executing the braking maneuver, which was, in his opinion, the cause of Whitaker's accident.

The testimony of Clyde Reaves, one of the two state troopers who responded to the accident, is of limited value. He remembered very little about the accident and testified, contrary to the testimony of Tucker and Edwards himself, that the truck was still jackknifed in the road when he arrived at the scene. He also testified that he was not the state trooper who investigated the accident, but, instead, that he was assigned to direct traffic at the scene. He also stated that he did not recall the other state trooper's measuring the distances involved with a tape measure or a "walking stick"; he believed that the other state trooper "walked off" the distance.

In order to prove contributory negligence, Edwards and Coca-Cola had to show that Whitaker: (1) had knowledge of the condition: (2) had an appreciation of the danger under the surrounding circumstances and, (3) failed to exercise reasonable care by placing himself in the way of danger. Edwards and Coca-Cola attempted to meet this burden by arguing that Whitaker's collision with the bridge resulted from a failure on his part to exercise reasonable care to maintain control over his truck. Whitaker, however, argued that he should not be held to the ordinary "reasonable-care" standard because, as he said, Edwards's jackknifing truck presented him with a sudden emergency from which he attempted, and failed, to extricate himself. Edwards and Coca-Cola argued that, if there was a sudden emergency, it was of Whitaker's own making and, therefore, that the sudden-emergency doctrine did not apply.

The sudden-emergency doctrine is available to explain why in certain situations a person is not held to the strict standard of care required of a reasonably prudent person acting under ordinary circumstances. Under that doctrine, a person faced with a sudden emergency calling for quick action is not held to the same standard of correctness of judgment and action that would apply if he had the time and opportunity to consider fully and choose the best means of escaping peril or preventing injury. For the sudden-emergency doctrine to be applicable, there must be a sudden emergency and the sudden emergency must not be the fault of the one seeking to invoke the doctrine.

Although many, if not all, sudden-emergency-doctrine cases involve the propriety of a trial court's choice to charge the jury on the doctrine, the Appeals Court found the underlying legal principles in those cases persuasive. Alabama law requires that a trial court give the charge if the jury has heard evidence from which it could conclude that there was a sudden emergency, and it is a question for the finder of fact as to whether the doctrine is properly applicable. Logically, then, if there is substantial evidence of disputed material facts upon which a factfinder, a jury, can base a determination that a sudden emergency existed, a summary judgment on the issue is inappropriate.

After reviewing the extensive record, the Appeals Court concluded that the facts and opinions presented at trial would permit a fact-finder to conclude that Whitaker was faced with a *sudden emergency* not of his own making and that he was not to be held to the same standard as one acting under ordinary circumstances. Although Edwards and Coca-Cola argued that Whitaker created the *sudden emergency* by failing to have his truck under control when he applied his brakes, the conflicting evidence concerning the accident does not compel a finding that Whitaker was not in control of his truck at the time he began to apply his brakes. Even though Whitaker obviously lost control of his truck at some point, the mere fact that he did is, in the words of the supreme court, "the very point of the doctrine." In any event, whether the *sudden-emergency doctrine* was applicable in this case was for a jury, not a court, to determine. The case was remanded for trial.

Chapter 5. The Rescue Doctrine

The thought behind the *rescue doctrine* is that a party who comes to the rescue of a person in need of help and is injured as a result can bring a claim in negligence against the party who was in need of assistance, unless the party rendering assistance is an on-duty emergency medical technician, a fireman, or policeman or such a person with an on-duty obligation to give assistance. The *rescue doctrine* holds that one who sees a person in imminent peril as a result of negligence cannot be charged with contributory negligence, providing the attempt at rescue is not foolhardy or rash.

The *rescue doctrine* provides that a party sustaining an injury as the result of a rescue attempt may recover damages from the person responsible for negligently creating a situation that precipitated a rescue attempt. The doctrine facilitates the natural human disposition to come to the aid of one in need of help. When a rescuer is injured attempting to come to another's aid, then, the injury is considered a product of the party requiring assistance, notwithstanding the fact that the immediate cause may be an intervening act of negligence by another.

An off-duty EMT worker was traveling home one evening when she came upon an auto accident. The accident was mostly off the road in the left-hand lane. While the EMT worker was rendering emergency assistance, another car hit her vehicle, causing an injury to her person. The EMT worker brought a negligence claim against the accident party (the party she was assisting) for damages for medical expenses and pain and suffering. At trial the defendant moved for judgment as a matter of law, citing a rule of law that excludes EMTs, firemen, and policemen from claiming under the *rescue doctrine*. The trial court granted the victim's motion and the case was dismissed.

The off-duty EMT appealed the trial court decision and the appeals court reversed and remanded.

The appeals court held that off-duty emergency personnel were not excluded from the benefit of the rescue doctrine. On remand, the off-duty EMT received an award in damages. The case that follows gives another aspect of the *rescue doctrine.*

JERRY TRAPP V. JERRY VESS
SUPREME COURT OF ALABAMA
847 SO. 2D 304 (2002 AL.)
SEPTEMBER 27, 2002

Legal Considerations

Torts / Vicarious Liability / Rescue Doctrine

The rescue doctrine arose as a way to establish a causal relation between the action of a defendant and the harm to a rescuer and to prohibit a negligent defendant (the party being rescued) from using the affirmative defenses of assumption risk and contributory negligence against the rescuer for the rescuer's efforts. *The rescue doctrine* allows a person who sustains an injury when he or she comes to the aid of another in peril to recover damages based upon the negligence of the party being rescued.

Torts / Vicarious Liability / Rescue Doctrine

In order to claim the status of a rescuer, a party must establish that he had a reasonable belief that the person he was trying to rescue was in a dangerous position. The person being rescued does not need to be in actual peril so long as there is a reasonable belief that a person is in imminent peril.

Civil Procedure / Summary Judgment

When a movant for summary judgment makes a prima facie showing that the two conditions of (1) no genuine issue of material fact and (2) entitlement to judgment as a matter of law are satisfied, the burden then shifts to the non-moving party to present substantial evidence creating a genuine issue of material fact. Evidence is substantial if it is of such weight and quality that fair-minded persons in the exercise of impartial judgment could reasonably infer the existence of the fact sought to be proved.

Civil Procedure / Summary Judgment

In reviewing a motion for summary judgment, an appeals court applies the same standard the trial court applied. The review is subject to the caveat that the court must review the record in a light most favorable to the non-moving party and must resolve all reasonable doubts against the moving party.

Torts / Transportation Torts

The mere skidding of an automobile on an icy street does not necessarily prove negligence of the driver of the car. Alabama law also states that the mere possibility that negligence caused an injury, without evidence, is not sufficient to support a verdict.

PROCEDURAL POSTURE: Appellant injured party sued appellees, motorist and motorist's insurer, in the Franklin Circuit Court (Alabama) for injuries he received when removing the motorist's car from a ditch. The trial court granted appellees' summary judgment motion, and the injured party appealed.

OVERVIEW: A motorist lost control of his car on an icy road while taking his daughter to the hospital for tests, and the car went into a ditch. A rescuer party was hurt while helping remove the car from the ditch. The supreme court held that to recover under the *rescue doctrine*, the injured party, the rescuer, had to show negligence on the part of the other motorist, but he presented no evidence of the other motorist's speed or that the speed was unreasonable. The trial court held that the injured party had to show a reasonable belief that the person he was trying to help was in peril. The only pertinent evidence was that the other motorist said he was taking his daughter to the hospital for tests. Instead of taking the other motorist's daughter to the hospital, the injured party pulled the motorist's car out of the ditch because he did not reasonably believe the daughter was in peril. The injured party did not present enough evidence to create a genuine issue of material fact as to whether he was a rescuer under the *rescue doctrine*. Even if he reasonably believed the other motorist's daughter was in peril, there was no evidence of negligence on the part of the uninjured motorist.

OUTCOME: The trial court's judgment was affirmed.

OPINION: Jerry Trapp appeals from a summary judgment for Jerry Vess and Cotton States Insurance Company. The Appeals Court affirmed the trial court decision.

Facts and Procedural History

On January 28, 2000, the weather conditions in Franklin County included freezing temperatures and two to three inches of snow. Jerry Vess and his daughter left their home that morning to take Vess's daughter to the Russellville Hospital where she was scheduled to undergo medical tests. Along the way, Vess applied the brakes on an icy portion of a road, and his car skidded into a ditch. Neither Vess nor his daughter were injured; however, Vess's car was stuck in the ditch.

A few minutes later Trapp drove by and stopped to help. Vess says that he informed Trapp that he and his daughter were not injured and that they were on their way to Russellville Hospital where his daughter was to undergo some tests. Trapp offered to get a truck with a trailer hitch to pull Vess's car out of the ditch. Trapp left and later returned with a truck and five or six men to aid in getting Vess's car out of the ditch.

The men attached a chain to the front of Vess's car and proceeded to pull the car from the ditch. During this process, Trapp and some of the men were standing in the ditch pulling on the car while the truck pulled from the road. As Trapp pulled on the car, he tore his right distal biceps tendon. The men successfully removed the car from the ditch. Trapp sought medical attention for his injury a few days later and eventually underwent surgery on his arm.

Trapp sued Vess alleging that the injury to his arm resulted from Vess's negligence and/or wantonness in driving his car into the ditch. Vess filed a motion for a summary judgment. After Trapp responded to the motion, the trial court entered a summary judgment for Vess. Trapp appealed.

The principles of law applicable to the review of a motion for a summary judgment are well settled. To grant such a motion, the trial court must determine that the evidence does not raise a genuine issue of material fact and that the moving party is entitled to the judgment as a matter of law. When the moving party makes a prima facie showing that those two conditions are satisfied, the burden then shifts to the nonmoving party to present substantial evidence creating a genuine issue of material fact. Evidence is "substantial" if it is of "such weight and quality that fair-minded persons in the exercise of impartial judgment can reasonably infer the existence of the fact sought to be proved."

In reviewing a summary judgment, an Appeals Court applies the same standard the trial court applied. The review is subject to the caveat that the Appeals Court must review the record in a light most favorable to the nonmoving party and must resolve all reasonable doubts against the party bringing the motion.

Analysis

Trapp argued that the record contained substantial evidence creating a genuine issue of material fact as to whether Trapp's injury was caused by Vess's negligence and/or wantonness. Trapp argued that he was entitled to a recovery from Vess based on the "rescue doctrine" of tort law. The Appeals Court recently described the purpose of the rescue doctrine as follows:

"The rescue doctrine arose as a way of establishing a causal relationship between the action of a party being rescued and harm to a rescuer so as to prohibit the negligent party, the party being rescued, the defendant, from claiming that his rescuer assumed the risk that went with his rescue attempt or that, in the alternative, the rescuer was contributorily negligent. The rescue doctrine allows a person who sustains an injury when he or she comes to the aid of another in peril to recover damages based upon the negligence of the party being rescued.

Trapp maintained there was a genuine issue of material fact as to whether Vess's driving his car in such a manner that it landed in a ditch constituted negligence. He points to the hazardous weather conditions and to Alabama law which provides that: "No person shall drive a vehicle at a speed greater than is reasonable and prudent under prevailing conditions, bearing in mind the actual and potential hazards then existing." Trapp also relied on *Nelson v. Meadows*, 684 So. 2d 145 (1996 AL). In that case, the Court of Civil Appeals, applying the summary-judgment standard, held that the mere fact that an individual was abiding by the speed limit at the time of an accident was not sufficient evidence to indicate that the driver acted reasonably and with prudence under the conditions present at the time of the accident.

Despite Trapp's accurate description of the standard of care imposed on a driver in Alabama, his argument contained no factual support to show that Vess acted negligently in causing his car to enter the ditch. Trapp testified in his deposition that he did not see Vess's car go into the ditch; it was already in the ditch when Trapp arrived on the scene. He presented no evidence indicating Vess's speed at the time of the accident or that the speed, although unknown, was unreasonable. Trapp presented no evidence to show that Vess's use of his brakes on an icy road was not reasonable. The only evidence the trial court had before it as to the events that occurred before the car left the road was Vess's testimony. In his deposition, Vess testified that the road was "slick and iced-over from prior traffic" and that he was not driving too fast when he applied his brakes and lost control of his car.

The Appeals Court noted that: "The mere skidding of an automobile on an icy street does not necessarily prove negligence of the driver of the car." Alabama law also states that "the mere possibility that negligence caused an injury, without evidence, is not sufficient to support a verdict." The Court held that, in the absence of any evidence sufficient to raise a genuine issue of material fact as to Vess's negligence, the trial court correctly entered summary judgment for Vess.

The Court also held that summary judgment for Vess was appropriate because there was no genuine issue of material fact as to Trapp's claim that the rescue doctrine was applicable in this case. Alabama courts have never directly addressed the issue of when a person qualifies as a rescuer under the rescue doctrine. In order to claim the status of a rescuer, a party must establish that he had a reasonable belief that the person he was trying to rescue was in a dangerous position. The person being rescued does not need to be in actual peril so long as there is "a reasonable belief that some person is in imminent peril."

In this case, the only fact that could have led Trapp to a "reasonable belief that some person was in imminent peril" was Trapp's statement in his affidavit indicating that Vess told Trapp that he needed to get his daughter to the hospital to have medical tests performed. However, there is absolutely no other evidence that Vess indicated that he and his daughter were in peril or that he requested Trapp's assistance. There was no evidence indicating that Trapp, seeing what he perceived to be an emergency, offered to take Vess's daughter immediately to the hospital or telephoned for an ambulance. Instead, he went to get a truck that could pull the car from the ditch and then returned to the scene. On the record, the court concluded that, as a matter of law, Trapp did not have a "reasonable belief that some person was in imminent peril" and, as a result, he was not entitled to the application of the rescue doctrine. There was a factual dispute as to whether Vess told Trapp that the situation was not an emergency, but that was not a material fact in light of all of the other circumstantial evidence defeating Trapp's claim that he had a reasonable belief that Vess's daughter was in peril.

CONCLUSION

The trial court properly entered a summary judgment in favor of Vess. Trapp did not present sufficient evidence to create a genuine issue of material fact as to whether Trapp was a rescuer under the rescue doctrine. Even assuming that Trapp had a reasonable belief that Vess's daughter was in imminent peril, so as to qualify as a rescuer, there was no evidence indicating that Vess acted negligently and/or wantonly in causing his car to go into the ditch. Accordingly, the Appeals Court affirmed the judgment in favor of Vess.

Chapter 6. The Doctrine of Comparative Negligence

The *Doctrine of Comparative Negligence* is the legal facilitation whereby comparative fault and its consequences are determined. As a rule, a "less than or equal to" *comparative negligence* rule determines the respective degrees of negligence attributable to a plaintiff and a defendant where conflicting inferences of responsibility may be drawn, presenting a question of fact for jury deliberation. The apportionment of negligence between plaintiff and defendant determines both whether the plaintiff is barred from recovery or can recover some of his damages.

The concept of *comparative negligence* has a long history that harks back to the days of Roman and Medieval-European maritime law. Given those antecedents, the concept probably first found its way into American maritime law and then into the American *corpus juris*. In 1910 Mississippi was the first state to enact a *comparative negligence* statute. Today most state jurisdictions have enacted *comparative negligence* provisions into their bodies of law. Recovery under a *comparative negligence* regime is usually limited to the degree to which a plaintiff's responsibility is less than a defendant's. Most comparative fault laws are a result of legislative enactment.

Mr. D (the defendant) operated a state DOT road-maintenance vehicle for a northern state and had been called out to help remove an eighteen wheeler that had jackknifed on an interstate artery, partially blocking an eastbound lane. Mr. D was driving west, pulling a trailer loaded with a small Caterpillar tractor.

As Mr. D approached the location of the eighteen wheeler, he slowed to a crawl, signaled a left turn for the median crossover and commenced his turn. Before Mr. D's trailer had cleared the left-hand lane from which he was turning, Mr. P (the plaintiff) came along and slammed into the rear of the trailer Mr. D was towing. Mr. P's car was seriously damaged and Mr. P was seriously injured. When Mr. P was healed, he brought a lawsuit against Mr. D and the Department of Transportation, citing negligence as a claim for damages.

There was a law in this particular state that held that state vehicles were exempt from claims of negligence when they were engaged in road repair. The same law, however, held that when such vehicles were traveling to and from work locations, they enjoyed no such immunity. Mr. P's attorney predicated his legal action on a claim of negligence per se. (Negligence per se rises from state-law violations.)

When the DOT and Mr. D's lawyer petitioned the court for summary judgment, arguing work-progress statutory immunity, Mr. P's attorney argued that no such immunity accrued because Mr. D and the DOT vehicle were en route to a work site.

At the heart of Mr. P's argument was the issue of negligence per se. Counsel argued that the essential purpose of the relevant traffic statute was to protect motorists from the kind of accident-engendered harm his client had suffered, and that his client was a member of the class of persons (motorists) the statute was meant to protect. That said, counsel went on to claim that Mr. D and the DOT owed his client a duty of care and that they had violated that duty and that, such being the case, negligence per se was implicated. Plaintiff's counsel argued that defendant's negligence was the responsible cause for plaintiff's injuries and that, consequently, an award of damages was rightfully contemplated. The Trial court agreed with Mr. P's counsel that issues of material fact existed and therefore refused summary judgment. Mr. D and the DOT appealed.

On appeal, defense counsel argued, all issues having been properly preserved for appeal, that state case law recognized that a violation of a traffic statute did not constitute negligence per se under explanatory or excusatory circumstances (The DOT vehicle had, after all, slowed to a crawl to make a median-strip turn to assist in a situation to which it had been summoned). Defense counsel also pointed out that a finding of a statutory violation does not automatically lead to the recovery of damages: That the plaintiff must prove that the alleged violation must have been the proximate cause of plaintiff's damages. Proximate cause requires both causation in fact and legal causation. Causation in fact is proved by establishing that "but for" the defendant's negligence no injury would have occurred, and legal causation is established by proving that plaintiff's injury was a foreseeable consequence of the defendant's negligent conduct.

The appeals court remanded for trial.

At trial the jury determined that under the doctrine of *comparative negligence*, negligence per se had been proven; however, the plaintiff was 40% negligent and could therefore receive an award of no more that 10% of the damages sought. The plaintiff should have slowed his vehicle in time to avoid hitting the DOT trailer if, as testified, he could not merge into the right-hand lane.

BRIAN W. ROWE, PLAINTIFF, APPELLEE, V. SISTERS OF THE PALLOTTINE
MISSIONARY SOCIETY, A NON-PROFIT CORPORATION, DEFENDANT, APPELLANT.
SUPREME COURT OF APPEALS OF WEST VIRGINIA
560 S.E.2D 491, (2001 W. VA.)
DECEMBER 11, 2001, FILED

LEGAL CONSIDERATIONS

Negligence / Comparative Negligence

Under the *comparative-negligence doctrine*, a plaintiff is not entitled to recover from a negligent tortfeasor if the plaintiff's own contributory negligence equals or exceeds the combined negligence or fault of the other party or parties involved in the accident or occurrence.

Negligence / Comparative Negligence

A party is not barred from recovering damages in a tort action so long as his negligence or fault does not equal or exceed the combined negligence or fault of the other party or parties involved in the incident.

Negligence / Comparative Negligence

In operation, the jury must apportion the comparative fault of parties. The plaintiff's percentage of fault is then deducted from the gross award of the jury, and the defendants may seek contribution from other defendants in accordance with their percentage of fault.

Negligence / Comparative Negligence

A majority of courts hold that a healthcare provider cannot compare the plaintiff's negligent conduct that triggered the plaintiff's need for treatment with the healthcare provider's later negligence in treating the plaintiff. The reason for this rule is simple and obvious: A physician simply may not avoid liability for negligent treatment by asserting that the patient's injuries were originally caused by the patient's own negligence. Those patients who may have negligently injured themselves are entitled to subsequent non-negligent medical treatment.

Negligence / Comparative Negligence

In the context of medical-malpractice actions, courts usually place extreme limits upon a health-care provider's use of the defense of *comparative negligence*. Courts do this because of the disparity in medical knowledge between the patient and the physician, and because of the patient's justifiable reliance on the physician's recommendations and care. The doctrine of *contributory negligence* has a limited use in the medical-negligence field. It is the duty of the patient to cooperate with the physician and to conform to his prescriptions and directions, and if he neglects to do so, he can not hold the physician responsible for his own neglect. On the other hand, he has a right to rely upon the instructions and directions of his physician and incurs no liability by doing so.

Negligence / Comparative Negligence

In any action, medical malpractice or otherwise, the defendant carries the initial burden of proving an affirmative defense such as *comparative negligence*. Contributory negligence on the part of the plaintiff is an affirmative defense. (An affirmative defense is a defense that, if proven, disposes of the action. An alibi is an affirmative defense.) There is a presumption of ordinary care in favor of the plaintiff, and where the defendant relies upon *contributory negligence*, the burden of proof rests upon the defendant to show such negligence unless it is disclosed by the plaintiff's evidence or may be fairly inferred by all of the evidence and circumstances surrounding the case.

Negligence / Comparative Negligence

In order to obtain a proper assessment of the total amount of the plaintiff's contributory negligence under the *comparative-negligence* rule, negligence must be ascertained in relation to all of the parties whose negligence contributed to the accident, and not merely those defendants involved in the litigation. The *comparative-negligence doctrine* applies only when a plaintiff has been contributorily negligent i.e., when the negligence of the plaintiff in causing his or her injury is ascertained in relation to all other tortfeasors.

Negligence / Joint & Several Liability / Comparative Negligence

Between tortfeasors who have asserted claims for contribution, an instruction allowing a jury to apportion fault may be necessary so as to allow the tortfeasors to ascertain their degrees of joint and several liability. The concept of joint and several liability is a doctrine separate from the *comparative-negligence doctrine*. Joint and several liability among joint tortfeasors was not changed by the adoption of the *comparative-negligence doctrine*. When contribution claims have been asserted between joint tortfeasors, the relative fault of the various tortfeasors is relevant, and a jury could be properly instructed to assess the fault of the joint tortfeasors.

Negligence / Negligence Generally / Comparative Negligence

To establish the defense of *comparative negligence* in a medical-malpractice claim, the defendant must prove (1) that the plaintiff owed herself a duty of care, (2) that she breached that duty and that (3) the breach was the proximate cause of the (4) damages she sustained. Proximate cause means that the alleged wrong of the party caused the damage. There must be such a natural, direct and continuous sequence between the negligent act and the injury that it can reasonably be said that but for the act, the injury would not have occurred.

Statutory Interpretation

Generally the words of a statute are to be given their ordinary and familiar meanings. It is not for an appellate court to arbitrarily read into a statute that which it does not say. Just as courts are not to eliminate through judicial interpretation words that were purposely included, the appellate court is obliged not to add to statutes something the Legislature purposely omitted.

OVERVIEW: A hospital contended that a trial court erred in refusing to instruct the jury on the principles of *comparative negligence* in a medical malpractice suit. The trial court held that a healthcare provider was not entitled to a *comparative-negligence* instruction requiring a jury to consider the plaintiff's negligent conduct that triggered a need for medical treatment. There was no evidence indicating that the patient breached any duty of care he may have owed himself. Had the patient's parents not called other physicians, and arranged for the patient to be promptly seen the following morning, it is possible he might have lost his leg. There was nothing to indicate the patient was negligent in the time he took to go to another emergency room, nor was there any evidence that the passage of time was a responsible cause of any portion of his damages. There was no requirement, without some proof of negligence, that the jury be instructed to ascertain or apportion fault between a defendant and non-party tortfeasor (the doctor who treated the plaintiff, i.e., the doctor had settled before trial and was dismissed from the action and was, therefore, a non-party tortfeasor). None of the other alleged tortfeasors was brought into the litigation.

OUTCOME: The judgment was affirmed.

OPINION: In a medical malpractice action from the Circuit Court of Cabell County, The West Virginia Appeals Court was asked to examine a judgment of a trial court's jury verdict awarding damages to an appellee, Brian W. Rowe ("Mr. Rowe"). The appellant was the Sisters of Pallottine Missionary Society, which does business as St. Mary's Hospital. The appellant hospital contends that the trial court erred in refusing to instruct the jury on the principles of *comparative negligence*. The Appeals Court found that the trial court correctly refused to give *comparative-negligence* instructions to the jury, and the lower court finding was affirmed.

Factual and Procedural Background

On the afternoon of Sunday, September 6, 1987, 17-year-old appellee Brian W. Rowe lost control of his motorcycle while participating in a motocross event. During the crash, the motorcycle tumbled onto Mr. Rowe's left leg, injuring his knee. Mr. Rowe was transported by ambulance to the emergency room of the appellant St. Mary's Hospital.

Mr. Rowe arrived at St. Mary's Hospital at approximately 4:05 p.m., where his left leg was examined by emergency room nurses. Over the course of the next 2 1/2 hours, the nurses made extensive notes in Mr. Rowe's patient file. The notes indicate that Mr. Rowe complained of severe pain in his left knee and numbness in his foot. The nurses were repeatedly unable to find a pulse in Mr. Rowe's lower left leg and foot either by palpitation or with the assistance of a portable Doppler ultrasound device.

Mr. Rowe was also examined by a St. Mary's Hospital emergency room physician, Dr. Willard F. Daniels, a defendant in the court below. Dr. Daniels noted tenderness and swelling in the left knee and lower left leg, and had difficulty finding, but claimed he did find, a pulse in Mr. Rowe's lower leg and foot. A nurse testified that she told Dr. Daniels that she was unable to detect a pulse in Mr. Rowe's foot, that she asked Dr. Daniels why she wasn't getting a pulse, and that Dr. Daniels replied, "I don't know." While x-rays showed fragments of bone in Mr. Rowe's knee joint, Dr. Daniels noted in the patient file that Mr. Rowe had a "severe sprain, to his left knee."

Mr. Rowe was discharged at 6:20 p.m. to be taken home by his mother. He was given instructions to elevate his left leg and apply ice to the knee. Mr. Rowe was also told that the nurses could not find a pulse in his lower leg, but that such a condition was probably caused by the swelling, and that a pulse would return when the swelling went down. Mr. Rowe was instructed to make an appointment with an orthopedist and was told that in the meantime, if his pain continued or became worse, he should return to St. Mary's emergency room.

That night, Mr. Rowe's knee and leg continued to swell, and the pain intensified. His parents called several physicians by phone, and one agreed to see Mr. Rowe at 10:00 a.m. the next morning at Cabell Huntington Hospital's emergency room. An examination revealed that Mr. Rowe had a dislocated knee and a lacerated political artery, an artery which passes behind the knee joint and provides circulation to the lower leg. Because of the loss of blood flow, the physician contemplated amputation of the lower left leg. However, after extensive surgery to repair the knee and artery, to relieve pressure on the leg and to remove dead tissue, the lower leg was saved. Mr. Rowe was hospitalized for 35 days, and was left with significant impairment to the use of his left leg.

The appellee, Mr. Rowe, subsequently brought a lawsuit against Dr. Daniels and against appellant St. Mary's Hospital for negligence. In October 1996, after 8 years of litigation, the appellee settled his cause of action against Dr. Daniels for $270,000.00, and the case against the hospital proceeded to trial. At trial, the appellee asserted that St. Mary's nurses had breached the standard of care by not adequately advocating his interests when he was discharged with unexplained and unaddressed symptoms. The appellee presented evidence that St. Mary's policy, and the guiding standard of care for all emergency room nurses, was that when a nurse "believed that appropriate care was not being administered to a patient by a physician," the nurse was to report the situation to a supervisor who would discuss it with the doctor. If that did not correct the problem, the matter was to be referred up the chain of command so that another doctor could evaluate the problem.

The appellee argued that St. Mary's nurses repeatedly found no pulse in his lower left leg or foot, and that when Dr. Daniels did not address this serious symptom, the nurses did not properly report the problem to a supervisor, or otherwise seek another medical opinion. As the plaintiff's expert stated:

The nurses at St. Mary's Hospital failed to advocate for Brian Rowe in the sense that they knew that he had compromised circulation to his left leg and had no pulse. He was not able to move his foot, and he had no sensation in his foot. The nurses did not intervene with the physician and try to influence the administration of his care so that he would have gotten appropriate medical care addressing his serious problems. The evidence showed that, instead of following the hospital's policy, the emergency room nurses simply made notes of their findings in Mr. Rowe's medical file to, as one nurse stated, "basically cover myself."

A jury returned a verdict against the appellant hospital for $880,186.00. A judgment order adopting the jury's verdict, with an offset for Dr. Daniels' $270,000 settlement, was entered on September 13, 1999. The hospital then appealed the circuit court's judgment order.

II. Standard of Review

In such a case an appeals court is asked to review the trial court's refusal to give certain instructions to the jury, and it was held that: As a general rule, the refusal to give a requested jury instruction is reviewed for an abuse of discretion. By contrast, the question of whether a jury was properly instructed is a question of law, and the review is de novo.

III. Discussion

Under the comparative-negligence doctrine, a plaintiff is not entitled to recover from a negligent tortfeasor if the plaintiff's own contributory negligence equals or exceeds the combined negligence or fault of the other parties involved in the accident or occurrence. As the Appeals Court stated in *Bradley v. Appalachian Power Co.*, 256 S.E.2d 879 (1979):

A party is not barred from recovering damages in a tort action so long as his negligence or fault does not equal or exceed the combined negligence or fault of the other parties involved in the accident. In operation, the jury must apportion the comparative fault of the parties. The plaintiff's percentage of fault is then deducted from the gross award of the jury, and the defendants may seek contribution from other defendants in accordance with their percentage of fault, if any.

The appellant contended that the jury should have been instructed to consider the contributory negligence of the appellee and apportion comparative fault between the appellee and the appellant hospital. The appellant argues that the appellee's own conduct in crashing his motorcycle caused many of his injuries. Furthermore, when the appellee was discharged at 6:20 p.m., he and his mother were told that if his condition persisted or became worse, he should be brought back to St. Mary's emergency department. When his condition did not improve later that night, and the appellee's parents did not return him to the emergency room, the appellant argues the appellee was negligent and contributed to his injury. The Appeals Court began by addressing the appellant's first argument, that the appellee's own conduct in crashing his motorcycle contributed to his injury, and that the jury should have been instructed to consider whether this conduct was the responsible cause of the appellee's damages. the Court found nothing in the record to suggest that the appellee's crash was caused by negligence, but for purposes of that argument, the Court assumed the appellee's conduct was negligent.

A majority of courts have held that a healthcare provider cannot compare the plaintiff's negligent conduct that triggered the plaintiff's need for treatment with the healthcare provider's later negligence in treating the plaintiff. The reason for this rule is simple and obvious: A physician simply may not avoid liability for negligent treatment by asserting that the patient's injuries were originally caused by the patient's own negligence. Those patients who may have negligently injured themselves are nevertheless entitled to subsequent non-negligent medical treatment and to an undiminished recovery if such subsequent non-negligent treatment is not afforded.

The Court therefore held that in a medical malpractice claim, a healthcare provider is not entitled to a comparative-negligence instruction requiring a jury to consider the plaintiff's negligent conduct that triggered the plaintiff's need for medical treatment. Plaintiffs who negligently injure themselves are entitled to subsequent, non-negligent medical treatment. If a healthcare provider renders negligent medical treatment, regardless of the event that triggered the need for medical treatment, plaintiffs are entitled to an undiminished recovery in a legal action for any damages proximately caused by negligent medical treatment. The Appeals Court held that the trial court did not abuse its discretion in refusing to give an instruction on that issue.

Next, the Court examined the appellant's argument that it was entitled to an instruction requiring the jury to consider whether the plaintiff was contributorily negligent in not returning to the St. Mary's emergency room. In the context of medical malpractice actions, courts usually place extreme limits upon a healthcare provider's use of the defense of comparative negligence. Courts do this because of the disparity in medical knowledge between the patient and the physician, and because of the patient's justifiable reliance on the physician's recommendations and care. The physician-patient relationship differs substantially from that of the ordinary plaintiff and defendant. This is so because of the great disparity in medical knowledge between doctor and patient. The Appeals Court recognized over a century ago that the doctrine of contributory negligence has a limited use in the medical negligence field when it stated: "It is the duty of the patient to co-operate with the physician, and to conform to his prescriptions and directions, and if he neglect to do so, he can not hold the physician responsible for his own negligence. On the other hand, he has a right to rely upon the instructions and directions of his physician and incurs no liability by doing so."

In any action, medical malpractice or otherwise, a defendant carries the initial burden of proving an affirmative defense such as comparative negligence. Contributory negligence on the part of the plaintiff is an affirmative defense, also. There is a presumption of ordinary care in favor of the plaintiff, and where the defendant relies upon contributory negligence, the burden of proof rests upon the defendant.

To establish the defense of comparative negligence in a medical malpractice claim, the defendant must establish that the plaintiff committed each of the elements of negligence: that (1) the plaintiff owed herself a duty of care, that (2) she breached that duty and that (3) the breach was the proximate cause of the (4) damages sustained. Proximate cause means that the alleged wrong of the party caused the damage. There must be such a natural, direct and continuous sequence between the negligent act and the injury that it can reasonably be said that but for the act, the injury would not have occurred. The court therefore held that for a healthcare provider to establish the defense of comparative negligence, the healthcare provider must prove, with respect to plaintiff's conduct after medical treatment is initiated, that: (1) the plaintiff owed himself a duty of care; (2) the plaintiff breached that duty; and (3) the breach was a proximate cause of the damages the plaintiff sustained.

The Appeals Court found no evidence in the record indicating that Mr. Rowe breached any duty of care he may have owed himself. It appears that Mr. Rowe and his family were told he had no pulse in his lower left leg and foot, but they were also told that the pulse would return when the swelling went down. Dr. Daniels' erroneous diagnosis was a sprain to the left knee. Mr. Rowe was advised to keep ice on the knee and elevate his leg. He was advised to return to the appellant's emergency room if his condition worsened without being given any timetable for making that evaluation. He was advised to see an orthopedic specialist later in the week. Had Mr. Rowe's parents not called other physicians, and arranged for Mr. Rowe to be promptly seen the following morning, it is possible he would have lost his leg.

The Appeals Court stated in 1892, in Lawson v. Conaway, that a patient "has a right to rely upon the instructions and directions of his physician and incurs no liability by so doing." Mr. Rowe appears to have followed the instructions of his physician, and returned to an emergency room the next day. The Court could not, on the record, find that Mr. Rowe had breached any duty of care."

Additionally, the Appeals Court noted that when contributory negligence by the patient arises as an issue in a medical-malpractice context, there is often a need for the defendant to offer expert testimony on the issue; usually only experts can testify regarding the proximate effect that a patient's negligence may have had to aggravate the patient's medical condition. In much the same way that laymen on a jury are not qualified to judge whether a doctor has been negligent, patients also are not qualified from a medical standpoint to determine the effects of the negligent acts of a physician.

The Court found no affirmative evidence in the record, and the appellant directed the Court to none indicating that Mr. Rowe was negligent in the time he took to go to another emergency room, nor did the Court find any evidence that the passage of time was a proximate cause of any portion of the plaintiff's damages. The Court therefore concluded that the circuit court, the trial court, did not abuse its discretion, and correctly refused to instruct the jury to consider whether Mr. Rowe was contributorily negligent.

The appellant hospital also contended that the jury should have been instructed to consider the negligence of Dr. Daniels, and to have considered the negligence of the other doctors telephoned by Mr. Rowe's parents the night of his injury. The appellant argued that the circuit court erred by refusing to instruct the jury that it could apportion comparative negligence between these non-party tortfeasors and the appellant hospital.

In Bowman v. Barnes, 282 S.E.2d 613 (1981), the Appeals Court held that: "In order to obtain a proper assessment of the total amount of a plaintiff's contributory negligence under West Virginia's comparative-negligence rule, negligence must be ascertained in relation to all of the parties whose negligence contributed to the accident and not merely to those defendants involved in the litigation."

As Bowman made clear, the comparative-negligence doctrine applies only when a plaintiff has been contributorily negligent, and the negligence of the plaintiff in causing his or her injury is ascertained in relation to all other tortfeasors. In those instances where a defendant intends to shift some degree of fault to a non-party tortfeasor, one court proposed the following rule in a medical malpractice action:

> To prove a nonparties' negligence, a defendant must show that (1) the nonparties owed the patient a duty recognized by law, that (2) the nonparties breached the duty by departing from the proper standard of medical practice recognized in the community, and that (3) the acts or omissions complained of proximately caused the patient's aggravation of injury or death.

Additionally, when a tortfeasor seeks contribution or otherwise seeks to share liability with other tortfeasors, the Court has said:

> West Virginia jurisprudence favors the consideration of all claims regarding liability and damages arising out of the same transaction, occurrence or nucleus of operative facts, and the joinder in such trial of all parties who may be responsible for the relief that is sought in the litigation.

In the instant action, appellant St. Mary's Hospital was the sole party tortfeasor. It did not appear from the record that any cross or counter-claims for contribution were asserted.

The appellant contended that certain arguments made by the appellee's counsel during closing argument were prejudicial. The appellant's counsel did not make a contemporaneous objection to any of these arguments, nor did the appellant ask for a curative instruction before the jury retired for its deliberations. Instead, after the jury began deliberating, the appellant made a motion for a mistrial which was denied by the circuit court. The Appeals Court held that a party's failure to make a timely objection to improper closing argument, and to seek a curative instruction, waived the party's right to raise the question on appeal. The appellant also contended that the verdict was excessive. In light of the evidence in the record regarding the extensive nature of the appellee's injuries, the Appeals Court declined to address that argument.

IV. CONCLUSION

Finding no error in the circuit court's rulings, the Appeals Court affirmed the September 13, 1999 judgment order for the appellee.

Chapter 7. The Doctrine of Unjust Enrichment

Unjust Enrichment comes into play whenever equity requires compensation be given for services rendered or consideration made. Under the doctrine of unjust enrichment, justice requires that benefit be denied to one who has profited unduly at the expense of another.

Suppose you sign a one-year lease on an apartment and make a required security deposit of $4000. You live out the term of the lease and give the landlord a one-month notice that you will not be renewing the lease agreement as you have bought a house in an adjoining township. The landlord inspects your apartment, and, finding no damage, takes your new address for the purpose of forwarding your security deposit refund. Six weeks go by and no refund. You try to get in touch with your former landlord but without results. Finally, it is obvious your former landlord is avoiding you and has no intention of returning your deposit.

The state you're living in requires such tenant-landlord disputes to first go to arbitration before going to court, and you file the necessary papers to comply. As a result of arbitration, it is determined that your former landlord does in fact owe you $4000 on a theory of *unjust enrichment* and is given thirty days to pay up. Instead of returning your money to you, however, your former landlord appeals the decision to a civil court.

The civil-court justice upholds the arbitration decision and tacks on a $4000 penalty award plus interest and costs, so what was once a mere $4000 controversy is now an award of over $10,000. The court upholds the arbitration decision verbatim, explaining that normally a court will not disturb such a decision unless there is an obvious error of law or the evidence relied upon will simply not support the finding.

The following AmeriPro case expands on the theory of *unjust enrichment.*

AMERIPRO SEARCH, INC., APPELLEE V. FLEMING STEEL COMPANY, APPELLANT
SUPERIOR COURT OF PENNSYLVANIA
787 A.2D 988, (2001 PA.)
NOVEMBER 16, 2001

LEGAL CONSIDERATIONS

Unjust Enrichment

The elements of *unjust enrichment* are benefits conferred on a defendant by a plaintiff, appreciation of such benefits by defendant, and acceptance and retention of such benefits under such circumstances that it would be inequitable for the defendant to retain the benefit without payment of value.

Implied-in-Fact Contracts

A contract implied in fact is an actual contract arising when there is an agreement, but the parties' intentions are inferred from their conduct in light of the circumstances.

Quasi-Contracts

A quasi-contract imposes a duty, not as a result of any agreement, whether express or implied, but in spite of the absence of an agreement when one party receives *unjust enrichment* at the expense of another. In determining if the doctrine applies, a court focuses not on the intention of the parties, but rather on whether the defendant was unjustly enriched.

PROCEDURAL POSTURE: Appellant company challenged the judgment against it in favor of appellee corporation in an action brought by the corporation seeking a commission from the appellant company, Fleming Steel.

OVERVIEW: The AmeriPro Corporation referred a job seeker to the Fleming Steel Company, but Fleming did not hire the individual because the his salary request was too high. Later, after the job seeker was laid off from his job with another company, he contacted Fleming on his own behalf and Fleming hired him. AmeriPro sent an invoice to Fleming claiming entitlement to a placement fee. Fleming refused to pay the demanded fee, and AmeriPro filed an action claiming entitlement to an employment-commission fee. The trial court found there was a contract implied in law, or what is termed a quasi-contract. On appeal, the Appeals Court found that there was no express contract because the parties never agreed to the terms of the fee, and there was no contract implied in fact: the Appeals Court found no unjust enrichment. The Appeals Court reasoned that the events leading to the hiring of the job seeker were separate from actions taken by AmeriPro. In addition, regardless of any benefit the company received by the

AmeriPro action of first introducing the job seeker to the company, the Appeals Court concluded the enrichment of Fleming was not unjust.

OUTCOME: The Superior Court reversed the judgment of the trial court.

OPINION: This lawsuit involved a commission sought by AmeriPro from Fleming. AmeriPro is an employment referral firm that places professional employees with interested employers. Fleming is a steel fabricator. In May of 1993, Elaine Brauninger, an agent of AmeriPro, contacted Fleming and inquired about Fleming's need for professional employees. Ms. Brauninger spoke to Mr. Dahlberg, Vice President of Engineering for Fleming, and during the conversation Mr. Dahlberg stated that Fleming was seeking an employee with an engineering background. In further conversations with Mr. Dahlberg, Ms. Brauninger was advised that in order to move forward with hiring such an employee, Ms. Brauninger would have to speak to Seth Kohn, president of Fleming who alone made all decisions relating to employment and salaries.

Ms. Brauninger then contacted Mr. Kohn. In their initial discussion, Ms. Brauninger advised Mr. Kohn that if her services were accepted she would be entitled to a fee equal to 30% of the candidate's first year's salary. Mr. Kohn did not agree because he believed the fee was too high. Mr. Kohn told Ms. Brauninger that the fee would be as determined by him and AmeriPro only after an agreement to hire a candidate was made. Ms. Brauninger agreed and told Mr. Kohn that she would work with him on the amount of the fee. Ms. Brauninger thereafter sent Mr. Kohn resumes of potential candidates and a copy of AmeriPro's Fee Agreement.

One of the candidates referred to Fleming by AmeriPro was Dominic Barracchini. Ms. Brauninger had contacted Mr. Barracchini in November of 1993 to determine whether Mr. Barracchini would be interested in a position at Fleming. At the time Mr. Barracchini was employed by Boardman Molded Products in the sales division. As a result of the contact, Mr. Barracchini informed Ms. Brauninger that he would be interested. Despite Mr. Barracchini's statement of interest, an interview could not be arranged with Fleming and Mr. Barracchini took employment with another company. In April of 1994, Ms. Brauninger again contacted Mr. Barracchini and informed him that she could arrange an interview with Fleming. Mr. Kohn interviewed Mr. Barracchini on April 8, 1994. Fleming did not hire Mr. Barracchini because Mr. Barracchini's salary request was too high.

In February of 1995, Mr. Barracchini was laid off and was again in the market for a job. Mr. Barracchini called Ms. Brauninger to inquire whether Fleming was still trying to fill the position for which he had previously interviewed. Ms. Brauninger never got back to Mr. Barracchini regarding his inquiry. Mr. Barracchini then contacted Fleming on his own. Mr. Kohn interviewed Mr. Barracchini in June of 1995. Fleming hired Mr. Barracchini as an engineer on June 19, 1995.

On September 6, 1995, AmeriPro sent an invoice to Fleming claiming entitlement to $14,400.00 for placement of Mr. Barracchini with Fleming, and Fleming refused to pay the demanded fee. AmeriPro then filed its lawsuit, claiming entitlement to the commission fee, and a non-jury trial followed. The trial court found in favor of AmeriPro in the amount of $15,981.76, finding that the parties had entered into both an express verbal contract and one by implication of law. Fleming filed post-trial motions. After considering the post-trial motion, the trial court rendered another decision. The trial court, in its second decision, concluded that it had erred in finding that an express contract had been formed. The trial court, however, denied the post-trial motions of Fleming and upheld its previous ruling in favor of AmeriPro but on the basis that there was a contract implied in law. The trial court determined that there was no express contract formed in this case. The trial court also concluded that there was no contract implied in fact because Fleming repeatedly stated its refusal of AmeriPro's fee of 30% of the candidate's annual salary. The trial court did, however, find that there was a contract implied in law, or a quasi-contract, because Fleming had been unjustly enriched. It was on this basis that the trial court ordered Fleming to pay AmeriPro the fee for placement of Barracchini.

Fleming then filed an appeal.

Upon review, the Appeals Court found that there was no contract, express or implied, i.e., the Appeals Court agreed with the trial court that there was no express contract in this case because the parties never agreed to the terms of the fee. Furthermore, the Appeals Court agreed that there was no contract implied in fact. A contract implied in fact is an actual contract arising when there is an agreement between the parties, but the parties' intentions are inferred from their conduct in light of the circumstances. See *Birchwood Lakes Community Assoc. v. Comis*, 442 A.2d 304, 308 (Pa. Super. 1982). Again, there was no agreement which could be inferred from the conduct of the parties in this case regarding a material element of the arrangement, specifically the fee agreement. The Appeals Court disagreed, however, with the trial court's determination that there was a contract implied in law, or a quasi-contract.

A quasi-contract imposes a duty, not as a result of any agreement, whether express or implied, but in spite of the absence of an agreement when one party receives unjust enrichment at the expense of another.

In determining if the doctrine of unjust enrichment applied, the Appeals Court focused not on the intention of the parties but rather on whether the defendant had been unjustly enriched. The elements of unjust enrichment are benefits conferred on a defendant by a plaintiff, appreciation of such benefits by the defendant, and acceptance and retention of such benefits under such circumstances that it would be inequitable for the defendant to retain the benefit without payment of value. The most significant element of the doctrine is whether the enrichment of the defendant is unjust; the doctrine does not apply simply because the defendant may have benefited as a result of the actions of the plaintiff. Where unjust enrichment is found, the law implies a quasi-contract which requires the defendant to pay to the plaintiff the value of the benefit conferred. In other words, the defendant makes restitution to the plaintiff in *quantum meruit*.

The Appeals Court could not find that Fleming was unjustly enriched. Mr. Barracchini was referred to Fleming and the first interview was arranged by AmeriPro. Fleming did not hire Mr. Barracchini at that time because the candidate's salary requirement was too high. Approximately ten months after Mr.

Barracchini's initial interview with Fleming, he was laid off. He contacted Ms. Brauninger to inquire about the job at Fleming and whether it was still open. Ms. Brauninger never responded to Mr. Barracchini's inquiry. As a result, Mr. Barracchini contacted Fleming directly to determine whether the position for which he had previously interviewed was still available. The parties, working directly with one another, arranged for the interview, and Fleming hired Mr. Barracchini after interviewing him in June of 1995.

The Appeals Court held that the events leading to the hiring of Mr. Barracchini were separate from any actions taken by Ms. Brauninger and AmeriPro on his behalf. While it is true that AmeriPro and Brauninger first introduced Barracchini to Fleming and the available position, that connection was broken when Fleming refused to hire Barracchini after the interview in April of 1994. After being laid off by his previous employer in February of 1995, Mr. Barracchini contacted Mr. Kohn directly. Mr. Barracchini's subsequent independent interaction with Mr. Kohn, which led to his actual employment by Fleming, was removed from previous actions taken by AmeriPro on his behalf.

While it may be argued that Fleming received a benefit from AmeriPro because Barracchini would not have known about the position at Fleming without the initial interaction involving AmeriPro, the doctrine of quasi-contract does not apply simply because the defendant may have benefited as a result of the actions of the plaintiff. Regardless of any benefit Fleming received by AmeriPro's action of first introducing Mr. Barracchini to Fleming, the enrichment of Fleming was not unjust. Mr. Barracchini approached Fleming the second time on his own and the two parties came to an agreement regarding Mr. Barracchini's employment without any involvement by AmeriPro. Fleming did nothing to wrongly secure the benefit of Mr. Barracchini's employment. Moreover, the arrangement regarding Mr. Barracchini's employment by Fleming was not under such circumstances that it would be inequitable or unconscionable for Fleming to retain the benefit without payment of value, here the placement fee. Because Fleming was not unjustly enriched, the Appeals Court found there was no quasi-contract, or contract implied in law. Thus, Fleming owes AmeriPro nothing in restitution.

The elements of *unjust enrichment* are benefits conferred on a defendant by a plaintiff, appreciation of such benefits by defendant, and acceptance and retention of such benefits under such circumstances that it would be inequitable for the defendant to retain the benefit without payment of value. The most significant element of the doctrine is whether the enrichment of the defendant is unjust; the doctrine does not apply simply because the defendant may have benefited as a result of the actions of the plaintiff. Where *unjust enrichment* is found, the law implies a quasi-contract which requires the defendant to pay to a plaintiff the value of the benefit conferred. In other words, the defendant makes restitution to the plaintiff in *quantum meruit*.

The Judgment of the trial court was reversed and Fleming was not required to make restitution.

CHAPTER 8. THE DOCTRINE OF UNCLEAN HANDS

There was a case concerning a man who feared that his assets would be seized to pay his bills. His only substantial asset was the house he owned, and he decided to transfer ownership of his house to his girlfriend and her parents in a effort to avoid losing the house to his creditors. As things developed, he was able to satisfy his creditors and they didn't come after his house, or what had been his house. Well, don't you know that while he was getting everyone off his back, he and his girlfriend had a falling out and she refused to give him back the house.

What was the poor man to do? He thought he'd go to court and petition for the return of the house which, he maintained, was rightfully his.

Surprise, surprise! Courts don't like being used to further illegal enterprises, and the court ruled sternly in this case, saying: "Under the doctrine of *unclean hands* this court will refuse recognition and relief to those guilty of unlawful conduct in a matter for which relief is sought. The doctrine of unclean hands protects the integrity of the court and the judicial process by denying relief to those persons whose very presence before the court is the result of some fraud or inequity." So, the poor man lost his house, but he'd made his ex-girlfriend deliriously happy!

The next example is a bit more complex.

MONETARY FUNDING GROUP, INC. V. JOHN PLUCHINO
APPELLATE COURT OF CONNECTICUT
867 A.2D 841
FEBRUARY 15, 2005

LEGAL CONSIDERATIONS

Civil Procedure / Pleading & Practice / Unclean-Hands Doctrine

Foreclosure is an equitable and not a common-law action. Those seeking equitable redress in our courts must come with clean hands. The doctrine of unclean hands expresses the principle that where a plaintiff seeks equitable relief,
he must show that his conduct has been fair, equitable and honest as to the particular controversy in issue. For a complainant to show that he is entitled to the
benefit of equity he must establish that he comes into the court of equity with
clean hands. The clean-hands doctrine is applied not for the protection of the
parties but for the protection of the court. It is applied for the advancement of
right and justice.

Civil Procedure / Standards of Review / Unclean-Hands Doctrine

Application of the doctrine of unclean hands rests within the sound discretion of the court. The exercise of such equitable authority is subject only to limited review on appeal. The only issue on appeal is whether the lower court acted
unreasonably and in clear abuse of its discretion.

Civil Procedure / Standards of Review / Clean-Hands Doctrine

The question of whether the clean-hands doctrine may be applied to the facts
found by the court is a question of law. Appellate courts must therefore engage
in a plenary review (a complete, exhaustive review) to determine whether a trial
court's conclusions were legally and logically correct and whether they are supported by the facts appearing in the record. The lower court's factual findings
underlying the special defense of unclean hands are reviewed pursuant to the
clearly erroneous standard.

Civil Procedure / Pleading & Practice / Clean-Hands Doctrine

A party seeking to invoke the clean-hands doctrine to bar equitable relief must
show that his opponent engaged in willful misconduct with regard to the matter
in litigation. The trial court enjoys broad discretion in determining whether the
promotion of public policy and the preservation of the courts' integrity dictate
that the clean-hands doctrine be invoked.

Contracts Law / Remedies on Default

Special defenses and counterclaims alleging a breach of an implied covenant
of good faith and fair dealing are not equitable defenses to a mortgage foreclosure.
(A court of equity, while sitting at the same bench as a court of law, decides matters from the bench on legal principle without the involvement of a jury.)

Real & Personal Property Law / Remedies on Default

Foreclosure is peculiarly an equitable action, and a court of equity may entertain such questions as are necessary to be determined in order that complete

justice may be done. Because a mortgage foreclosure action is an equitable proceeding, a court of equity may consider all relevant circumstances to ensure that complete justice is done.

Real & Personal Property Law / Remedies on Default

Foreclosure may be withheld by the court on the grounds of equitable considerations and principles.

Civil Procedure / Appeals / Standards of Review

Appellate courts apply the clearly erroneous standard of review to challenges of a trial court's factual findings.

Civil Procedure / Clearly Erroneous Review / Unconscionability

The question of unconscionability is a matter of law to be decided by the court based on all the facts and circumstances of the case. An appellate court's review on appeal is not limited to determining whether there has been clear error. The ultimate determination of whether a transaction is unconscionable is a question of law, not a question of fact, and the trial court's determination on that issue is subject to a plenary review on appeal. It also means, however, that the factual findings of the trial court that underlie that determination are entitled to the same deference on appeal that other factual findings command. Thus, those findings must stand unless they are clearly erroneous.

Contracts Law / Unconscionability

As applied to real estate mortgages, the doctrine of unconscionability draws heavily on its counterpart in the Uniform Commercial Code which, although formally limited to transactions involving personal property, furnishes a useful guide for real estate transactions. The basic test is whether, in the light of the general commercial background and the commercial needs of the particular trade or case, the clauses involved are so one-sided as to be unconscionable under the circumstances existing at the time of the making of the contract.

Torts / Unfair Business Practices

Connecticut courts, when determining whether a practice violates the Connecticut Unfair Trade Practices Act, will consider (1) whether the practice, without necessarily having been previously considered unlawful, offends public policy as it has been established by statutes, the common law, or, otherwise, and whether it is within at least the penumbra of some common-law, statutory, or other established concept of unfairness; (2) whether it is immoral, unethical, oppressive, or unscrupulous; (3) whether it causes substantial injury to consumers (or competitors or other businessmen).

Torts / Unfair Business Practices

A violation of the Connecticut Unfair Trade Practices Act may be established by showing either an actual deceptive practice or a practice amounting to a violation of public policy.

Civil Procedure / Pleading & Practice

Pleadings have their place in our system of jurisprudence. While they are not held to the strict and artificial standard that once prevailed, no orderly administration of justice is possible without pleadings. The purpose of a complaint or counterclaim is to limit the issues at trial, and such pleadings are calculated to inform an adversary of the issue(s) involved.

Civil Procedure / Pleadings

The principle that a plaintiff may rely only upon what he has alleged is basic. It is fundamental in our law that the right of a plaintiff to recover is limited to the allegations of his complaint.

Real & Personal Property Law / Remedies on Default

It is well established that a mortgagee is entitled to pursue its remedy at law on the notes, or to pursue its remedy in equity upon the mortgage, or to pursue both. A note and a mortgage given to secure it are separate instruments executed for different purposes. In a state action for foreclosure of the mortgage and upon the note are regarded and treated, in practice, as separate and distinct causes of action, although both may be pursued in a foreclosure suit.

PRIOR HISTORY: (Appeal from Superior Court, judicial district of Fairfield). Action to foreclose a mortgage on certain real property and for other relief, brought to the Superior Court in the judicial district of Fairfield where the defendant filed a counterclaim; thereafter, the matter was tried to the court of equity; judgment in favor of the defendant on the complaint, from which the plaintiff appealed to the Appeals Court.

DISPOSITION: Judgment affirmed.

PROCEDURAL POSTURE: Plaintiff brought an action against defendant to foreclose a mortgage on certain real estate. Defendant filed a counterclaim alleging the special defenses of *unclean hands* and *unconscionability*, and alleging a violation of the Connecticut Unfair Trade Practices Act, Connecticut General Statute §42-110a et sequitur (following). The Superior Court in the Judicial District of Fairfield (Connecticut), entered judgment for defendant. Plaintiff appealed.

OVERVIEW: Defendant had shown successfully that plaintiff engaged in intentional misconduct with respect to the various transactions in order to obtain excessive fees and costs as well as to foreclose on the defendant's property. Despite the fact that the note was a commercial transaction, defendant was an unsophisticated borrower and was unrepresented by counsel, plaintiff charged an arbitrarily high annual percentage rate of interest and misrepresented the rate to defendant, and plaintiff failed to conduct a "bona fide evaluation" of defendant's ability to repay the loan. Thus, the superior court properly applied the *unclean-hands doctrine*. Also, the lower court's underlying factual findings with respect to unconscionability were not clearly erroneous. As the superior court properly applied the doctrines of unclean hands and unconscionability, judgment was proper on the Connecticut Unfair Trade Practices Act counterclaim as entered by defendant. Finally, because plaintiff failed to bring an action at law as to the note and sought, instead, the equitable proceeding of foreclosure, the issue of whether an appropriate remedy included repayment of the loan plus the interest was not before the court (an equitable proceeding of foreclosure does not involve trial by jury). Plaintiff was not entitled to a remedy it did not request.

OUTCOME: The judgment of the court of equity was affirmed by the Appeals Court in favor of the defendant.

OPINION: The plaintiff, Monetary Funding Group, Inc., appealed from the judgment of the trial court, rendered after a hearing in equity, in favor of the defendant, John Pluchino. On appeal, the plaintiff claimed the court improperly (1) determined that it, the plaintiff, had *unclean hands*, (2) determined that it had made an unconscionable loan, (3) determined that it had violated the Connecticut Unfair Trade Practices Act and (4) imposed a remedy precluding it from collecting principal and interest.

The Appeals Court found the following facts relevant to the plaintiff's appeal. In the spring of 2000, the defendant, who previously had owned and operated a gasoline station and radiator business for more than thirty years, sought to obtain financing to purchase a convenience store and Laundromat business (business). He applied for a loan from a bank, but was turned down as a result of concerns regarding the stability of a new restaurant, another business, with which he had recently replaced his radiator business.

The defendant, who was not represented by counsel, contacted Paul Dwyer, the president of the plaintiff corporation. He informed Dwyer that he needed to borrow $20,000 in order to purchase the Laundromat business. On April 13, 2000, the defendant executed a ninety day promissory note in favor of the plaintiff, secured by a mortgage on the defendant's unencumbered property located at 621 Washington Avenue in Bridgeport. The interest rate disclosed on the ninety day note was 15 percent. Additional terms included a $3000 origination fee, a $400 processing fee, $937.50 in prepaid interest, $550 for attorney's fees and $112.50 for a courier fee. In short, the defendant incurred a liability of $25,000 and received a net amount from the note of $20,000. The plaintiff also indicated an annual interest rate of 28 percent. After ninety days, the loan was to be restructured through a refinancing into an installment loan. Dwyer was aware that the defendant lacked any other means to repay the note, except for refinancing at the conclusion of the ninety days. Dwyer planned to broker the second loan and receive additional broker fees.

In January 2001, approximately five months after the defendant had defaulted on the note, the plaintiff located a lender willing to refinance the defendant's debt. At the closing, the defendant for the first time learned that the refinancing consisted of an $80,000 loan from an entity known as InterBay Funding. According to the proposed terms of the second loan, the defendant would receive only $38,721.25 of the $80,000. A total of $28,678.31 would pay off the original note to the plaintiff, who also would receive a broker fee of $4,800. In summary, considering both the original $25,000 note and the second proposed loan in the amount of $80,000, the defendant would receive in hand a total of $58,721.25 and incur up-front costs of $21,278.75 ($5000 for the first transaction and $16,278.75 for the second transaction).

The defendant expressed concern regarding the $80,000 loan. He requested time to have an attorney review the proposed arrangement, but was told that was not necessary. The defendant, already in default with respect to the original note, never executed the second loan, nor did he ever repay the original note. The plaintiff commenced the present foreclosure action on April 23, 2001. In its prayer for relief, the plaintiff sought a judgment of strict foreclosure. The defendant answered the complaint and, on April 10, 2002, set forth eleven special defenses and a counterclaim alleging a Connecticut Unfair Trade Practices Act violation. The court found that the defendant had demonstrated that the plaintiff had unclean hands and that the loan transaction was unconscionable. Additionally, it found in favor of the defendant with respect to the Connecticut Unfair Trade Practices Act counterclaim and awarded attorney's fees in the amount of $6750 to the defendant. The instant appeal followed.

As a general matter, the Appeals Court noted that it is well established that foreclosure is peculiarly an equitable action, and the trial court may entertain such questions as are necessary to be determined in order that complete justice may be done. Because a mortgage foreclosure action is an equitable proceeding, the trial court may consider all relevant circumstances to ensure that complete justice is done. Foreclosure may be withheld by the court on the grounds of equitable considerations and principles. With those legal principles in mind, the Appeals Court turned to the plaintiff's specific claims.

I

The plaintiff first claimed that the court improperly determined that it had unclean hands. Specifically, the plaintiff argues that several of the court's factual findings were clearly erroneous and that the court improperly applied the doctrine of unclean hands. The Appeals Court was not persuaded.

The starting point for the resolution of that issue was the determination of the appropriate standard of review. The Appeals Court turned to the Connecticut Supreme Court's decision in *Thompson v. Orcutt*, 257 Conn. 301, 777 A.2d 670 (2001), for guidance in resolving the issue. In Thompson, the Supreme Court stated: "Application of the doctrine of unclean hands rests within the sound discretion of the trial court. The exercise of such equitable authority is subject only to limited review on appeal. The only issue on appeal is whether the trial court has acted unreasonably and in clear abuse of its discretion. In determining whether the trial court abused its discretion, the Appeals Court must make every reasonable presumption in favor of the trial court's action. Whether the trial court properly interpreted the doctrine of unclean hands, however, is a legal question distinct from the trial court's discretionary decision whether to apply it." Similarly, the Appeals Court stated that "the question of whether the clean-hands doctrine may be applied to the facts found by the court of equity is a question of law. We must therefore engage in a plenary review to determine whether the court's conclusions were legally and logically correct and whether they are supported by the facts appearing in the record." The court's factual findings underlying the special defense of unclean hands, however, are reviewed pursuant to the clearly erroneous standard. See *Willow Funding Co., L.P. v. Grencom Associates*, 63 Conn. App. 832, 840, 779 A.2d 174 (2001).

The Appeals Court reiterated that foreclosure is an equitable action. "Our jurisprudence has recognized that those seeking equitable redress in our courts must come with clean hands. The doctrine of unclean hands expresses the principle that where a plaintiff seeks equitable relief, he must show that his conduct has been fair, equitable and honest as to the particular controversy in issue. For a plaintiff to show that he is entitled to the benefit of equity he must establish that he comes into court with clean hands. The clean-hands doctrine is applied not for the protection of the parties but for the protection of the court. It is applied for the advancement of right and justice. The defendant seeking to invoke the clean-hands doctrine to obtain equitable relief must show that his opponent, the plaintiff, engaged in willful misconduct with regard to the matter in litigation. The court of equity enjoys broad discretion in determining whether the promotion of public policy and the preservation of the courts' integrity dictate that the clean-hands doctrine be invoked."

The court found the following facts that, *in toto*, supported a determination that the plaintiff had unclean hands. Despite the fact that the note was a commercial transaction, the defendant was an unsophisticated borrower and was unrepresented by legal counsel. The plaintiff charged an arbitrarily high annual percentage rate of interest and misrepresented the rate to the defendant. Dwyer testified that he arbitrarily charged the defendant a 15 percent origination fee in the amount of $3000, which was significantly higher than the 2 to 6 percent customarily applied to commercial loans. The plaintiff failed to conduct a "bona fide evaluation" of the defendant's ability to repay the loan, and Dwyer conceded that he was aware that repayment by the defendant was impossible but for a subsequent refinancing. Lastly, the plaintiff, knowing the defendant's dire financial situation with respect to the note, did not offer him an opportunity to discuss or to evaluate the terms of the second loan. In short, the court found that the plaintiff misled the defendant, who thought he was borrowing a net of $20,000 in exchange for fees totaling $4000 to $5000 when, in reality, the terms consisted of an $80,000 loan with the defendant receiving approximately $ 59,000 and the plaintiff and InterBay Funding receiving approximately $21,000 in fees. The court specifically credited the defendant's testimony that Dwyer had represented that the fees would not exceed the $4000 to $5000 range. "The court finds that the reasonable implication from the evidence is that the transaction was structured by the plaintiff for its own benefit in order for it to acquire an origination fee, a loan processing fee, as well as a finder's fee, all of which the plaintiff could not have ordinarily demanded as part of a single loan transaction." Essentially, the court found a single transaction that required two steps to completion: first, the initial ninety day note for $20,000 and, second, the refinancing that consisted of an $80,000 loan for the purpose of maximizing fees for the plaintiff.

A

The plaintiff challenged certain of the court's factual findings. The Appeals Court applied the clearly erroneous standard of review to those challenges. First, the plaintiff argued that contrary to the court's memorandum of decision, there was evidence as to why the transaction was structured so that a refinancing would be necessary. According to the plaintiff, the defendant was unable to obtain a bank loan because his restaurant business was not yet established. That claim, however, failed to account for the testimony of the defendant that he sought to borrow only $20,000 to purchase another business. Although he discussed a subsequent purchase of the buildings that would require an additional $80,000 at the time of the loan, the defendant requested only a $20,000 loan. Moreover, the clear import of the defendant's testimony, which the court credited, was his belief that the plaintiff would simply turn the existing note into a monthly installment loan, and not obtain funds from a new lender with all of the accompanying fees and costs. Further, the defendant testified that he relied on Dwyer's representation that the only costs associated with borrowing the $20,000 consisted of the $4000 to $5000 in fees that the two had discussed. The Appeals Court determined that it could not say the findings of the court of equity were clearly erroneous.

The plaintiff also argued that there was no evidence that the defendant would be able to obtain an installment loan. There was evidence that the defendant's application to a bank had been denied. The defendant, however, testified that there were no time constraints on when the purchase of the businesses would occur. Thus, the defendant had no immediate need for the funds that would warrant the exorbitant fees generated by the plaintiff's proposed two step transaction. The Appeals Court concluded, therefore, that there was evidence in the record to support the findings underlying the special defense of unclean hands and, accordingly, that such findings were not clearly erroneous.

B

The plaintiff also claimed that on the basis of the facts found by the court, the doctrine of unclean hands was applied improperly. That claim implicates the plenary standard of review. The court stated that "under these particular circumstances, where the borrower was unsophisticated, the borrower was misled and was unquestionably unable to comply with the terms of the note, the plaintiff has attempted to take advantage of the defendant in order to charge arbitrarily high fees as part of a transaction structured by the plaintiff precisely for that purpose. The court's enforcement of this loan according to its terms would involve the court in this unfair transaction in a manner that would run afoul of the unclean hands doctrine."

The Appeals Court reviewed the entire record before it and determined that the defendant had shown successfully that the plaintiff engaged in intentional misconduct with respect to the various transactions in order to obtain excessive fees and costs, as well as to foreclose on the Washington Avenue property. On that basis, particularly with respect to the facts that were set forth, the Court determined that the trial court properly concluded the plaintiff violated the clean-hands doctrine because the plaintiff's conduct was not fair, equitable and honest. Accordingly, the court's application of the unclean-hands doctrine was legally and logically correct and supported by the record.

II

The plaintiff next claimed that the court improperly determined that it made an unconscionable loan. Specifically, the plaintiff argued that several of the court's factual findings underlying the determination of unconscionability were clearly erroneous. The Appeals Court disagreed.

"Our first consideration is the standard of review for a claim of unconscionability. The question of unconscionability is a matter of law to be decided by the court based on all the facts and circumstances of the case. Our review on appeal is not limited to determining whether there has been clear error. The ultimate determination of whether a transaction is unconscionable is a question of law, not a question of fact, and the court of equity's determination on that issue is subject to a plenary review on appeal. It also means, however, that the factual findings of the trial court, the court of equity, that underlie that determination are entitled to the same deference on appeal that other factual findings command. Thus, those findings must stand unless they are clearly erroneous.

"The purpose of the doctrine of unconscionability is to prevent oppression and unfair surprise. As applied to real estate mortgages, the doctrine of unconscionability draws heavily on its counterpart in the Uniform Commercial Code which, although formally limited to transactions involving personal property, furnishes a useful guide for real property transactions. As Official Comment 1 to §2-302 of the Uniform Commercial Code suggests, the basic test is whether, in the light of the general commercial background and the commercial needs of the particular trade or case, the clauses involved are so one-sided as to be unconscionable under the circumstances existing at the time of the making of the contract. Unconscionability is determined on a case-by-case basis, taking into account all of the relevant facts and circumstances." Because the plaintiff challenged only the factual findings that related to the court's finding of unconscionability, the Appeals Court employed the clearly erroneous standard of review.

The plaintiff again argued that there was no evidence the defendant was misled with respect to the refinancing of the note not exceeding $5000, but the Appeals Court had already rejected that argument. The plaintiff then claimed that the defendant's failure to complain at the closing about the amount of the loan indicated that he wanted the loan. The plaintiff contended that the defendant objected only to the cost and fees associated with the second part of the transaction, and not the actual amount offered. The Appeals Court held that that argument failed to account for the direct testimony of the defendant, who stated that although that amount was discussed in a preliminary fashion, he wanted to borrow only $20,000 until he determined the viability of the new businesses.

III

The plaintiff next claimed that the court improperly determined that it violated the Connecticut Unfair Trade Practices Act (CUTPA). Specifically, the plaintiff argued that the trial court's finding of a CUTPA violation, as alleged in the defendant's counterclaim, was based on improper findings of unclean hands and an unconscionable transaction. In parts I and II, the Appeals Court determined that the court of equity properly applied the doctrines of unclean hands and unconscionability and, accordingly, the plaintiff's argument with respect to the CUTPA counterclaim was fatally flawed.

"Connecticut courts, when determining whether a practice violates CUTPA, will consider (1) whether the practice, without necessarily having been previously considered unlawful, offends public policy as it has been established by statutes, the common law, or otherwise whether, in other words, it is within at least the penumbra of some common-law, statutory, or other established concept of unfairness; (2) whether it is immoral, unethical, oppressive, or unscrupulous; (3) whether it causes substantial injury to consumers (or competitors or other businessmen). Thus, a violation of CUTPA may be established by showing either an actual deceptive practice or a practice amounting to a violation of public policy. Whether a practice is unfair and thus violates CUTPA is an issue of fact. The facts found must be viewed within the context of the totality of circumstances which are uniquely available to the trial court. Additionally, our Supreme Court has stated that all three criteria do not need to be satisfied to support a finding of unfairness. A practice may be unfair because of the degree to which it meets one of the criteria or because to a lesser extent it meets all three criteria. Thus a violation of CUTPA may be established by showing either an actual deceptive practice or a practice amounting to a violation of public policy."

It was determined that the lower court decided the plaintiff acted with unclean hands and engaged in an unconscionable transaction. The conduct of the plaintiff, therefore, was unfair, oppressive and unscrupulous, and constituted a violation of the Connecticut Unfair Trade Practices Act (CUTPA) Accordingly, the court awarded the defendant $ 6750 in attorneys' fees.

On appeal, the plaintiff challenged only the court's conclusions with respect to the special defenses of unclean hands and unconscionability. Because the Appeals Court had already determined that the trial court properly resolved those issues, the plaintiff's challenge to the judgment on the CUTPA counterclaim also failed.

IV

The plaintiff's final claim was that the court of equity improperly imposed a remedy precluding it from collecting principal and interest on the $20,000 note. Specifically, the plaintiff argued that it was entitled to recover the balance of the note plus interest. The Appeals Court disagreed.

At the outset of the Court's discussion, it noted that "pleadings have their place in our system of jurisprudence. While they are not held to the strict and artificial standard that once prevailed, we still cling to the belief that no orderly administration of justice is possible without them. The purpose of a complaint (a pleading) or counterclaim is to limit the issues at trial, and such pleadings are calculated to prevent surprise. It is fundamental in our law that the right of a party to recover is limited to the allegations in his pleading. Facts found but not claimed cannot be made the basis for a recovery. Thus, it is clear that the court is not permitted to decide issues outside of those raised in the pleadings. A judgment in the absence of written pleadings defining the issues would not merely be erroneous, it would be void. Put another way, the principle that a plaintiff may rely only upon what he has alleged is basic. It is fundamental in our law that the right of a plaintiff to recover is limited to the allegations of his complaint."

The only count in the plaintiff's complaint sought to foreclose the defendant's property. The plaintiff elected the equitable proceeding of foreclosure rather than to pursue an action at law (common law) for the amount due on the note. The Appeals Court stated "It is well established that the mortgagee is entitled to pursue its remedy at law on the notes, or to pursue its remedy in equity upon the mortgage, or to pursue both. A note and a mortgage given to secure a loan are separate instruments, executed for different purposes and in this State action for foreclosure of the mortgage and upon the note are regarded and treated, in practice, as separate and distinct causes of action, although both may be pursued in a foreclosure suit. In the present case, the plaintiff failed to bring an action at law as to the note and sought, instead, the equitable proceeding of foreclosure. On that basis, the court was limited either to foreclose the property in favor of the plaintiff or to find in favor of the defendant. The issue of whether an appropriate remedy would include repayment of the loan plus the interest simply was not before the court. The plaintiff is not entitled to a remedy that it did not plead."

The judgment of the court of equity was affirmed in favor of the defendant.

CHAPTER 9. THE DOCTRINE OF UNCONSCIONABILITY

The foremost aspect of the *Doctrine of Unconscionablility* has to do with contracts that are not freely bargained by the parties. Such contracts are called contracts of adhesion. The contract you sign with a credit card company, for example, is a contract of adhesion in as much as the terms in their entirety are dictated by the credit card company: Take it or leave it! Courts across the country have upheld such contracts except when they impose provisions that "shock the conscience," that are *unconscionable*, in other words.

The doctrine has both a procedural and a substantive element. The former focuses on oppression , i.e., a subscriber must accept the terms of the agreement as presented, and the latter focuses on the harshness of the terms as presented by the agreement. For a contract to be unconscionable it must have both a procedural and a substantive component. A court may refuse to enforce an unconscionable clause of a contract and enforce the remainder of the contract, or it may refuse to enforce the entire contract if there are two or more unconscionable clauses

In the many situations in which the doctrine of *unconscionability* has been applied are cases of home-improvement contracts, rent-to-buy agreements, equipment leases, gasoline-station leases, etc.

There was a case where a young lady had purchased an annuity from an insurance company with funds she had received as the result of an automobile accident. The young lady happened to meet a young man with whom she fell in love around the time the value of her annuity reached an amount in excess of $200,000. It so happened that her lover was an ex-con who promptly introduced her to hard drugs. The ex-con saw an opportunity for enrichment and convinced the young lady to sell her annuity for $60,000 and proceeded set things up with some underworld acquaintances of his. The acquaintances hired a lawyer and did everything legally. The ex-con made out handsomely! It seems he owed his friends $10,000 which they deducted from the $60,000 when payment to the young lady was made.

The young lady finally came to her senses and brought a lawsuit seeking to void the agreement. Upon repayment of the money she had received, the court voided the agreement and the young lady got her annuity back. The case that follows illustrates how *unconscionability* can come into play when a large national corporation decides to trim operating costs by getting rid of employees who are high on the salary-benefits scale.

SHO-PRO OF INDIANA, INC., APPELLANT-PLAINTIFF
V. ROGER J. BROWN, APPELLEE-DEFENDANT
COURT OF APPEALS OF INDIANA, THIRD DISTRICT
585 N.E.2D 1357
FEBRUARY 11, 1992

LEGAL CONSIDERATIONS

Contracts Law / Unconscionability

Indiana Code Annotated §26-1-2-302 provides that if the court as a matter of law finds the contract or any clause of the contract to have been unconscionable at the time it was made, the court may refuse to enforce the contract, or it may enforce the remainder of the contract without the unconscionable clause, or it may so limit the application of any unconscionable clause as to avoid any unconscionable result.

Contracts Law / Unconscionability

The Indiana Supreme Court has defined an unconscionable contract to be one which no sensible man not under delusion, duress or in distress would make, and such as no honest and fair man would accept. A contract may be declared unconscionable when there is a great disparity in bargaining power which leads the party with the lesser power to sign a contract unwillingly or unaware of its terms.

Contracts Law / Unconscionability

Pursuant to Indiana Code Annotated §35-43-6-8, a home improvement contract is unconscionable if an unreasonable difference exists between the fair market value of the services, materials, and work performed or to be performed and the home improvement contract price.

Contracts Law

The question whether a document, a contract, has been assented to by the parties as a complete expression of their intent is an ordinary question of fact, and no relevant evidence on this question is excluded on the mere ground that it is offered in the form of oral testimony.

Contracts Law

The expressions contained in a document purporting to be a sales contract require a meeting of the minds, the absence of which prevents the formation of a contract. The intention of the parties is a factual matter to be determined by the trier of fact from all the circumstances, and a party relying on an express contract bears the burden of proving its existence. Where there is probative evidence to support the conclusion that there was no meeting of the minds between the parties, the Court will not disturb that conclusion.

PRIOR HISTORY: APPEAL FROM THE DELAWARE CIRCUIT COURT.

PROCEDURAL POSTURE: Plaintiff home improvement company appealed from the judgment of the Delaware Circuit Court (the trial court) entered in favor of defendant consumer, asserting the trial court erred in finding no binding contract between the parties, and in finding that even if there was a binding contract, such contract was unconscionable and therefore unenforceable.

OVERVIEW: Plaintiff home improvement company visited the residence of defendant consumer in order to sell him replacement windows. After a five hour sales pitch, the consumer signed several documents without reading them. Several days later, the company notified him that he had purchased replacement windows on credit for $4,322. The consumer protested that he had not purchased any windows. The matter was next called to the consumer's attention when he received a copy of the complaint instituting this action to collect the contract price, attorneys fees, and prejudgment interest. The court found that because the consumer did not read the documents, misunderstood their purpose, and was twice assured that he had no obligation to purchase windows, the finding that there was no meeting of the minds was not clearly erroneous. A finding that there were elements of unconscionability in the contract price was also not clearly erroneous as $3,241 of the $4,322 purchase price was assigned as costs, commissions, and profits.

OUTCOME: The judgment of the trial court was in all respects affirmed in favor of the defendant.

OPINION: Sho-Pro of Indiana, Inc. (Sho-Pro) appeals a negative judgment entered in favor of Roger J. Brown, raising two issues for our review, which we restate as follows:

I. Whether the trial court erred in finding that there was no binding contract between the parties.

II. Whether the trial court erred in finding that, even if there was a binding contract between the parties, such contract was unconscionable and therefore unenforceable.

We affirm.

The evidence most favorable to the judgment reveals that representatives of Sho-Pro visited the residence of Roger J. Brown in order to sell him replacement windows. They obtained Brown's name through a "lead card" obtained as a result of Brown's entry in a "sweepstakes contest" to win a house full of windows or $500, with no obligation. The entrant was also entitled to a "turkey platter" merely for entering. After a four-to-five-hour sales pitch, Brown signed a number of documents and received a tin platter.

Three days later, a representative of Sho-Pro left a card at Brown's door. Upon contacting Sho-Pro and inquiring about the card, Brown was informed by the woman who answered the phone that he had purchased four replacement windows on credit for $4,322. Brown protested that he had not purchased any windows, that he could not afford $4,322, and that he did not even own the house in which he resided. The woman then told him that there would be no problem and that the order would be stopped.

No windows were ever installed, but a week or two later a representative of Sho-Pro arrived to measure windows. When Brown again protested that he did not order any windows, the representative assured him that he was not measuring because Brown was buying the windows, but in case Brown changed his mind about the windows or someone else moved into the house. On that basis, Brown assented to the measurements. He again signed a document stating that the man had been to his house because the man said he needed Brown's signature in order to get paid for measuring the windows.

The next time the matter was called to Brown's attention was when he received a copy of the complaint instituting this action to collect the contract price, attorneys fees, and prejudgment interest. The case was tried to a judge, who entered findings of fact concluding that there was no contract between the parties, and even if there were a contract, the bargaining process rendered the contract unconscionable and therefore unenforceable. Judgment was entered in favor of Brown and Sho-Pro appealed.

The trial court entered findings of fact and conclusions of law on some but not all issues litigated. When such occurs, two separate and distinct standards of review are applied to the judgment of the trial court. A general judgment standard of review is applied to those issues not supported by findings of fact. Issues supported by findings of fact are treated differently on review. On those issues where the Court has entered findings, the Court employs the following standard of review: the Court first must determine whether the evidence supports the findings; then determine whether the findings support the judgment. The judgment of the trial court will be affirmed if the Appeals Court concludes that the special findings support the judgment and are not clearly erroneous. A judgment is clearly erroneous where a review of the record leaves the Court with a firm conviction that a mistake has been made.

I. Contract

Sho-Pro argued that Brown's defense that he misunderstood the transaction was not a defense under Indiana law. Sho-Pro argued that the parol evidence rule prevents the trial court from examining the circumstances surrounding the transaction, and that "there is not even a scintilla to support the conclusion that Roger Brown didn't know what he was doing." (The parol evidence rule does not allow for oral amendment of contractual terms except in circumstances of fraud, duress, or mutual mistake.)

Initially, the Court noted that Sho-Pro's argument regarding the parol evidence rule lacked merit. The plain language of the Uniform Commercial Code requires a writing "intended by the parties as a final written expression of their agreement" before the parol evidence rule becomes applicable. Simply stated, the rule presumes a valid written contract between parties. The question of whether a document has been assented to by the parties as a complete expression of their intent is an ordinary question of fact, and no relevant evidence on this question is excluded on the mere ground that it is offered in the form of oral testimony. No evidence was introduced in the incident case which purported to vary the terms of the written document offered; rather, the question was whether there was a meeting of the minds between the parties as regards the installation of windows. The Court held that the parol evidence rule had no application, and that Sho-Pro's argument lacked merit.

The expressions contained in a document purporting to be a sales contract require a meeting of the minds, the absence of which prevents the formation of a contract. *Continental Grain Co. v. Followell*, 475 N.E.2d 318, 321. The intention of the parties is a factual matter to be determined by the trier of fact from all the circumstances, and a party relying on an express contract bears the burden of proving the existence of same. Where there is probative evidence to support the conclusion that there was no meeting of the minds between the parties, the Court will not disturb that conclusion.

In the incident case, the evidence revealed that Brown had not read the documents he signed. Moreover, there was evidence that he misunderstood the purpose of the documents:

> Q. Why did you sign those documents if you couldn't afford the windows? Why did you sign the different documents that you signed?
>
> A. One of them was for the day they came out to my house and showed me a demonstration. I was at my residence and they performed a demonstration.

Thus, Brown testified that he thought he was signing a document certifying that the salesman had performed a demonstration for him. In addition, Brown personally told two employees of Sho-Pro that he did not intend to buy replacement windows, and was twice assured that he had incurred no obligation. The Court held that these facts supported an inference that Brown never intended to incur an obligation to purchase windows.

Sho-Pro argued that Brown had to have known that he was applying for windows because he applied for financing. However, the record revealed that he did not fill out the financing form, but was asked a number of questions regarding the ownership of his house and his debts in the course of the "demonstration". He merely signed the document where he was told. Even if he had filled out the financing form, it would not necessarily follow that he had agreed to purchase the windows. Parties to sales transactions often secure financing before they agree to go through with the transaction, the real estate sales industry is just one such example.

The Appeals Court determined that there was probative evidence to support the trial court's finding that there was no meeting of the minds between Brown and Sho-Pro, and the Court could not say that the findings on the issue were clearly erroneous. Accordingly, the trial court did not err in concluding that there was no binding contract between the parties.

II. Unconscionability

The Court that the trial court did not err in concluding there was no binding contract between the parties. Nonetheless, The Court also addressed Sho-Pro's arguments concerning the trial court's finding on the issue of unconscionability. Sho-Pro essentially argued that there was no evidence to support the trial court's finding of unconscionability. However, Indiana Code 26-1-2-302 provides in relevant part that: "If the court as a matter of law finds the contract or any clause of the contract to have been unconscionable at the time it was made, the court may refuse to enforce the contract, or it may enforce the remainder of the contract without the unconscionable clause, or it may so limit the application of any unconscionable clause as to avoid any unconscionable result."

The Indiana Supreme Court has defined an unconscionable contract to be one which no sensible man not under delusion, duress or in distress would make, and such as no honest and fair man would accept. *Weaver v. American Oil Co.,* 276 N.E.2d 144, 146. *Weaver* also stands for the proposition that a contract may be declared unconscionable when there is a great disparity in bargaining power which leads the party with the lesser power to sign a contract unwillingly or unaware of its terms. Finally, the trial court also made reference to the statutory provisions on unconscionability of home improvement contracts: "A home improvement contract is unconscionable if an unreasonable difference exists between the fair market value of the services, materials, and work performed or to be performed and the home improvement contract price."

The evidence here revealed that Brown responded to a contest which purported to award a free "house full of windows" or $500 and promised a "turkey platter" while the contestant incurred "no obligation." For his participation, Brown was subjected to a four-to-five-hour "demonstration" of the replacement windows conducted by two Sho-Pro representatives, including an inquiry into his financial background. He assumed after the demonstration that he did not order any windows, only to later find out that he had purchased four replacement windows at a price of $4,322. The sales contract was prepared by Sho-Pro and filled out by representatives of Sho-Pro. Brown did not read the contract before signing it and did not read any of the "fine print" on the back. The evidence also reveals that the windows cost Sho-Pro a total of $1,080.50. The remaining $3,241.50 was assigned as "lead costs" of $432.20, "sales management costs" of $600.61, "administrative costs" of $379.99, sales commissions of $648.30, and profit of $648.30. Sho-Pro's president was cross-examined at length regarding his justification for these various costs. These figures total $3,789.90. Presumably, the remaining $532.10

would represent the installation costs for the four windows (the windows were never delivered nor installed).

The Appeals Court could not conclude that the trial court was clearly erroneous in finding elements of unconscionability in both the circumstances surrounding the signing of the contract and the contract price itself. Upon finding that the contract (if a contract existed) was unconscionable, the trial court could decline to enforce it. The Appeals Court found no error and, finding none, affirmed the trial court's judgment in favor of the defendant.

A concurring opinion was entered, concurring in the result on the basis that the contract with Sho-Pro was unconscionable. The evidence not only demonstrated that the contract was unconscionable, but that the contract was void due to fraud and misrepresentation on the part of Sho-Pro.

Chapter 10. The Doctrine of the Fruit of the Poisonous Tree

This doctrine has to do with evidence gathered in the course of an illegal search and seizure in violation of rights against such searches as guaranteed by the Fourth Amendment to the United States Constitution. The principle is that such evidence is tainted as a result of being illegally obtained and is therefore excluded from consideration as evidence, the so called "exclusionary rule" as applied to *fruit of the poisonous tree.* The exclusionary rule is calculated to discourage law-enforcement personnel from disregarding the constitutional mandate against "trumped" searches and seizures. The bedrock of the exclusionary rule is the *doctrine of the poisonous tree.*

There was a case in the Eastern United States recently that involved an illegal stop by a campus-police patrol car off campus at the time of the stop. It seems that the campus police thought another vehicle was driving in a hazardous way and flashed the patrol car's blue light. The car stopped and the driver got out of his car and the campus policeman approached the individual. The campus policeman thought he smelled alcohol and called in the city police. In the course of events, the city police asked for permission to search the vehicle and its two passengers and, finding marijuana, arrested both occupants of the vehicle. At trial, the marijuana evidence was thrown out because it was developed from an illegal stop, *fruit of the poisonous tree!*

STATE OF WASHINGTON, RESPONDENT, V. FLOYD TAKESGUN, APPELLANT.
COURT OF APPEALS OF WASHINGTON, DIVISION THREE, PANEL FOUR
949 P.2D 845, (1998 WASH.)
JANUARY 22, 1998

LEGAL CONSIDERATIONS

Constitutional Law / Search & Seizure

A proponent of a motion to suppress evidence must show that the challenged governmental action infringed upon his own fourth amendment rights.

Passengers without a possessory interest in a stopped vehicle have no legitimate privacy interest in it and cannot, therefore, challenge its search.

A police officer's act of stopping a vehicle and detaining its occupants constitutes a seizure under the fourth amendment of the U.S. Const. and such act must be reasonable.

Criminal Law & Procedure / Search & Seizure / Standing

A passenger has standing to challenge a stop that constitutes his own seizure, regardless of whether he has standing to challenge a subsequent search of the vehicle. Standing to challenge a stop presents issues separate and distinct from standing to challenge a search.

Constitutional Law / Search & Seizure / Vehicle Searches

Whereas a search of an automobile does not implicate a passenger's U.S. Constitution fourth amendment rights, a stop results in the seizure of the passenger and driver alike. Thus, the passenger of a stopped automobile does have standing to challenge the seizure as unconstitutional.

Constitutional Law / Warrantless Searches

If a stop was unreasonable, the seized contraband is subject to exclusion under the *"fruit-of-the poison-tree"* doctrine.

PROCEDURAL POSTURE: Police officers found cocaine on defendant, a passenger, while they were conducting a search incident to the illegal arrest of the vehicle's driver. After denying defendant's motion to suppress, the Superior Court of Yakima County (Washington) convicted defendant of illegal possession of cocaine, holding that defendant lacked standing to challenge the driver's detention. Defendant appealed.

OVERVIEW: The Appeals Court found that the driver's detention was illegal. Defendant contended that the cocaine evidence found on him should have been suppressed as fruit of an illegal search and seizure. The Court reversed. A passenger had standing to challenge a stop that constituted his own seizure, regardless of whether he had standing to challenge a subsequent search of the vehicle. The trial court found that the initial stop was warranted, but the continued detention of the driver ripened into an unlawful seizure, which tainted his consent to search the vehicle. The trial court acknowledged the driver was entitled to suppression of the cocaine in the trunk but concluded that defendant was not because he could not assert the driver's constitutional rights. The trial court's analysis, however, ignored the fact that defendant's detention also became unlawful when the officer exceeded the scope of the investigatory stop. The fruits of the unreasonable seizure of the car's occupants, the cocaine in the trunk, both arrests, and the cocaine in defendant's shoe, were all inadmissible and should have been suppressed.

OUTCOME: The Appeals Court reversed and vacated defendant's conviction.

OPINION: Police officers found cocaine on a passenger while they were conducting a search incident to the illegal arrest of the vehicle's driver. The Court was asked whether the passenger had standing to challenge the legality of the search and to suppress the fruits of that search.

Floyd Takesgun was a passenger in a vehicle pulled over in July 1994 for failure to dim its bright lights. The officer ascertained the vehicle's lights were merely out of adjustment, but because the driver seemed nervous and his eyes were bloodshot, the trooper engaged him in conversation. He asked if there was alcohol in the car, where the car was going, and where it had been. During this contact, the trooper noticed Mr. Takesgun also had bloodshot eyes and appeared nervous.

The trooper suspected the two young men were up to something. He had the driver step out of the car, obtained permission to search the vehicle and found cocaine in the trunk. Both driver and passenger were placed under arrest. Before being transported to jail, Mr. Takesgun admitted he had cocaine in his shoe.

The trial court found that the detention of the driver was illegal, but denied Mr. Takesgun's motion to suppress. On its own initiative, the court ruled Mr. Takesgun lacked standing to challenge the driver's detention and found him guilty of illegal possession of the cocaine in his shoe. Mr. Takesgun contends the evidence should have been suppressed as fruit of an illegal search and seizure. The Appeals Court reversed and vacated the conviction, finding in Mr. Takesgun's favor.

Fourth Amendment rights are personal, and a proponent of a motion to suppress must prove that the challenged governmental action infringed upon his own Fourth-Amendment rights. *United States v. Soule*, 908 F.2d 1032, (1st Cir. 1990). Here, the trial court accepted the State's argument that this case was indistinguishable from its decision in which the Appeals Court held that passengers without a possessory interest in the stopped vehicle had no legitimate privacy interest in it and could not, therefore, challenge its search. In that case, however, as the concurring opinion emphasized, the passengers did not challenge the constitutionality of the stop. Thus, the Court's decision was limited to the issue of whether the passenger's legitimate expectation of privacy was invaded by a search of the vehicle, and not of the stop thereof. Rakas, 439 U.S. at 150-51 Here, Mr. Takesgun did challenge the stop. And that was a crucial difference.

A police officer's act of stopping a vehicle and detaining its occupants constitutes a seizure. Under the Fourth Amendment that seizure must be reasonable. *Delaware v. Prouse*, 440 U.S. 648, 653. A passenger has standing to challenge a stop that constitutes his own seizure, regardless of whether he has standing to challenge a subsequent search of the vehicle. "Standing to challenge a stop presents issues separate and distinct from standing to challenge a search." *United States v. Erwin*, 875 F.2d 268, 269 (10th Cir. 1989). In other words, "whereas the search of an automobile does not implicate a passenger's fourth amendment rights, the stop results in the seizure of the passenger and driver alike. Thus, the passenger of a stopped automobile does have standing to challenge the seizure as unconstitutional." If the stop was unreasonable, the seized contraband is subject to exclusion under the "fruit-of-the-poisonous-tree" doctrine. *United States v. McKneely*, 6 F.3d 1447, 1450 (10th Cir. 1993).

The trial court found that the initial stop was warranted, as was a further brief detention to determine whether the driver was intoxicated. But the continued detention of the driver ripened into an unlawful seizure which tainted his consent to search the vehicle. The court acknowledged the driver was entitled to suppression of the cocaine in the trunk, but concluded Mr. Takesgun was not because he could not assert the driver's constitutional rights. The trial court's analysis ignored the fact that Mr. Takesgun's detention also became unlawful when the trooper exceeded the scope of the investigatory stop. The Appeals Court held that the fruits of the unreasonable seizure of the car's occupants, i.e., the cocaine in the trunk, both arrests and the cocaine in Mr. Takesgun's shoe, were all inadmissible and suppressed the same.

The Appeals Court reversed and vacated the conviction.

CHAPTER 11. THE ATTRACTIVE NUISANCE DOCTRINE

As a general rule, a landowner owes no duty of care to a trespasser on his property other than to refrain from causing willful and wanton injury. There is an exception to this rule for child trespassers, however. The exception is encompassed by the *Attractive-Nuisance Doctrine.*

There are five elements to the *Attractive-nuisance doctrine,* and a plaintiff must prove all five elements of the doctrine to prevail in a court of law. If proven, the landowner is liable in damages for any physical injury caused by artificial conditions impacting a trespassing child/children.

The five elements are: (1) The instrumentality or condition must be dangerous in itself, i.e., it must be an agency which is likely to, or probably will, result in injury to those attracted to it and coming in contact with it. (2) The nuisance must be attractive and alluring or enticing to young children. (3) Children must have been incapable, by reason of their youth, of comprehending the danger involved. (4) The instrumentality or condition must have been left unguarded and exposed at a place where children of tender years are accustomed to resort, or where it is reasonable to be expected they will resort for play or amusement or for the gratification of youthful curiosity. (5) It must have been reasonably practical and feasible either to prevent access to the instrumentality or condition, or else render it innocuous without obstructing any reasonable purpose or use for which the instrumentality was intended. The doctrine is usually applied on an ad hoc basis (case-by-case basis).

Courts have ruled that certain common objects such as ladders, fences, and trees possess dangers that are obvious and well known, at least to a 12-year-old child. For that reason objects such as ladders, fences and trees cannot be interpreted as *attractive nuisances* as a matter of law. As a rule, any child who climbs knows that if he falls, he will be hurt. To hold that such objects as ladders, fences and trees could be interpreted as *attractive nuisances* would be to require every property owner having a ladder, fence or tree accessible to children to maintain constant vigilance. Courts have been reluctant to be so over inclusive.

A young man, call him James, lived across the street from a small parking lot. One day James went into the parking lot to play with some friends who were skate boarding. In the course of his play, James climbed a waist high fence at the back of the parking lot and jumped to an overhanging limb of a small maple tree. The limb snapped under James' weight and he fell to the ground, hitting his head on a line of cinder blocks that had been placed two or three feet in front of the fence as a parking barrier.

James' friends waited for him to get up but he didn't. Twelve-year-old James was dead.

James' parents brought a wrongful death lawsuit against the property owner, call him Mr. P, based on premises liability. Once things were under way, Mr. P's lawyer motioned for summary judgment, claiming the tree and the fence were not a dangerous condition and the trial court agreed and dismissed the case. James' parents appealed.

In their appeal, James' parents sought to prove all five elements of the *doctrine of attractive nuisance*. In proving the first element James' parents maintained that the interplay of the parking blocks, the fence and the tree, all in proximity, made the parking lot dangerous. They argued that although an object in itself may not be dangerous, it may become dangerous when closely aligned with other non-dangerous instrumentalities. To establish the second element of *attractive nuisance*, that the instrumentality be alluring, James' parents were able to introduce testimony at trial from one of James' friends that he and James went to the parking lot two or three times a week and swung on the limb that caused James' fall.

In establishing the third element of liability, counsel argued that the mere fact that James regularly went to the parking lot to swing from the limb of the tree was evidence that James did not understand the danger he was in. To establish the fourth element that a hazardous condition was left unguarded at a place where children of tender years were accustomed to congregate, counsel submitted many declarations showing that children often loitered or played in the parking lot.

Finally, in proving the fifth element of the doctrine, that it was reasonably practical and feasible to prevent access to the hazardous condition the parking lot presented without obstructing the purpose for which the parking lot was intended, counsel for James' parents argued signs declaring "No Trespassing" or "No Loitering" could have been posted. The only posted sign was a "Customer Parking Only" sign.

The appellate court agreed with counsel's arguments and reversed and remanded the case to the district court for jury trial where the parents prevailed.

BENNETT, ADMR., APPELLANT, V. STANLEY ET AL., APPELLEES.
SUPREME COURT OF OHIO
748 N.E.2D 41
JUNE 13, 2001

LEGAL CONSIDERATIONS

Torts / General Premises Liability / Attractive Nuisance

Elements such as knowledge of children's presence, the maintenance of a potentially dangerous feature, and an exercise of care by the owner commensurate with the danger of the feature are a part of the *attractive- nuisance doctrine* in most states.

Torts / General Premises Liability / Attractive Nuisance

Under the *attractive-nuisance doctrine*, a possessor of land is subject to liability for physical harm to children trespassing thereon caused by an artificial condition upon land if: the place where the condition exists is one upon which the possessor knows or has reason to know that children are likely to trespass,

Torts / General Premises Liability / Attractive Nuisance

The *attractive-nuisance doctrine* will not extend tort liability to the owner of a residential swimming pool where the presence of a child who is injured or drowns therein is not foreseeable by the property owner.

Torts / General Premises Liability / Attractive Nuisance

One of the key elements of the *attractive-nuisance doctrine* is that the place where the condition exists is one upon which the possessor knows or has reason to know that children are likely to trespass.

Torts / General Premises Liability / Attractive Nuisance

The *attractive-nuisance doctrine* balances society's interest in protecting children with the rights of landowners to enjoy their property.

Torts / General Premises Liability / Attractive Nuisance

The requirement of foreseeability is built into the *attractive-nuisance doctrine*.

Torts / General Premises Liability / Attractive Nuisance

The *attractive-nuisance doctrine* effectively harmonizes the competing societal interests of protecting children and preserving property rights.

Torts / General Premises Liability / Attractive Nuisance

While the *attractive-nuisance doctrine* is not ordinarily applicable to adults, it may be successfully invoked by an adult seeking damages for his or her own injury if the injury was suffered in an attempt to rescue a child from a danger created by the defendant's negligence.

Torts / General Premises Liability

Ohio has long recognized a range of duties for property owners vis-à-vis persons entering their property. Currently, to an invitee the landowner owes a duty to exercise ordinary care and to protect the invitee by maintaining the premises in a safe condition. To licensees and trespassers, on the other hand, a landowner owes no duty except to refrain from willful, wanton, or reckless conduct which is likely to injure the licensee or trespasser.

Torts / Special Care

The Supreme Court of Ohio has consistently held that children have a special status in tort law and that duties of care owed to children are different from duties owed to adults.

Torts / General Premises Liability

Recognizing the special status of children in the law, the Supreme Court of Ohio has even accorded special protection to child trespassers by adopting the "dangerous-instrumentality" doctrine. The dangerous- instrumentality exception to non-liability of trespassers imposes upon the owner or occupier of a premises a higher duty of care to a child trespasser when such owner or occupier actively and negligently operates hazardous machinery or other apparatus, the dangerousness of which is not readily apparent to children.

Torts / General Premises Liability

The public interest in the possessor's free use of his land for his own purposes is of great significance. A particular condition is, therefore, regarded as not involving unreasonable risk to trespassing children unless it involves a grave risk to them which could be obviated without any serious interference with the possessor's legitimate use of his land.

PROCEDURAL POSTURE: Plaintiff, husband and father, filed a wrongful death and personal injury action against defendants, homeowners, in his capacity as administrator of his wife and son's estates and as custodial parent. The trial court granted defendants' motion for summary judgment, and the father appealed. The Court of Appeals for Washington County (Ohio) affirmed the trial court's judgment, and the state Supreme Court granted leave to appeal.

OVERVIEW: Homeowners purchased a home with a swimming pool. The pool was enclosed by fencing and a brick wall, and was covered by a tarp. Homeowners removed the tarp and fencing on two sides of the pool, and although they drained the pool, they allowed rainwater to collect in the pool to a depth of over six feet. The pool became a pond. It contained no ladders, the sides were slick with algae, and frogs and tadpoles lived in the pool. Plaintiff's family rented the house next to homeowners several months after homeowners purchased their house. Plaintiff was married and the father or stepfather of three young children. Homeowners were aware that children lived next door and evidence showed that there was some fencing between the properties but such as there was had an eight-foot gap. In March 1997, plaintiff arrived home to find his stepson and wife unconscious in homeowners' pool. Both later died. The state Supreme Court used this case to adopt the *attractive-nuisance doctrine* as the law of Ohio and also held that an adult who attempted to rescue a child from an attractive nuisance assumed the status of the child and was owed a duty of ordinary care by a property owner.

OUTCOME: The state Supreme Court reversed the intermediate appeals court's judgment and remanded the case to the trial court for findings consistent with its ruling.

SYLLABUS:

1. A possessor of land is subject to liability for physical harm to children trespassing thereon caused by an artificial condition upon the land if: (a) the place where the condition exists is one upon which the possessor knows or has reason to know that children are likely to trespass, and (b) the condition is one of which the possessor knows or has reason to know and which he realizes or should realize will involve an unreasonable risk of death or serious bodily harm to children, and (c) children, because of their youth, do not discover the condition or realize the risk involved in intermeddling with it or in coming within the area made dangerous by it, and (d) the utility to the possessor of maintaining the condition and the burden of eliminating the danger are slight as compared with the risk to children involved, and (e) the possessor fails to exercise reasonable care to eliminate the danger or to otherwise protect the children. (See Restatement of the Law 2d, Torts [1965], Section 339.)

2. While the *attractive-nuisance doctrine* is not ordinarily applicable to adults, it may be successfully invoked by an adult seeking damages for his or her own injury if the injury was suffered in an attempt to rescue a child from a danger created by the defendant's negligence.

OPINION: In this case the Supreme Court was called upon to determine what level of duty a property owner owed to a child trespasser. The Court resolved the question by adopting the attractive-nuisance doctrine as set forth in the Restatement of the Law 2d, Torts (1965), Section 339. The Court also held that an adult who attempts to rescue a child from an attractive nuisance assumes the status of the child, and is owed a duty of ordinary care by the property owner.

Factual and Procedural Background

When Rickey G. Bennett, plaintiff-appellant, arrived home in the late afternoon of March 20, 1997, he found his two young daughters crying. The three-year-old, Kyleigh, told him that "Mommy" and Chance, her five-year-old half-brother, were "drowning in the water." Bennett ran next door to his neighbors' house to find his wife and son unconscious in the swimming pool. Both later died.

The Bennetts had moved next door to defendants (the appellees), Jeffrey and Stacey Stanley, in the fall of 1996. The Stanleys had purchased their home the previous June. At the time of purchase, the Stanleys' property included a swimming pool that had gone unused for three years. At the time of purchase, the pool was enclosed with fencing and a brick wall. After moving in, the Stanleys drained the pool once, but thereafter they allowed rainwater to accumulate in the pool to a depth of over six feet. They removed a tarp that had been on the pool and also removed the fencing that had been around two sides of the pool. The pool became pond-like and contained tadpoles and frogs, and Mr. Stanley had seen a snake swimming on the surface. The pool contained no ladders, and its sides were slimy with algae.

Rickey and Cher Bennett were married in 1995. They had two daughters, born in 1993 and 1995. Cher brought her son, Chance Lattea, into the marriage. The Bennetts rented the house next to the Stanleys. The houses were about one hundred feet apart. There was some fencing between the two properties that displayed an eight-foot wide gap.

The Stanleys were aware that the Bennetts had moved next door and that they had young children. They had seen the children outside unsupervised. Stacey Stanley had once called Chance onto her property to retrieve a dog. The Stanleys testified, however, that they never had any concern about the children getting into the pool. They did not post any warning or "no trespassing" signs on their property.

Rickey Bennett testified that he had told his children to stay away from the pool on the Stanleys' property. He also stated that he had never seen the children playing near the pool.

Kyleigh told her father that she and Chance had been playing at the pool on the afternoon of the tragedy. The sheriff's department concluded that Chance had gone to the pool to look at the frogs and somehow had fallen into the pool. His mother apparently drowned trying to save him.

Bennett, in his capacity as Administrator of the Estate of Cher D. Bennett, as Administrator of the Estate of Chance C. Lattea, and as custodial parent of Kyleigh D. Bennett, filed a wrongful death and personal injury suit against the Stanleys. The complaint alleged that appellees (The Stanleys) had negligently maintained an abandoned swimming pool on their property and that appellees' negligence proximately caused the March 20, 1997 drowning of Chance and Cher. Appellant averred that appellees had created a dangerous condition by negligently maintaining the pool and that appellees reasonably should have known that the pool posed an unreasonable risk of serious harm to others. Appellant specifically alleged that appellees' pool created an unreasonable risk of harm to children who, because of their youth, would not realize the potential danger. Appellant further asserted that appellees' conduct in maintaining the pool constituted willful and wanton misconduct such as to justify an award of punitive damages.

Appellant sought damages for the beneficiaries of the deceased, for Kyleigh's mental anguish for witnessing the drownings, for mental anguish for Cher before her death, and for punitive damages. Appellees denied any negligence and asserted affirmative defenses of contributory negligence and assumption of risk.

The appellees, the Stanleys, filed a motion for summary judgment, which the trial court granted on September 4, 1998. The trial court found that Chance and Cher were trespassers on appellees' property and that appellees therefore owed them only a duty to refrain from wanton and willful misconduct. The trial court further rejected appellant's (The Bennets) argument that appellees' maintenance of the swimming pool amounted to a dangerous active operation, creating for them a duty of ordinary care pursuant to *Coy v. Columbus, Delaware & Marion Elec. Co.* (1932), 181 N.E. 131.

On appeal, the appellate court affirmed the trial court's granting of summary judgment. It, too, held that the appellees owed the decedents only a duty to refrain from wanton and willful misconduct, and added that there was no evidence of such misconduct. The appellate court also addressed the issue of appellees' duty to Cher Bennett. The court held that even if she were on the Stanleys' property in an attempt to rescue her son, she would still have the status only of a licensee, who is owed no greater duty of care than a trespasser.

The Supreme Court allowed a discretionary appeal.

Law and Analysis

Ohio has long recognized a range of duties for property owners vis-à-vis persons entering their property. A recent discussion of Ohio's classification system can be found in *Gladon v. Greater Cleveland Regional Transit Auth.* (1996), 662 N.E.2d 287, 291. Currently, to an invitee the landowner owes a duty "to exercise ordinary care and to protect the invitee by maintaining the premises in a safe condition." To licensees and trespassers, on the other hand, "a landowner owes no duty except to refrain from willful, wanton or reckless conduct which is likely to injure the licensee or trespasser." The Supreme Court entertained the question of whether child trespassers should become another class of users who are owed a different duty of care.

The Court held that "The Ohio Supreme Court has consistently maintained that children have a special status in tort law and that duties of care owed to children are different from duties owed to adults: The amount of care required to discharge a duty owed to a child of tender years is necessarily greater than that required to discharge a duty owed to an adult under the same circumstances." This was the approach long followed by the Court and the Court saw no reason to abandon it. Children of tender years, and youthful persons generally, are entitled to a degree of care proportioned to their inability to foresee and avoid the perils that they may encounter. The same discernment and foresight in discovering defects and dangers cannot be reasonably expected of children as can be expected of older and more experienced persons. Therefore greater precaution should be taken where children are exposed potential danger.

"Recognizing the special status of children in the law, the Court has been obliged to accord special protection to child trespassers by adopting the 'dangerous-instrumentality' doctrine: The dangerous- instrumentality exception imposes upon the owner or occupier of a premises a higher duty of care to a child trespasser when such an owner or occupier actively and negligently operates hazardous machinery or other apparatus, the dangerousness of which is not readily apparent to children." *McKinney v. Hartz & Restle Realtors, Inc.* (1987), 510 N.E.2d 386, 390.

The Court noted that the doctrine was developed in *Coy v. Columbus, Delaware & Marion Elec. Co.* (1932), 181 N.E. 131, a case where a six-year-old boy was injured when he touched a high voltage transformer owned by a defendant and located in a vacant lot known to be frequented by children. The court applied a negligence standard to the behavior of the property owner despite the fact that the child had been trespassing. "A deadly, hidden instrumentality should not be left easily accessible to children whose frequent presence was known to the property owner. Care must be commensurate with danger!"

Thus, the Ohio Supreme Court adopted as early as 1932 some of the hallmarks of the attractive-nuisance doctrine. Elements such as knowledge of children's presence, the maintenance of a potentially dangerous feature or instrumentality, and an exercise of care by the owner commensurate with danger.

The Court held that "The attractive-nuisance doctrine will not extend tort liability to the owner of a residential swimming pool where the presence of a child who was injured or drowned was not foreseeable by the property owner."

That ruling is not contradictory to the attractive-nuisance doctrine as set forth in the Restatement of Torts. One of the key elements of the doctrine as defined in the Restatement of Torts is that "the place where the condition exists is one upon which the possessor knows or has reason to know that children are likely to trespass."

The Court held that in the incident case there was at least a genuine issue of fact regarding the foreseeability of one of the Bennett children entering onto the Stanley property. The fact that three young children lived next door to the Stanleys would allow reasonable minds to conclude that it was foreseeable that one of the children would explore around the pool.

For that reason, the Court could not decline to adopt the attractive-nuisance doctrine because of a lack of foreseeability. Any failure to adopt attractive nuisance would be to reject its philosophical underpinnings and would keep Ohio in the small minority of states that do not recognize some form of the doctrine.

The Court held that adopting the attractive-nuisance doctrine would be merely an incremental change in Ohio law, not out of line with the law that has developed over time. It was, thus, an appropriate evolution of the common law.

On remand, if the evidence is established that Cher's status was that of a rescuer, then the injury should be attributed to the party that negligently, or wrongfully, exposed to danger the person who required assistance. While the attractive-nuisance doctrine is not ordinarily applicable to adults, it may be successfully invoked by an adult seeking damages for his or her own injury if the injury was suffered in an attempt to rescue a child from a danger created by the defendant's negligence. Therefore, the Court held that if Cher Bennett entered the Stanleys' property to rescue her son from an attractive nuisance, the Stanleys owed her a duty of ordinary care.

Accordingly, the Ohio Supreme Court reversed the judgment of the court of appeals and remanded the cause to the trial court for a finding consistent with their opinion.

CHAPTER 12. THE DOCTRINE OF MITIGATED DAMAGES

Under the *doctrine of mitigated damages,* any award in damages is reduced if it can be shown that the party claiming damages failed to reduce the effect of the negligence sued upon when it was within that party's wherewithal to do so. Mitigation of damages is an affirmative defense and applies when a plaintiff fails to make a reasonable effort to lessen his injuries or the effects thereof. A recent case involving a large, national, discount retailer is illustrative.

Mrs. P (the plaintiff) went to the retailer's local store to buy a fishing pole for her husband's birthday. The pole she wanted was displayed eight or nine feet above floor level, and Mrs. P had to get a sales clerk to retrieve it. As the sales clerk was descending his utility ladder, he lost control of the fishing pole and it hit Mrs. P on her cheek, just below her eye. Mrs. P reported the incident to the store manager, complaining of pain to the left side of her face.

That evening Mrs. P went to the E.R. of the local hospital. The attending physician could find no physical reason for the pain Mrs. P was experiencing but prescribed a medication and a therapeutic regimen and told her to consult her regular doctor. She was told, for example, to stop cigarette smoking because the effect of the smoke could be irritating the injured tissue around her eye.

In the months that followed, Mrs. P periodically complained of experiencing pain and consulted a couple of different pain specialists but never followed through on their recommendations. Finally she initiated a lawsuit claiming negligence on the part of the store's sales clerk. At trial, Mrs. P received an award in damages but a greatly reduced award compared to what she was asking because she had failed to reasonably reduce the effect of her injury. She had accumulated medical bills in excess of $10,000. The award she received was less than half of her documented medical expenses.

In its decision on a jury instruction for mitigated damages, the jury found that Mrs. P had (1) failed to stop smoking as recommended by her doctors, had (2) failed to obtain non-invasive follow-up treatment, and, (3) had failed to document her claims of pain and had incurred substantial medical expenses after being told she had no medical problem. All in all, Mrs. P was no match for the doctrine of mitigated damages. The following gives a little different spin to the concept.

ANTOINETTE WALTER V. WAL-MART STORES, INC.
SUPREME JUDICIAL COURT OF MAINE
748 A.2D 961 (ME 2000)
JANUARY 5, 2000, ARGUED
APRIL 12, 2000, DECIDED

LEGAL CONSIDERATIONS

Torts / Mitigated Damages

A classic application of the avoidable consequences, *mitigated damages*, doctrine is made when the plaintiff fails to seek medical treatment after being injured by a defendant.

Torts / Mitigated Damages

A defendant is not entitled to a double reduction of damages; that is, the same action or inaction of the plaintiff that justifies a comparative negligence instruction should not also authorize a reduction of damages under the *doctrine of mitigation of damages* or avoidable consequences.

Torts / Mitigation of Damages, Avoidable Consequences

Traditionally, one of the distinctions between contributory negligence and the doctrine of mitigation of damages, or avoidable consequences, has been a temporal one. Contributory negligence is generally unreasonable behavior by a plaintiff before or concurrent with the injury imposed by the defendant, whereas the avoidable consequences doctrine (Mitigation of Damages) is applied to plaintiff's action or inaction after the defendant's negligent act.

Civil Procedure / Summary Judgment

In reviewing a trial court's disposition of a motion for judgment as a matter of law, the court views the evidence together with all justifiable inferences in the light most favorable to the party opposing the motion. If a reasonable view of the evidence would sustain a verdict for the nonmoving party, the motion must be denied.

Evidence / Admissions by Party Opponent

Statements made by counsel during an opening statement or closing argument can result in a judicial admission. In order to be considered a judicial admission the statements must be deliberate, clear, and unambiguous. When made in an opening statement, the alleged judicial admission must be considered in the context of the entire statement. The statement must be unequivocal and pertain to a factual matter.

Torts / Duty

Pharmacists owe their customers a duty of ordinary care, but ordinary care for a pharmacist means the highest practicable degree of prudence, thoughtfulness, and vigilance.

Torts / Proximate Cause

In order to establish liability, a plaintiff in any negligence action must show that the defendant's negligence was the proximate cause of the plaintiff's harm.

Torts / Proximate Cause

Causation means that there be some reasonable connection between the act or omission of the defendant and the damage which the plaintiff suffered. The defendant's conduct must be a substantial factor in bringing about the plaintiff's harm in order for there to be proximate cause.

Torts / Negligence

Under Maine's comparative negligence statute, the damages owing to a plaintiff may be reduced when the plaintiff's harm is partly the result of the plaintiff's own fault, and fault is defined as the negligence that would give rise to the defense of contributory negligence. If the plaintiff's fault is equal to or greater than that of the defendant, the plaintiff cannot recover damages.

Torts / Comparative & Contributory Negligence

Contributory negligence is negligence by a plaintiff that unites with the negligence of the defendant to make the damage the direct result of both the defendant's negligence and the plaintiff's contributory negligence.

Torts / Comparative & Contributory Negligence

Contributory negligence has to antedate or be concurrent with the defendant's negligence.

Torts / Comparative & Contributory Negligence

When the plaintiff commits negligence after the defendant's negligence or fails to take steps to avoid the consequences of defendant's negligence, the amount of damages may be affected, but not the plaintiff's right of recovery.

Evidence / Expert Testimony

Where professional negligence and its harmful results are sufficiently obvious as to lie within common knowledge, no expert testimony is necessary.

Civil Procedure / Relief From Judgment

When a court refuses to grant a new trial on the ground of an excessive damage award, the ruling will not be reversed except for clear and manifest abuse of discretion.

Civil Procedure / Damages Generally

Evidence must be construed in the light most favorable to the jury verdict, and a damage award will not be overturned unless it is without rational explanation.

CASE SUMMARY

PROCEDURAL POSTURE: Defendant appealed from a judgment entered in the Superior Court, Knox County, Maine, following a jury trial awarding damages to plaintiff in the amount of $550,000 for her claim of pharmacist malpractice.

OVERVIEW: Plaintiff suffered from cancer, and her doctor prescribed a chemotherapy medication. Plaintiff had the prescription filled at defendant store. Defendant's pharmacist gave plaintiff the wrong medication, causing plaintiff serious physical problems requiring hospitalization. Plaintiff sued defendant for pharmacist malpractice. Although defense counsel apparently conceded there was no fault on plaintiff's part, the mention of plaintiff's delay in obtaining a blood test after taking the new medication rendered the concession ambiguous. The court could not conclude that there was a judicial admission in the defendant's opening statement that defendant was liable for plaintiff's damages. Further, the trial court did not err: in granting judgment as a matter of law to plaintiff on causation, in refusing to instruct the jury on comparative negligence, in giving the *mitigation-damages* jury instruction, and in denying defendant's motions for judgment as a matter of law, mistrial, or for a new trial.

OUTCOME: The judgment was affirmed in favor of the plaintiff since the evidence supported the verdict, and there was no error in the trial court's rulings on defendant's motions for judgment as a matter of law, mistrial, or for a new trial.

OPINION: Wal-Mart Stores, Inc. appeals from a judgment entered in the Superior Court (Knox County, Marsano, J.) following a jury trial awarding damages to Antoinette Walter in the amount of $550,000 for her claim of pharmacist malpractice. Wal-Mart contended that the Superior Court erred in (1) granting Walter's motion for judgment as a matter of law on liability; (2) or in denying Wal-Mart's motion for judgment as a matter of law. Wal-Mart also appealed on the ground that the jury verdict was excessive and the result of bias and prejudice.

I. FACTS

Walter, an eighty-year-old resident of Rockland, was diagnosed with a type of cancer which attacks the lymphatic system. Dr. Stephen Ross, Walter's treating physician and a board-certified oncologist, termed her condition treatable with the proper medication. Dr. Ross prescribed Chlorambucil, a chemotherapy drug, for Walter. On the prescription slip, he explicitly called for Chlorambucil, the generic name, because he feared that the drug's brand name, Leukeran, could be confused with other drugs with similar trade names.

Walter took the prescription for Chlorambucil to the pharmacy in the Wal-Mart store in Rockland on May 7, 1997. Henry Lovin, a Maine licensed pharmacist and an employee of Wal-Mart, was on duty at the pharmacy. Instead of giving Walter Chlorambucil, as called for in the prescription, Lovin gave her a different drug with the brand name of Melphalen. The generic name for Melphalen is Alkeran. Lovin did not speak with Walter at the time he filled the prescription, but he provided her with an information sheet which described the effects of Melphalen. Melphalen is also a chemotherapy drug, but it is a substantially more powerful medication than Chlorambucil. Melphalen is typically given in smaller doses over shorter periods of time than is Chlorambucil, and doctors monitor it more closely. Melphalen has a very toxic effect on the body, and it substantially suppresses bone marrow. It has a longer life in the body than Chlorambucil, which means that any side effects from it last longer.

To the extent that Walter noticed that the information sheet and bottle label read Melphalen, it did not make an impression on her. She assumed that the drug she had been given was the same as Dr. Ross had prescribed, and she began taking the prescribed dosage. Within seven to ten days of starting the drug treatment, Walter began to suffer from nausea and lack of appetite. When she referred to the information sheet, Walter saw that such side effects are common for chemotherapy drugs. She continued to take the Melphalen. During the third week after starting the medication Walter noticed bruises on her arms and legs, and during the fourth week she developed a skin rash on her arms and legs. Although the information sheet warned that bruises and rashes should prompt a call to the doctor, Walter waited a few days before attempting to contact Dr. Ross.

Dr. Ross testified at trial that his notes indicated that Walter should have had blood tests two weeks after starting medication and that she was to have scheduled an appointment with him within four weeks of beginning the medication. He also testified that because Chlorambucil is slow-acting, he does not insist that his patients have blood tests done in fourteen days but only that they have blood work periodically. Walter testified that she understood she was to have a follow-up appointment with Dr. Ross in four weeks and blood tests sometime before that appointment.

On the twenty-third day after starting the medication, Walter had blood tests done. She attempted to reach Dr. Ross by phone to tell him about the side effects, but she was unsuccessful until June 3, 1997. On that day Dr. Ross told her that her blood levels were low and to stop taking the medication immediately. He scheduled an appointment for June 5. Walter, however, was rushed to the hospital later in the day on June 3 when she suffered gastrointestinal bleeding. Following her emergency admission, Walter remained in the hospital five weeks and received numerous blood transfusions. She suffered several infections, and a catheter was placed in her chest. The bruising and skin rash continued. For a period of time, she was unable to eat because of bleeding gums and an infection in her mouth. Because of her weakened immune system, Walter's visitors could not come within ten feet of her.

Prior to receiving the Melphalen, Walter lived independently and was active. Following her hospital discharge on July 7, 1997, she was physically weak. She initially had to make daily trips to the hospital but later went less frequently. She had to have additional transfusions after she left the hospital. Melphalen did have the effect of causing her cancer to go into remission. Walter's total medical bills for her treatment came to $71,042.63.

The two-day jury trial was held in February 1999. Wal-Mart moved for judgment as a matter of law at the close of Walter's case on the grounds that she had failed to present expert testimony on the standard of care by pharmacists, but the motion was denied. At the close of the evidence Walter moved for a judgment as a matter of law, and the court granted Walter's motion concluding that she was entitled to judgment on liability. During Walter's closing argument, Wal-Mart moved for a mistrial arguing that certain comments by Walter's counsel were improper, but the motion was denied. The jury awarded Walter $550,000 in damages. Wal-Mart's post-trial motion for judgment as a matter of law or a new trial was denied.

II. WALTER'S MOTION FOR JUDGMENT ON LIABILITY

The court granted Walter's motion for judgment on the issue of liability. "In reviewing a trial court's disposition of a motion for judgment as a matter of law, we view the evidence together with all justifiable inferences in the light most favorable to the party opposing the motion." *Lewis v. Knowlton*, 688 A.2d 912, (ME 1997). If a reasonable view of the evidence would sustain a verdict for the non-moving party, the motion must be denied.

The effect of the court's grant of Walter's motion was a determination, as a matter of law, that Wal-Mart had a duty to Walter which it breached; that the breach caused Walter harm; and that Walter was not negligent, or if she was negligent, her negligence did not proximately cause her harm. The only issue left for the jury was the amount of damages caused by Wal-Mart's negligence and whether those damages should be reduced because of any action or inaction by Walter to take reasonable steps to reduce the extent of her injuries.

A. Wal-Mart's Representations to the Jury

Wal-Mart argued that the court erred in granting Walter's motion for judgment as a matter of law because it should have submitted the issues of negligence, proximate cause, and comparative negligence to the jury. Walter contended that Wal-Mart judicially admitted liability in its opening statement to the jury. The clear import of Wal-Mart's opening statement was that liability was not an issue, and the only question that the jury would have to decide was the amount of damages.

Statements made by counsel during an opening statement or closing argument can result in a judicial admission. Wal-Mart's opening statement admitted the error made by its pharmacist in filling the prescription, but because negligence consists of both law (whether a duty exists and what that duty is) and facts (whether the duty was breached), there was no judicial admission of negligence. Furthermore, the statement taken in its entire context, did not contain an unequivocal admission that the mistake in filling the prescription caused Walter's harm. While Wal-Mart appeared to concede that there was no fault on the part of Walter, the mention of the delay in obtaining the blood test rendered the concession ambiguous. For these reasons, The Appeals Court could not conclude that there was a judicial admission that Wal-Mart was liable for Walter's damages.

B. Wal-Mart's Negligence

Walter had the burden to prove that Wal-Mart, through its pharmacist employee, owed a duty to Walter that it breached, thereby causing her harm. In *Tremblay v. Kimball*, 107 Me. 53, 77 A. 405 (1910), The Appeals Court held that pharmacists owe their customers a duty of ordinary care, but that "ordinary care" for a pharmacist means "the highest practicable degree of prudence, thoughtfulness, and vigilance.

Lovin, the Wal-Mart pharmacist, readily admitted that he made an error in filling Walter's prescription. He testified that he thought that the brand name for Chlorambucil was Alkeran, and he filled the prescription with Alkeran, which is Melphalen. Lovin said that he made a "serious error" that did not "satisfy the proper standard of care for a pharmacist." He admitted that he would have discovered the error if he had followed the standard four-step process utilized to check for errors. He acknowledged that to comply with the standard of pharmacy care he should have checked the stock bottle against the prescription. He further admitted that the standard of practice required that he counsel Walter when she picked up the prescription, at which time he would have showed her the drug and discussed it with her. He testified that he did not counsel her, but if he had done so, he would have discovered the error. He also said that Walter would have no reason to suspect that she was given the wrong drug.

Pursuant to the standard of "the highest practicable degree of prudence, thoughtfulness, and vigilance and the most exact and reliable safeguards" as set forth in *Tremblay v. Kimball*, Lovin's testimony established that the standard was breached. Lovin's testimony established the standard and the breach of it. None of the evidence was disputed. A jury, acting reasonably, could not have found that Wal-Mart was not negligent.

C. Causation

In order to establish liability a plaintiff in any negligence action must show that the defendant's negligence was the proximate cause of the plaintiff's harm. Wal-Mart argued that Walter's motion should have been denied because she failed to prove that Wal-Mart's negligence in filling the prescription was the cause of her injury. Causation means "that there be some reasonable connection between the act or omission of the defendant and the damage which the plaintiff suffered." *Wheeler v. White*, 714 A.2d 125 (ME 1998). The defendant's conduct must be a "substantial factor" in bringing about the plaintiff's harm in order for there to be proximate cause. Wal-Mart specifically requested a jury instruction on proximate cause.

There was uncontroverted medical evidence that Melphalen, which Wal-Mart provided Walter erroneously, caused damage to her body. Although she had lymphoma, the disease did not limit her functioning. Witnesses described her as a very active person until her hospitalization occurred. Dr. Ross testified that the Melphalen made Walter seriously ill, to the point that he was not sure she would survive, and that her lack of energy after her release from the hospital was the result of the illness caused by the wrong medication. Wal-Mart's expert oncologist also testified that the side effects of Melphalen caused the lengthy hospitalization, and the hospitalization itself likely caused Walter's malaise and depression after her discharge.

Wal-Mart argued that the jury should have been instructed on proximate cause because its expert speculated that if a blood test had been done fourteen days after starting the medication it might have shown lowered blood levels and, depending on how low those levels were, Walter's physician might have stopped the medication, and if the medication had been stopped sooner, the harmful effect may have been less. Wal-Mart's expert did not testify that there would have been no damage if a blood test had been done on the fourteenth day. In fact, in his description of Melphalen, he noted it has a long life in the body and that its side effects last longer. No jury acting rationally could determine that Walter's failure to have a blood test in fourteen days broke the chain of causation between the pharmacist's negligence and Walter's injuries. No reasonable factfinder could have found that Wal-Mart's negligent act in misfilling the prescription was not a substantial cause in bringing about Walter's suffering. "When the totality of the evidence adduced in any particular case is so overwhelming that it leaves open to a fact-finder, acting rationally, only one conclusion on the issue, the issue is then determined as a matter of law." The trial court did not err in granting judgment as a matter of law to Walter on the issue of causation.

The court twice, in its instructions to the jury, stated that it was Walter's burden to prove to them by a preponderance of the evidence that Wal-Mart's negligence caused Walter's damages: (1) "Any damages that you award in this case must be based upon a finding by you that the plaintiff, who is the one seeking damages, has convinced you by a preponderance of the evidence that the particular injury and pain and suffering for which she seeks compensation was caused by the defendant's negligence, and, (2) You must determine the damages to which the plaintiff is entitled as a result of the injury proximately caused by the defendant."

D. Comparative Negligence and Mitigation of Damages

Wal-Mart argued that Walter's motion for judgment on liability should have been denied because Wal-Mart raised the defense of comparative negligence and it was entitled to have the jury decide whether Walter was negligent. Wal-Mart claimed that Walter should have realized that the drug name on the medicine container did not match the medication that she had discussed with Dr. Ross. Wal-Mart also argued that Walter was negligent when she did not contact Dr. Ross immediately upon noticing the rash and bruising.

Under Maine's comparative negligence statute, the damages owing to a plaintiff may be reduced when the plaintiff's harm is partly the result of the plaintiff's own fault, and fault is defined as the negligence that would give rise to the defense of contributory negligence. If the plaintiff's fault is equal to or greater than that of the defendant, the plaintiff cannot recover damages.

1. Walter's Failure to Discover Wal-Mart's Error

The Court turned first to Wal-Mart's contention that Walter was contributorily negligent in failing to discover that she had been given the wrong medication. The Court concluded that a jury, acting rationally, on this evidence could not find that she was negligent. Lovin testified that Walter "would have no way of knowing" that she had been given the wrong medication, and there was no evidence that Walter should have been expected to discover Wal-Mart's negligence. Thus, it was not error to refuse to instruct the jury on comparative negligence concerning Walter's failure to discover Wal-Mart's error.

2. Walter's Failure to Notify her Doctor Immediately of Side Effects

Wal-Mart claimed that Walter's delay in calling her doctor to report the skin rash and bruising was negligence on her part that contributed to her suffering. Walter contends that any inaction on her part goes to mitigation of damages and not comparative negligence.

Traditionally, one of the distinctions between contributory negligence and the doctrine of mitigation of damages, or avoidable consequences, mitigated damages, has been a temporal one. Contributory negligence is generally unreasonable behavior by a plaintiff before or concurrent with the injury imposed by the defendant, whereas the avoidable consequences doctrine is applied to plaintiff's action or inaction after the defendant's negligent act. For example, the Court has said that contributory negligence is negligence by a plaintiff that unites with the negligence of the defendant to make the damage the direct result of both the defendant's negligence and the plaintiff's contributory negligence. The Court has also stated that contributory negligence has to antedate or be concurrent with the defendant's negligence. When the plaintiff commits negligence after the defendant's negligence or fails to take steps to avoid the consequences of defendant's negligence, the amount of damages may be affected, but not the plaintiff's right of recovery.

A classic application of the avoidable consequences doctrine is made when a plaintiff fails to seek medical treatment after being injured by a defendant. It has been held that if a plaintiff's failure to follow the reasonable instructions of a defendant doctor directly contributes to the plaintiff's damages, the plaintiff's contributory negligence will bar recovery. The majority of courts appear to hold that contributory negligence for a patient's noncompliance with medical treatment decisions will bar recovery completely only if the patient's negligent acts are contemporaneous with the physician's negligent acts. Under the comparative negligence statute, the Appeals Court approved, without discussion, a jury instruction on comparative negligence when the plaintiff failed to keep a follow-up appointment with a defendant doctor. See *Hauser v. Bhatnager*, 537 A.2d 599, 601 (ME 1988). But there is no uniformity among other jurisdictions on the question of whether the patient's failure to follow a physician's instructions is comparative negligence or comes under the doctrine of mitigation or avoidable consequences.

The Court stated that "Although it is tempting to fully examine the rationale for applying comparative negligence as opposed to the doctrines of mitigation or avoidable consequences, we need not do so in this case. One principle that ought to be plain is that a defendant is not entitled to a double reduction of damages; that is, the same action or inaction of the plaintiff that justifies a comparative negligence instruction should not also authorize a reduction of damages under the doctrine of mitigation or avoidable consequences. The jury should not be instructed on both comparative negligence and mitigation of damages for the same act of the plaintiff. The major difference between the two instructions is that the jury is told in the comparative negligence instruction that if the plaintiff's fault is equal to or greater than the defendant's fault, the plaintiff recovers nothing. It is possible that with a mitigation instruction a jury could return a verdict for the defendant by finding that failure to avoid the consequences was so substantial that the damages should be reduced to nothing. The jury, however, should not be so instructed unless the facts warrant. In this case there were not sufficient facts from which a jury could find that Walter's inaction was so substantial as to allow a verdict for the defendant denying Walters damages.

> The jury was instructed on mitigation and told that every person who is injured has a duty to exercise reasonable care to reduce the extent of the injuries and to take reasonable and prudent steps to effect a cure or reduce the severity of the injury. Although the words "fault" or "negligence" are not used in the mitigation instruction, the practical effect is the same as though the words were used because of the reasonableness standard that the jury is told to apply. "The factors determining whether an injured person has used care to avert the consequences of a tort are in general the same as those that determine whether a person has been guilty of negligent conduct."

> With regard to the bruising and skin rash, the evidence is that the bruising appeared only a few days before Walter attempted to reach Dr. Ross. There is

no evidence that if the bruising and skin rash had been reported to Dr. Ross earlier, treatment could have been given immediately that would have reversed the effects of the wrong medicine. At best, the jury could infer that Dr. Ross would have stopped the medication a few days earlier and perhaps the effects of the wrong medication may have been lessened. A jury, acting rationally, could not have concluded that the negligence of Walter was equal to or greater than Wal-Mart's negligence.

3. Walter's Delay in Having Her Blood Tested

Although Wal-Mart did not argue that Walter's delay in obtaining the blood test was negligence, the same reasoning applied to the blood test as to the failure to report immediately the bruising and skin rash. Wal-Mart's expert testified that Walter could not be blamed for waiting twenty-three days for the blood test because she did not know the significance of a blood test. He testified that only if a patient is given a specific appointment for the blood test, which Walter was not, and then failed to keep that appointment could she be faulted. Dr. Ross did not tell Walter the importance of the blood test. Walter should not and could not have been expected to know the medical significance of the blood test. Thus, not only was there no evidence from which the jury could find that Walter was negligent in this regard, no jury, acting rationally, could have concluded that a delay in obtaining the blood test was negligence equal to or greater than Wal-Mart's negligence. That being so, the only possibility left to a jury was a reduction in damages, and the mitigation instruction fully gave the jury the ability to reduce damages.

III. WAL-MART'S MOTION FOR JUDGMENT AS A MATTER OF LAW

Wal-Mart moved for judgment as a matter of law on the ground that Walter failed to present any expert evidence on the pharmacist's standard of care. It pointed out that Lovin was not designated as an expert. In this case the testimony of an expert was not necessary. The Court has said that where professional negligence and its harmful results "are sufficiently obvious as to lie within common knowledge" no expert testimony is necessary. *Jim Mitchell and Jed Davis, P.A. v. Jackson*, 627 A.2d 1014, 1017 (Me. 1993) The negligence of the pharmacist and the harmful results were sufficiently obvious to be within the common knowledge of a lay person. It does not take an expert to know that filling a prescription with the wrong drug.

IV. WAL-MART'S MOTION FOR MISTRIAL

Wal-Mart moved for a mistrial because of three comments made by Walter's counsel during closing argument. First, Walter's attorney stated that the pharmacist attempted to accept responsibility but his employer, Wal-Mart, refused to accept responsibility for Walter's injury. Wal-Mart objected, and the objection was sustained. The court admonished counsel that the only issue was damages and told the jury that they were not to be swayed by any bias or predisposition towards one party or the other. Second, Walter's counsel said that Walter was sent home "not with the smiley face as we hear about at Wal-Mart, but with a bottle of poison, a bottle of medication that was not meant for her." Wal-Mart objected and moved for a mistrial. The motion was denied, and the judge told the jurors that the issue was damages. Third, while referring to the amount of damages the jury could award during rebuttal, Walter's counsel told the jury it should consider how much money professional basketball players are paid. Wal-Mart objected and the objection was sustained. Wal-Mart argued that the effect of the three comments was to prejudice the jury against Wal-Mart so that it would punish Wal-Mart by awarding greater damages.

The Appeals Court reviews a refusal to grant a motion for a mistrial for abuse of discretion. The trial judge sustained the objections to the comments, told the jurors to ignore the comments, and gave curative instructions. The trial judge did not abuse his discretion in refusing to grant a mistrial because of Walter's comments during closing argument.

V. WAL-MART'S MOTION FOR NEW TRIAL

After the verdict Wal-Mart moved for a new trial arguing that the verdict must be vacated because the damages amounted to an award of punitive damages. Wal-Mart further contended that the damages were excessive and the size of the verdict demonstrated that the judge and jury were biased against Wal-Mart.

The Court stated that "When a trial court refuses to grant a new trial on the ground of an excessive damage award, the ruling will not be reversed except for clear and manifest abuse of discretion." Evidence must be construed in the light most favorable to the jury verdict, and a damage award will not be overturned unless it "is without rational explanation." *Cope v. Sevigny*, 289 A.2d 682, 684 (ME 1972).

Walter's total medical bills and expenses equaled $71,042.63. The jury awarded Walter $550,000 in damages. Presumably, the additional $479,000 of Walter's recovery was in compensation for her pain and suffering. The jury heard several witnesses, including Walter herself, testify about the painful treatment she received in the hospital, the long recovery process, and the continuing difficulties she faces. In light of the evidence, which had to be considered favorably to Walter, the jury's award of damages was rational. Although the verdict may have seemed large, it reflected the considered opinion of the jury within the range of evidence of sufficient probative character

Punitive damages were never an issue in this case. They were not requested by Walter. They were not mentioned during the arguments of counsel, and no instructions were given from which the jury could have awarded any damages other than compensatory damages. The court did not abuse its discretion in refusing to grant a new trial because of the amount of damages.

CHAPTER 13. THE DOCTRINE OF QUANTUM MERUIT

Quantum meruit is a theory of recovery that operates when there is an implied or executory contract between parties. The term is directly from the Latin *Quantum*, meaning how much, and from the 2nd conjugation Latin verb *Mereo, Merere, Merui, Meritus*. Meruit is the 3rd person singular perfect (active) tense and translates "he deserved." The phrase *quantum meruit* means, then, "how much he deserved." So, if one party performs a labor for another where a contract exists and is not fully compensated, the performing party has legal recourse for fair compensation through the courts on a *quantum meruit* claim.

Take the situation where a party hired a law firm to prosecute a wrongful termination of employment claim. The plaintiff and the law firm entered into a contingency-fee agreement, plus costs, whereby the firm would receive 30% of any settlement or court award. Unhappy with the law firm's subsequent brokered agreement to settle the plaintiff's claim for $300,000, the plaintiff terminated the law firm's services. The law firm filed an attorneys lien against the proceeds of the plaintiff's wrongful termination lawsuit when the plaintiff received a jury award of several million dollars and, in so doing, sought to compel arbitration. The trial court that heard the request for arbitration found the contingency-fee agreement void and denied the law firm any recovery. The law firm appealed and the court of appeals reversed, holding that the law firm should have been allowed to proceed on a *quantum-meruit* claim, despite the plaintiff's rejection of the settlement offer in the lower court. On remand, the trial court proceeded on a *quantum meruit* claim and awarded the law firm an amount equal to 30% of the $300,000 rejected settlement offer plus costs.

BEVERLY HEEBSH, PLAINTIFF-APPELLANT, V. JENKS HOME MAINTENANCE
AND ZURICH NORTH AMERICA, DEFENDANTS-RESPONDENTS.
COURT OF APPEALS OF WISCONSIN, DISTRICT FOUR
693 N.W.2D 147
JANUARY 20, 2005

LEGAL CONSIDERATIONS

Contracts Law / Quantum meruit

When an owner wrongfully prevents a contractor from completing the work, after the contractor has gone to substantial expense in partial performance, the contractor may elect either to complete the contract and recover damages for the breach or may recover under the doctrine of *quantum meruit* for the reasonable value of the work already performed.

Civil Procedure / Appeals / Standards of Review

When an appellate court reviews the findings of fact made by a court sitting as trier of fact, a trial court, the appellate court accepts those findings unless they are clearly erroneous. The credibility of witnesses and weight of the evidence, as well as the inferences to be drawn from the evidence, are for the trial court to make not the appellate court.

Contracts Law

When one party to an executory contract prevents the performance of it, the other party may regard it as terminated and demand whatever damages he has sustained thereby. (An executory contract is a contract where some future act of performance is yet to be done.)

Civil Procedure / Damages

Under Wisconsin law, a person suffering pecuniary loss because of a contract violation may sue for damages in any court and shall recover twice the amount of such pecuniary loss, together with costs, including a reasonable attorney's fee.

Contracts Law / Contract Conditions & Provisions

Wisconsin law provides that if a "buyer" signs a written contract, the contract shall set forth "the dates or time period on or within which the work is to begin and be completed by the seller."

Contracts Law

Under Wisconsin law if a buyer believes that the seller has failed to provide the materials or services in a timely manner, and the home improvement contract specifies no deadline for the seller to provide the materials or services, the buyer may cancel the contract and demand return of all payments the seller has not yet expended on the home improvement project.

PRIOR HISTORY: APPEAL from a judgment of the circuit court (trial court) for La Crosse County: RAMONA A. GONZALEZ, Judge.

PROCEDURAL POSTURE: Plaintiff homeowner filed an action alleging that the fence erected by defendant company was deficient. The homeowner was awarded $58; she appealed and argued that the Circuit Court for La Crosse County, Wisconsin, erred in ruling that the company did not breach the contract, in applying the doctrine of *quantum meruit*, and in holding she was not entitled to remedies.

OVERVIEW: The homeowner hired the company to build a fence on her property and to build a hand railing on the steps and to install gutters with downspouts on the north side of her house. The fence proposal stated that the cost of labor and materials would be $1195, with $797 due on the start of the job and the balance upon completion; the railing/gutter proposal stated that the cost for labor and materials would be $ 1113, with $742 due at the start of the job and the remainder due upon completion. The homeowner paid the company $1,500. Neither proposal prepared by the company had a start date or completion date. The homeowner told the company to stop work on the fence after about a week and thereafter told the company to stop work on the railings because there were a number of problems with the fence. The appellate court affirmed the trial court's ruling and held: (1) the company did not breach the contract where it stopped construction at the owner's request; (2) the company was entitled to the *quantum meruit* value of its work as the homeowner prevented the company from completing its work; and (3) the homeowner was not entitled to statutory remedies under Wisconsin Statute §100.20(5) (2003-04).

OUTCOME: The appellate court affirmed the judgment, but denied the company's request for attorney fees.

Background and Opinion

Beverly Heebsh initiated a small claims action alleging that the fence erected by Jenks Home Maintenance (Jenks) was deficient in a number of ways. She appealed the judgment in her favor for $58.62, contending that the trial court erred in determining that Jenks did not breach the contract, that the trial court erred in applying the doctrine of *quantum meruit* to determine Jenks' damages, and in concluding she was not entitled to remedies under Wisconsin law. The Appeals Court concluded that:

(1) the evidence supported the trial court's determination that Jenks did not breach the contract because Heebsh, without sufficient justification, directed that all work stop before work was completed; (2) that the trial court's use of the doctrine of *quantum meruit* to compute Jenks' damages was proper; and that (3) Heebsh was not entitled to remedies under Wisconsin law.

The Appeals Court also concluded that the appeal was not frivolous as Jenks contended. Therefore, Jenks was not entitled to attorney fees.

Factual and Procedural Background

On October 4, 2002, Heebsh signed two proposals prepared by Jenks, one for the construction of a chain link fence on her residential property and the other for a hand railing on the steps and for gutters with downspouts on the north side of her house. The fence proposal stated that the cost of labor and materials would be $1195.22, with $797.22 due on the start of the job and the balance upon completion; the railing/gutter proposal stated that the cost for labor and materials would be $1113.38, with $742.38 due at the start of the job and the remainder due upon completion. Heebsh paid $1500 by check to Jenks on October 4.

Bert Jenks along with his brother began work on the fence approximately eight to eleven days after the proposal was signed. According to Heebsh's testimony at trial, after about a week she told Bert's brother they were to stop work and they did; at that point they had started work on the railings. Heebsh testified that she told them to stop work because there were a number of problems with the fence.

Heebsh filed a complaint with the Agriculture and Consumer Protection Agency, seeking a return of her down payment, removal of all materials, and repair of the cement on the sidewalk. When she was unable to reach a resolution with Jenks as a result of that complaint, she initiated this action, seeking $3000. Jenks answered alleging that he had not completed the work when Heebsh directed that work stop, and he counterclaimed for $641, allegedly the cost in excess of $1500 for labor and materials before work stopped.

At the trial Heebsh presented the testimony of John Kanpur, a contractor who installs chain link fences and who had inspected this fence about five or six months after Jenks had stopped working on it. Kamprud testified to a number of ways in which, in his opinion, the work on the fence was not properly done.

Jenks testified that the fence had not been completed when Heebsh directed them to stop working. When his brother told him that they were to stop working, Jenks asked Heebsh what the problems were; when she told him the problems she had with the fence, he explained the fence was not finished. Bert testified that they still needed to tighten the fence and patch the sidewalk for which he had already purchased the concrete and still needed to finish the railing, which they had already begun, and put up the gutters. He estimated this would take about a day. Bert Jenks also testified that the problems Kamprud described with the fence would be able to be fixed in about two hours.

Heebsh testified that she assumed the brothers were done with the fence, although neither told her they were, because they had started to work on the railing. She stated that after she told them to stop work, Bert asked to be able to finish the work but she did not allow it. Nothing further was done on either of the projects by anyone.

The circuit court found that Jenks had not completed the fence when Heebsh directed that work stop and that, although there were some problems with the fence at that time that needed to be fixed, they were not as serious as Heebsh contended. Because Heebsh prevented Jenks from completing the two projects without an adequate basis for doing so, the court determined that Jenks was entitled to relief based on the doctrine of *quantum meruit* for the labor provided and materials purchased. The court determined that the materials used or purchased for both projects cost $839.69 and that $500 was fair compensation for the work already performed. The court then deducted the sum of $1359.69 from the $1500 that Heebsh had already paid, finding that Heebsh was due the difference. Ultimately, however, the judgment entered in favor of Heebsh was for only $58.62.

Both after trial and in denying the motion for reconsideration, the court rejected Heebsh's position that the failure of the two proposals to contain start-and-completion dates entitled her to double damages and attorney fees. The basis for this ruling was the court's determination that there was no evidence that the failure of the two proposals to contain all the information required caused any pecuniary damage to Heebsh.

Discussion

Heebsh contends on appeal that the circuit court erred by (1) determining that Jenks did not breach the contract; (2) in applying the doctrine of *quantum meruit*; and by (3) concluding that the remedies of Wisconsin law did not apply.

When an Appeals Court reviews the findings of fact made by a court sitting as trier of fact, the Court accepts those findings unless they are clearly erroneous. The credibility of witnesses and weight of the evidence, as well as the inferences to be drawn from the evidence, are for the trial court to make, not an Appeals Court. The Court affirms the trial court's determination if, accepting the reasonable inferences from the evidence drawn by the fact finder, a reasonable fact finder could have come to the same conclusion. However, whether the circuit court (trial court) applied the correct legal standard presents a question of law which the Appeals Court will review de novo. That is also the standard of review for construing and applying statutes and regulations to the facts as found by the circuit court.

The Appeals Court first addressed Heebsh's contention that it was undisputed that Jenks materially breached the contract by erecting a defective fence. The Court did not agree that the evidence on that issue was undisputed. The Court credited Bert's explanation that the fence was not completed and that, had he and his brother been allowed to complete it, the problems Heebsh observed would have been remedied. Heebsh pointed to Kamprud's testimony (the expert witness) on how he, Kamprud, constructed a fence and his opinion that Jenks had completed construction. However, Kamprud also acknowledged that it was possible to put up a fence using a different order of tasks and that there were adjustments that still could be done to stretch the fence. In addition, Bert explained why he performed the tasks in the order he did and what he still intended to do. To the extent that Kamprud's testimony and Bert's testimony was in conflict, the circuit court could properly choose to credit the latter rather than the former. The Court concluded there was sufficient evidence to support the circuit court's determination that Jenks did not materially breach the contract because Heebsh prevented him and his brother from completing the fence.

The Court next addressed Heebsh's contention that the trial court erred in applying the doctrine of *quantum meruit* to compensate Jenks. Heebsh points to the court's comment that "the contract itself is silent on several significant issues and therefore is not subject to enforcement in its specific terms. The court will rely on *quantum meruit* with regard to the appropriate amounts due in this case." Heebsh contended this was error because there was an enforceable contract and the court was not free to set it aside.

Heebsh's position on this point is apparently based on a misunderstanding of the trial court's comments. The sentence preceding the two quoted above is: "Miss Heebsh violated the contract by ceasing the contract without any warning or prior knowledge or notice to Mr. Jenks." It was evident from this sentence and the findings the court had already made that the court meant that the terms of the contracts were not specific enough to provide a basis for compensating Jenks for the work he had done and, therefore, the court was going to apply the doctrine of *quantum meruit*. The trial court was not setting aside the contracts, but, rather, having determined that Heebsh, not Jenks, had breached the contracts, the court was deciding on the method of computing Jenks' damages for Heebsh's breach.

The trial court was correct that, because it had found that Heebsh had prevented Jenks from completing the contracts, Jenks was entitled to compensation for any damages he sustained. When one party to an executory contract prevents the performance of it, the other party may regard it as terminated and demand whatever damages he has sustained thereby. The Appeals Court also held that the trial court was correct that *quantum meruit* was a proper basis on which to compute damages. When a property owner wrongfully prevents a contractor from completing his work, after the contractor has gone to substantial expense in partial performance, the contractor may elect either to complete the contract and recover damages for breach of contract, or he may stop work and recover under the doctrine of *quantum meruit* for the reasonable value of the work already performed. The Court concluded the circuit court did not commit error in applying the doctrine of *quantum meruit* to determine Jenks' damages.

Finally, the Appeals Court turned to Heebsh's contention that she was entitled to remedies under Wisconsin law, and concluded the circuit court correctly decided she was not.

Wisconsin law provides that a person "suffering pecuniary loss because of a violation ... of any order issued under the law may sue for damages ... in any court ... and shall recover twice the amount of such pecuniary loss, together with costs, including a reasonable attorney's fee." The Court of Appeals concluded that if the buyer signs a written contract, the contract shall set forth "the dates or time period on or within which the work is to begin and be completed by the seller."

Heebsh contended that because the two proposals she signed did not contain start and completion dates for the work, she is entitled to double damages and attorney fees and remedies. Under Wisconsin law, if the "buyer believes that the seller has failed to provide the materials or services in a timely manner, and the home improvement contract specifies no deadline for the seller to provide the materials or services," the buyer may cancel the contract and demand return of all payments the seller has not yet expended on the home improvement project.

The Appeals Court held that the evidence supported the trial court's determination that Heebsh was dissatisfied with the work itself, not with the date on which Jenks began work nor with the time it took Jenks to do the work.

The Court next agreed with the circuit court that Heebsh did not establish that she suffered a pecuniary loss caused by the absence of start and completion dates in the two proposals. Heebsh first argued that the lack of a completion date allowed Jenks to "retain indefinitely some or all of the deposit that did not belong to him." However, based on the facts as found by the circuit court, supported by the record, the court determined that it was Heebsh's direction to stop work that caused Jenks to retain a portion of the deposit that had not yet been earned. Heebsh also argued that the extra funds that she would have to expend to have the defective fence remedied were a pecuniary loss. Again, however, based on the circuit court's findings, which are supported by the record, it was Heebsh's unjustified direction to stop work that resulted in a fence that was not completed or not properly completed; the lack of a completion date in the two proposals did not cause that result.

Although the Court affirmed the judgment, it denied Jenks' request for attorney fees in as much as it could not determine that Heebsh's arguments were frivolous.

The judgment was affirmed in the defendant's favor.

CHAPTER 14. THE DOCTRINE OF SOVEREIGN IMMUNITY

The history of sovereign immunity is most interesting. The history of the doctrine in this country is associated with the English common-law concept that "the king can do no wrong." That concept evolved from the personal prerogatives of the King of England who was considered the fount of justice and equity in English law. In the English feudal system, the lord of the manor was not subject to suit in his own courts. Under the doctrine of sovereign immunity, then, the sovereign is immune. That is to say the king cannot be sued, long live the king! This doctrine comes to us, we Americans, down through the English ages and originally was meant to prevent the king from being sued in his own court. How could you, after all, sue a king in his own court when originally the king was the court because it was the king's court. Although the notion of sovereign immunity is best suited to a government of royal power, American courts nonetheless accepted the doctrine in the early days of the republic. However, courts and commentators have remained mystified why the doctrine was ever accepted in this country. One commentator has expressed his bafflement this way: "Nothing seems more clear than that this immunity of the King from the jurisdiction of the King's courts was purely personal. How it came to be applied in the United States of America, where royal prerogative is unknown, is one of the mysteries of legal evolution." Admitting its application to the sovereign and its illogical ascription as an attribute of sovereignty, it is not easy to appreciate its application in the United States where undivided sovereignty as orthodox theory flies in the face of what we are. It is beyond doubt that the Executive in the United States is not historically the sovereign, and the legislature, which is perhaps the depository of the widest powers, is restrained by constitutional limitations. The federal government stands on delegated powers and the states are not sovereign according to the Constitution as demonstrated forcibly by the Civil War and the resulting Constitutional Amendments. That brings us to the only remaining alternative, that sovereignty resides in the American electorate."

Generally, the doctrine holds that citizens may not sue the government without the government's consent. It isn't that the government has no duty to protect its citizens, just that such a breach of duty is not actionable against the government.

Supreme Court Justice Oliver Wendell Holmes put it succinctly when, in *Kawananakoa v. Polyblank*, 205 U.S, 349 (1907), he said "A sovereign is exempt from suit not because of any formal conception or obsolete theory, but on the logical and practical ground that there can be no legal right against the authority that makes the law on which the right depends." There are those, of course, who would argue the point with Justice Homes, and who have, but sovereign immunity is still very much a force to be reckoned with as we shall see.

Take for example the case where an osteopathic physician in charge of a county-run nursing home in a rural southern state left explicit instructions with a nursing supervisor that a certain patient was no longer to be given a certain anti-diarrheic medication because the patient had developed an infection for which the anti-diarrheic was counter-indicated and might result in serious medical consequences. The nursing supervisor felt the doctor was wrong in his instructions and administered the medication anyway. As it turned out, the patient fell gravely ill and came close to dying. Because the nursing home was, as I have said, a county-run facility, the doctor was required by a state law to report the incident to the state agency whose responsibility it was to monitor state and county-run nursing homes

Well, it so happened that the particular nursing supervisor involved was a long time employee of the nursing home and had considerable clout with certain individuals who subsequently got together and, collectively, fired the doctor. The doctor, much chagrined I'm sure, was not one to turn his cheek. He initiated a legal action against the nursing home and its director, citing wrongful discharge, an actionable tort. The nursing home, the district, and the defendant filed a motion to dismiss for failure to state a claim upon which relief could be granted, a Rule 12(b)(6) motion, arguing that because the nursing home was a political sub-division of the state, all involved were immune under the doctrine of sovereign immunity. The trial-court judge agreed and the case was thrown out. The doctor appealed.

The appeals court reversed the trial court and remanded for retrial.

Citing the state regulation, the appeals court said that according to state law neither a nursing-home operator nor any person in authority in a state or county-run nursing home could retaliate against any employee who reports suspected incidents of patient abuse or neglect, and, additionally, that no person who directs or has authority in a such facility shall evict, harass, or retaliate against any resident or employee because such resident or employee or any member of such an individual's family has made a report of any violation of the laws, regulations or ordinances that apply to such state facilities, sovereign immunity notwithstanding.

NANCY CARTER, INDIVIDUALLY AND AS ADMINISTRATRIX OF THE ESTATE OF WILLARD
CARTER, MICHAEL BRIAN CARTER AND MARGARET ANN CARTER, MINOR CHILDREN,
BY THEIR NEXT FRIEND, NANCY CARTER, PLAINTIFFS BELOW, APPELLANTS,
V. BRAIN MCLAUGHLIN,
DELAWARE ADMINISTRATION FOR REGIONAL TRANSIT, INC., ST. PAUL MERCURY INS.
CO., AND DELAWARE TRANSIT CORPORATION, DEFENDANTS BELOW, APPELLEES.
SUPREME COURT OF DELAWARE
APRIL 14, 2000, DECIDED

LEGAL CONSIDERATIONS

Torts / Public Entity Liability / Sovereign Immunity

Under the doctrine of sovereign immunity, State agencies, including the Delaware Administration for Regional Transit, Inc. (DART), are protected from liability for damages caused by ordinary negligence. The State Tort Claims Act, Delaware Code Annotated title 10, $4001, however, waived sovereign immunity for claims alleging gross or wanton negligence. A more recent statute also waived DART's sovereign immunity for claims covered by liability insurance, but the statute limited recovery against DART to a maximum of $300,000.

Governments / Public Entity Liability / Sovereign Immunity

Delaware Code Annotated title 2, $1329 (amended 1999), creates a new, but limited, cause of action against the Delaware Administration for Regional Transit, Inc., (DART), for claims that otherwise were barred by the doctrine of sovereign immunity. Since sovereign immunity does not apply to claims for gross and wanton negligence, those claims are not newly created by, or otherwise within the scope of $ 1329.

Civil Procedure / De Novo Review

The appellate court reviews summary judgment decisions de novo (from anew, from scratch).

Civil Procedure / Summary Judgment

On cross-motions for summary judgment, neither party's motion will be granted unless no genuine issue of material fact exists and one of the parties is entitled to judgment as a matter of law.

Governments / Immunity

Under the State Tort Claims Act, Delaware Code Annotated title 10, §4001, there is no limit on the amount of recovery against a State agency for a claim of gross or wanton negligence.

Governments / Public Entity Liability

The $300,000 cap on liability under Delaware Code Annotated title 2, §1329 (amended 1999), now applies only to passenger rail carrier operations of the Delaware Transit corporation. For other claims against the Delaware Administration for Regional Transit, Inc. (DART), the statute allows recovery up to the amount of insurance purchased by DART, which must be at least $300,000 per occurrence.

Governments / Legislation

The General Assembly is presumed to be aware of existing law, and statutes are presumed to be consistent with prior law.

Governments / Interpretation

Repeal by implication is not favored in law, except when two provisions are irreconcilably inconsistent or repugnant to each other.

OVERVIEW: Plaintiffs, surviving spouse and children of decedent, sought damages from defendant state agencies and their insurer alleging that decedent's death from being struck by defendants' bus was the result of gross negligence. Defendants asserted that damages were subject to the monetary limit set out in Delaware Code Annotated title. 10, §1329 (amended 1999) while plaintiffs maintained that no such limitation was applicable under the waiver of *sovereign immunity* of the State Tort Claims Act (Act). The court held that the Act waived *sovereign immunity* for claims of gross negligence, and created a new, but limited, cause of action against defendants for claims that were otherwise barred by *sovereign immunity*. Since *sovereign immunity* did not apply to claims for gross and wanton negligence, the Court held that plaintiffs' claim was not within the scope of the law and was not subject to existing statutory monetary recovery limits.

OUTCOME: The order of the court was reversed by the Supreme Court; the statute limiting the amount of damages recoverable from defendant state agencies only applied to actions otherwise barred by *sovereign immunity*, and thus the limitation did not apply to plaintiffs' action alleging gross negligence which was specifically within the scope of the statutory waiver of sovereign immunity.

OPINION: In this appeal, The Supreme Court considered whether there is a limit on DART's liability for damages caused by its gross or wanton negligence. Under the doctrine of *sovereign immunity*, State agencies, including DART, are protected from liability for damages caused by ordinary negligence. The State Tort Claims Act, however, waived *sovereign immunity* for claims alleging gross or wanton negligence. A more recent statute also waived DART's *sovereign immunity* for claims covered by liability insurance, but the statute limited recovery against DART to a maximum of $300,000. The Court held that said damage cap does not apply to claims for gross and wanton negligence. Accordingly, the Court reversed the trial court's grant of summary judgment to DART and its denial of summary judgment to the Carters. (The Delaware Administration for Regional Transit, Inc. (DART) is a division of the Delaware Transportation corp. The two entities were referred to collectively throughout this opinion as "DART."

Factual and Procedural Background

For purposes of this appeal, the parties stipulated to the following facts. Appellants are the surviving wife and children of Willard Carter who died as a result of injuries sustained when his vehicle was struck by a DART bus operated by Brian McLaughlin. The accident occurred on February 8, 1996, at the intersection of Pennsylvania Avenue and Van Buren Street in the City of Wilmington. The DART bus went through a red light into the intersection where it struck the vehicle driven by Willard Carter. After striking Carter's vehicle, the bus jumped a curb and came to rest 298 feet from the point of initial impact. Carter's vehicle was pushed 82 feet to its final resting place. The bus left no skid marks. Willard Carter suffered massive injuries and remained in a coma for fifteen months. On April 25, 1997, Carter died as a result of the injuries sustained in the collision.

Willard Carter's wife and children filed the incident action seeking compensatory and punitive damages, charging DART and its employee with gross negligence. Both sides moved for summary judgment on the issue of whether Delaware Code Annotated title 2 §1329, which limits damages against DART to $ 300,000, applies to claims alleging gross negligence. The Superior Court, relying on the Supreme Court's decision in *Turnbull v. Fink*, 668 A.2d 1370 (1995), held that it does.

DISCUSSION

A. Standard of Review

The Supreme Court reviews summary judgment decisions de novo. On cross-motions for summary judgment, neither party's motion will be granted unless no genuine issue of material fact exists and one of the parties is entitled to judgment as a matter of law.

B. Waiver of DART's Sovereign Immunity

The parties agreed that DART, as a State agency, was protected by the doctrine of sovereign immunity unless the General Assembly had waived that immunity. The parties also agreed that immunity had been waived, at least in part. The question was whether, for the claim herein, the extent of the waiver was controlled by the State Tort Claims Act or by Delaware Code Annotated title 2 §1329. The State Tort Claims Act 5 provides, in relevant part:

"Except as otherwise provided by the Constitutions or laws of the United States or of the State of Delaware, no claim or cause of action shall arise, and no judgment, damages, penalties, costs or other money entitlement shall be awarded or assessed against the State or any public officer or employee . . . where the following elements are present: . . . . (3) The act or omission complained of was done in the absence of gross or wanton negligence."

By its terms, the statute excludes from the doctrine of sovereign immunity claims of gross or wanton negligence. As a result, under the State Tort Claims Act, there is no limit on the amount of recovery against a State agency for a claim of gross or wanton negligence.

The doctrine of sovereign immunity was also restricted in Delaware Code Annotated title 2 §1329, which was enacted by Section 68 of the 1989 Bond Act. At the time of the Carter accident, Section 1329 provided, in relevant part:

> Any operation, service or program provided by the Delaware Transportation Authority not covered by a general liability policy, self-insurance or other insurance policy as shall be legally established and funded by said Authority shall be covered and protected by the doctrine of sovereign immunity of the State. In the event that insurance has been provided, such claim, including any award for damages or costs assessed against the Authority, its administrators, subsidiaries, officers or employees either individually or on behalf of their employer shall not exceed the amount of said insurance covering the risk or loss or the amount of $300,000 whichever amount shall be lesser for any and all claims arising out of a single occurrence.

> Section 1329 was amended in 1999. The $300,000 cap on liability now applies only to passenger rail carrier operations of the Delaware Transit corporation. For other claims against DART, the statute allows recovery up to the amount of insurance purchased by DART, which must be at least $ 300,000 per occurrence.

C. Interpretation of §1329 in *Turnbull v. Fink*

The Supreme Court recently examined §1329 in connection with another tort claim against DART. In *Turnbull v. Fink*, like this case, the parties disputed the extent of DART's potential liability for damages arising out of bus accidents. The injured parties argued that, under Delaware Code Annotated title 8§ 6511, DART should be held liable up to the limits of its insurance coverage ($5 million), whereas DART contended that the $300,000 cap in §1329 controlled. Although the majority in Turnbull concluded that $ 1329 controlled, a careful reading of the decision revealed that the same result was not warranted here.

In Turnbull the alternative to §1329 was Delaware Code Annotated title 18 §6511, enacted in 1969 as part of a comprehensive act designed to provide insurance protection for the State. Section 6511 expressly waives sovereign immunity for "any risk or loss covered by the state insurance program or by self-insurance...." Other sections of the act establish a State Insurance Coverage Office, a committee to determine methods of insuring the State, and procedures by which insurance may be obtained either through a self-insurance fund or commercial insurance policies. Because the state insurance coverage program never was established or funded, however, this Court held, in 1985, that §6511 did not waive sovereign immunity. The Turnbull majority used the same reasoning to find that §6511 remained inoperative at the time of the accident at issue.

After determining that §6511 provided no waiver of sovereign immunity, the Turnbull majority considered the validity of §1329. It found that the statute was properly enacted and did not deprive injured parties of due process, equal protection of the laws, or the right to a jury trial. In responding to the jury trial argument, the majority noted that §1329 provided a new cause of action not available "heretofore":

> At common law and under the Delaware Constitution, lawsuits against the state have always been barred by the doctrine of sovereign immunity unless waived by the General Assembly. The enactment of Delaware Code Annotated title 2 §1329, therefore, represents a modification of the common law rule by allowing lawsuits against DART through a limited waiver of sovereign immunity. Section 1329 does not deprive petitioners of their existing right to a jury trial, rather, it creates a new right to sue. By enacting Delaware Code Annotated title 2 §1329, the General Assembly exercised its power to create, and at the same time, limit the new cause of action.

In sum, Turnbull held that the injured parties would have had no recourse against DART if not for the limited waiver of sovereign immunity provided by Delaware Code Annotated title 2 §1329.

D. Interpretation of §1329 in this case

In Turnbull this Court did not reconcile two arguably conflicting statutes. Rather, the majority held that one of the two statutes, §6511, was inoperative. Here, too, there is no conflict because only one of the two statutes under consideration addresses the parties' claim. The State Tort Claims Act waives sovereign immunity for claims of gross or wanton negligence. As noted in Turnbull, §1329 creates a new, but limited, cause of action against DART for claims that otherwise were barred by the doctrine of sovereign immunity.

Since sovereign immunity does not apply to claims for gross and wanton negligence, those claims are not newly created by or otherwise within the scope of §1329.

This common sense interpretation of the two statutes found support in established principles of statutory construction. The General Assembly was presumed to be aware of existing law, and statutes were presumed to be consistent with prior law. The corollary to these rules was that "repeal by implication is not favored in law except when two provisions are irreconcilably inconsistent or repugnant to each other. If §1329 were read to limit the recovery on a claim for gross or wanton negligence, it would be partially repealing the State Tort Claims Act, which has no limit on recovery for such a claim. Instead, the interpretation the Court adopts harmonizes the two statutes and gives effect to both."

CONCLUSION

Based on the foregoing, the decisions of the Superior Court were reversed in favor of the plaintiff and the matter was remanded to the trial court for further action consistent with the opinion herein.

Chapter 15. The Doctrine of Absolute Immunity

The doctrine of *absolute immunity* holds that a person or persons to whom the doctrine applies by virtue of statute or common-law precedent is absolutely immune from prosecution for tort liability. In other words, the doctrine of sovereign immunity applies to governmental entities and the doctrine of *absolute immunity* applies, when applicable, to individuals. An example of the workings of this doctrine is a situation that developed in a Western state a few years ago. A sheep rancher was moving his herd of a couple of thousand sheep from one pasture range to another. In order to do so, it was necessary that the sheep move along a traveled highway for a mile or so.

The sheepherder had attendants on foot accompanying his herd and also had vehicles with flashers operating preceding and following his herd. While the herd was moving along the highway Mr. A came up behind the herd and slowed his vehicle to a crawl. Shortly after gearing down another vehicle driven by Mr. B approached the herd at a high rate of speed and couldn't stop in time to avoid hitting Mr. A's vehicle in the rear. Mr. B. was seriously injured.

When Mr. B had recovered, he brought a negligence suit against the sheep rancher, claiming the rancher had been negligent in blocking the highway with his herd. The rancher's lawyer moved for dismissal as a matter of law. The court granted the motion. The court based its decision on the fact that state law allowed ranchers to move their herds and flocks along state highways so long as such movements were supervised, saying that under the doctrine of *absolute immunity*, negligence would absolutely not attach to a party doing something it was legally entitled to do. The following case is further illustrative of *Absolute Immunity*.

JULIE JOHNSON, INDIVIDUALLY, AND ROBIN JOHNSON, NICOLE JOHNSON,
AND ZACHARY CLEEK, MINORS, BY AND THROUGH JULIE JOHNSON, THEIR
NEXT FRIEND, MOTHER, AND NATURAL GUARDIAN, APPELLANTS,
v. NANCY SACKETT,
DEPARTMENT OF HEALTH AND REHABILITATIVE SERVICES (N/K/A DEPARTMENT OF
CHILDREN AND FAMILIES, CITY OF ST. PETERSBURG, AND L.A. CLEMENTO, APPELLEES,
793 SO. 2D 20
MARCH 28, 2001

LEGAL CONSIDERATIONS

Constitutional Law / Absolute Immunity

In the context of 42 U.S.C.S. §1983 claims, the United States Supreme Court has afforded prosecutors absolute immunity for their actions in initiating or litigating a criminal charge. Thereafter, the Supreme Court extended this protection to persons performing adjudicatory or quasi-judicial functions within federal agencies.

Constitutional Law / Public Officials / Absolute Immunity

Caseworkers enjoy *absolute immunity* from 42 U.S.C.S. §1983 claims in regard to their roles in filing and pursuing dependency petitions because these roles are quasi-judicial like the role of a prosecutor.

Constitutional Law / Absolute Immunity

Florida case law has never extended absolute immunity to caseworkers. In seeking such immunity, a heavy burden rests upon the caseworker to establish that public policy requires an exemption of this scope.

Constitutional Law / Public Officials

A police officer is entitled to only qualified immunity.

PROCEDURAL POSTURE: Appellant, individually and as the mother and guardian of her children, challenged an order of the Circuit Court for Pinellas County (Florida) granting appellee caseworker summary judgment on plaintiff's federal 42 U.S.C.S. §1983 and state common-law claims for malicious prosecution for actions arising from a child-dependency proceeding. (42 U.S.C.S. §1983 is the federal codification of the Fourteenth Amendment enacted following the Civil War to guarantee the slaves the rights of due process and equal protection of the law. Overtime these rights came to be recognized as applicable to all individuals as federal citizens.)

OVERVIEW: Appellee caseworker initiated a dependency proceeding regarding appellant's two children. The children were initially placed in the custody of appellant's mother, but appellee later sought to place them in protective custody when appellant's mother failed to abide by the trial court's orders.

Plaintiff-appellant gave birth to a third child and when appellee caseworker attempted to remove the children to protective custody, appellant parent resisted. Plaintiff was arrested and all three children were taken into protective custody. Defendant-appellee then filed a separate dependency proceeding regarding the youngest child. Ultimately, the dependency proceedings and the charges stemming from appellant mother's arrest were dropped. Appellant filed a lawsuit alleging appellee's actions violated her rights under 42 U.S.C.S. §1983, alleging various state common-law claims, including malicious prosecution (malicious prosecution is an action in criminal law addressing a criminal proceeding that was undertaken without probable cause). The trial court granted appellee's motion for summary judgment dismissing plaintiff's claims. The Appeals Court reversed in part, holding that appellee enjoyed *absolute immunity* from plaintiff's federal civil rights claims, but that the trial court erred in granting summary judgment on the malicious prosecution claim because appellee was not cloaked with *absolute immunity* to such a claim.

OUTCOME: The judgment was reversed in part because while appellee enjoyed absolute immunity from the federal civil rights violations alleged, that immunity did not extend to appellant's state law claim for malicious prosecution for the actions alleged in the petition for dependency regarding appellant's youngest son, rendering summary judgment inappropriate.

OPINION: Appellee, Nancy Sackett's motion for rehearing was granted. The opinion issued by the trial court December 8, 2000, was withdrawn, and the attached opinion was substituted in its stead.

Julie Johnson, individually and as the mother and guardian of her three minor children, appealed a summary judgment entered in favor of Nancy Sackett, an employee of the Department of Health and Rehabilitative Services, now known as the Department of Children and Families (the Department). The Appeals Court affirmed in part and reversed in part.

This case arises out of events culminating in January 1989, when Ms. Sackett and Officer L.A. Clemento, an employee of the City of St. Petersburg, forcibly took custody of Ms. Johnson's three children during a pending custody proceeding. The events leading up to this incident, however, began in early 1988, when Ms. Johnson's former husband had custody of their two children pursuant to a divorce decree. Ms. Johnson was pregnant with a third child and living at Alpha House. Then, in September 1988, the former husband was arrested for a serious felony. As a result, the Department initiated a dependency proceeding for the two older children. Ms. Johnson's third child was born November 8, 1988.

After an initial hearing in the custody proceeding on December 27, 1988, the trial court orally approved the placement of the two older children with the maternal grandmother. Ms. Johnson was allowed some contact with the children. Thereafter, an investigation conducted by Ms. Sackett caused her to believe that the grandmother was not adequately supervising the children and was allowing Ms. Johnson more contact with the children than the circuit court's oral order had authorized. After discussing the matter with the Department's counsel, Ms. Sackett decided to place the two older children in protective custody.

Ms. Johnson had custody of the children when Ms. Sackett located them. Ms. Sackett arranged for the police to assist in the change of custody. Ms. Johnson protested the pick-up and was ultimately arrested by Officer Clemento. At that point, Ms. Sackett also took protective custody of Ms. Johnson's infant child, Zachary. Although Ms. Sackett testified in deposition that the initial rationale for taking protective custody of the infant was the mother's arrest, the child was not returned to Ms. Johnson when she was released from jail the next day. Instead, five days later, and after a child protective team staffing, Ms. Sackett, on behalf of the Department, filed a dependency proceeding for Zachary, alleging as grounds that Ms. Johnson was "carrying the child in an unsafe manner, putting said child at risk."

Ten days after the children were taken into custody, a trial judge reviewed the case and ordered the Department to return all of the children to Ms. Johnson. Eventually, the Department dismissed the cases involving these children and the State decided not to pursue the criminal charges against Ms. Johnson for her actions at the time of the pick-up.

As a result of these events, Ms. Johnson filed suit in 1993 against the two employees, Ms. Sackett and Mr. Clemento, and the two governmental entities, the Department of Health and Rehabilitative Services, now known as the Department of Children and Families, and the City of St. Petersburg, for herself and on behalf of her three children.

Ms. Johnson's second amended complaint contained six separate theories in six separate counts. The theories included: (1) deprivation of constitutional rights under 42 U.S.C. §1983; (2) false arrest; (3) assault and battery; (4) intentional infliction of emotional distress; (5) negligence; and (6) malicious prosecution. Among the three children and Ms. Johnson, the pleading attempts to allege more than eighty separate causes of action. Initially, the trial court dismissed the entire lawsuit on a motion to dismiss. The Appeals Court affirmed the trial court in part and reversed in part. Following the last appeal, one or more claims remained pending against Ms. Sackett by one or more of the plaintiffs claims under each of the above theories.

On a later occasion, the Appeals Court reviewed an order that granted summary judgment in favor of Ms. Sackett on all remaining claims. The claims against Officer Clemento, the City, and the Department remained pending in the trial court at the time the incident appeal was filed. The Court emphasized that the claims against Ms. Sackett and those against the Department tended to be mutually exclusive in light of the law of sovereign immunity. Thus, the judgment in Sacket's favor did not determine the potential liability of the Department of Children and Families.

The Appeals Court could not affirm the trial court's order in its entirety. Although discovery put to rest many of the claims against Ms. Sackett, the Court concluded that the record did not resolve beyond a question of fact the claim for malicious prosecution arising out of the filing of the dependency petition naming the infant child, Zachary.

Although discovery in this case contained some factual disputes, there was a substantial core of undisputed facts. In light of those undisputed facts, the Court concluded that Ms. Sackett was entitled to immunity from all claims regarding her decision to initially take the three children into protective custody.

There was no evidence that Ms. Sackett acted in this regard with the type of bad faith or malice that shifts liability for the actions of government employees from the state agency to the individual employee. Ms. Sackett made her decision to take the older children into protective custody during the pendency of a lawful dependency proceeding after counsel for the Department advised her that this action was appropriate. Additionally, Sackett made her decision within the scope of her employment with the Department. Ms. Johnson's arrest necessitated the decision to shelter the youngest child, who was not a subject of the dependency proceeding. Thus, Ms. Sackett is entitled to qualified immunity for the $1983 claims arising out of her conduct in this respect. Likewise, she is also accorded immunity for the state tort claims involving these actions.

On the other hand, Ms. Johnson claimed that Ms. Sackett thereafter maliciously and without a lawful basis made the decision to file a dependency proceeding naming Zachary, the infant. There are conflicting facts concerning this aspect of Ms. Sackett's conduct. This action forms the basis for Ms. Johnson's claims, individually and on behalf of Zachary, for malicious prosecution and for civil rights violations.

Ms. Sackett maintained she was entitled to absolute immunity for her decision to file the dependency action involving Zachary. In the context of $1983 claims, the United States Supreme Court has afforded prosecutors absolute immunity for their actions in initiating or litigating a criminal charge. *Imbler v. Pachtman*, 424 U.S. 409, (1976). Thereafter, the Supreme Court extended this protection to persons performing adjudicatory or "quasi-judicial" functions within federal agencies. *Butz v Economou*, 438 U.S. 478, (1978). In *Imbler and Butz*, the Supreme Court analyzed the role of the official involved and whether policy considerations supported a grant of absolute immunity to that official for that role.

Applying that functional analysis, most federal courts have concluded that caseworkers like Ms. Sackett enjoy absolute immunity from $1983 claims in regard to their roles in filing and pursuing dependency petitions because these roles are "quasi-judicial" like the role of a prosecutor. See *Spielman v. Hildebrand*, 873 F.2d 1377 (10th Cir. 1989) (recognizing that social workers may enjoy absolute immunity when their actions have requisite connection to judicial process, but finding social worker defendants entitled to only qualified immunity for taking custody of children without prior hearing); *Malachowski v. City of Keene*, 787 F.2d 704 (1st Cir. 1986) (holding juvenile officer entitled to absolute immunity for filing of sworn juvenile delinquency petition). But see *Snell v. Tunnell*, 920 F.2d 673 (10th Cir. 1990) (declining to extend absolute immunity to caseworkers who, in part, sought court order allowing removal of children from home).

Although the Court recognized that there were certain distinctions between case workers in this context and prosecutors in criminal cases, the Court found no meaningful distinction between the role of the federal agency officials in Butz and the role of Ms. Sackett in this case. Thus, concerning the federal claim alleged under $1983, the Court held that Ms. Sackett was entitled to absolute immunity for filing the dependency petition involving Zachary, even if she intentionally misrepresented the factual basis for dependency in the petition. The Court therefore affirmed the dismissal of that claim.

Concerning the state law claim for malicious prosecution, however, the Court did not agree that absolute immunity should be extended to Ms. Sackett's actions in filing the sworn petition for dependency of Zachary. Florida case law has never extended absolute immunity to caseworkers such as Ms. Sackett. In seeking such immunity, a heavy burden rests upon Ms. Sackett to establish that public policy requires an exemption of such a scope. .

The Appeals Court found that Ms. Sackett's role in the dependency proceeding was not fully analogous to the role of a prosecutor. Ms. Sackett was not an attorney relying upon information provided to her by law enforcement. Instead, she investigated whether there was evidence that the child was dependent as defined in section 39.01(10), Florida Statutes (1987), and also decided whether the evidence was sufficient to support the filing of her sworn petition for dependency. Ms. Sackett's role in the institution of this proceeding was comparable to a blend of both that of a prosecutor and that of a police officer whose arrest affidavit results in prosecution. A police officer is entitled to only qualified immunity. Given the dual role of Ms. Sackett in investigating the claims and filing the dependency petition, and the immense power thus placed in her hands, the Court believed the best balance of the interests involved in the incident circumstances supported a grant of only qualified immunity: At the time Ms. Sackett filed the dependency action involving Zachary, section 39.404(1), Florida Statutes (1987), permitted a non-attorney agent of the Department to file the sworn petition subject only to a review of legal sufficiency by the state attorney. Thus, in future cases, the distinct roles of caseworker and department attorney will be more akin to that of an investigating officer and prosecutor, respectively.

Because Ms. Sackett was not entitled to absolute immunity from malicious prosecution by Florida's state common law, she was allowed to claim only the benefit of the qualified immunity provided to her by Florida Statutes (1987). This immunity did not protect her if her actions were taken with "malicious purpose." Thus, the Court concluded that the malicious prosecution claims by Ms. Johnson, individually and on behalf of Zachary, related specifically to the filing of this dependency petition were not appropriate for summary judgment at this time. Affirmed in part and reversed in part.

CHAPTER 16. THE DOCTRINE OF QUALIFIED IMMUNITY

The doctrine of *Qualified Immunity* grants immunity from tort liability to government officers performing discretionary functions within the scope of their employment (authority). Distinction is made here between discretional and ministerial functions. A ministerial function is a function that is essentially clerical or lock step, spelled out by established procedural dictates which involve obedience to instructions and no special discretion, judgment or skill. In other words, a ministerial function is a function or act that requires no use of judgment or discretion. Discretionary functions, on the other hand, do require judgment and that judgment may be spur-of-the-moment.

A public official is entitled to qualified immunity in the performance of a discretionary function if the constitutional or statutory right alleged to have been violated was not "clearly established" at the time of the official's conduct. The United States Supreme Court has explained that, in order to be "clearly established," it is not necessary that "the very action in question has previously been held unlawful." In order to allow officials to "know that they will not be held personally liable as long as their actions are reasonable in light of current American law," the Court has defined a "clearly established" right as one that has "sufficiently clear contours that a reasonable official would understand that what he [or she] is doing violates that right. In other words, in the light of pre-existing law, the unlawfulness of the governmental official's action must be apparent."

There was the situation, for example, where Lady X accused Officer Y of using excessive force in conducting an arrest of her person following an after-midnight traffic stop. According to Lady X, when she got out of her car and raised her arms in a surrender gesture, Officer Y grabbed her arms, slammed her up against her car and handcuffed her. In the process, Officer Y broke Lady X's arm.

Based on these allegations, Lady X initiated a lawsuit against Officer Y claiming that she was battered and that Officer Y's use of excessive force violated her rights under both the 14th-Amendment Due-Process Clause of the U.S. Constitution (protecting individuals from state actors)and her rights under the 4th Amendment of the U.S. Constitution (barring unreasonable search and seizure). Lady X also entered a civil-rights-violation claim under 42 U.S.C. (United States Code) §1983, (also a 14th- Amendment claim. Remember, in 1871 the U.S. Congress passed the 14th Amendment to the U.S. Constitution for the purpose of protecting Southern blacks from post-civil-war violations of their civil rights. Subsequently, through common-law court decisions, the provisions of those rights were codified and extended to all citizens as federal citizens.)

Officer Y subsequently filed a motion to dismiss Lady X's claims as a matter of law claiming qualified immunity, and the court granted his motion, ruling that Officer Y's alleged battery arose from the performance of his official duties as a correctional officer and that he was therefore immune from prosecution. Lady X appealed to the appellate law court.

The Law Court ruled that the matter of qualified immunity exists only "insofar as an officer's conduct does not violate clearly established statutory or constitutional rights of which a reasonable person would have known or should have known....The test for determining whether a defendant is protected from suit by the doctrine of qualified immunity is the objective reasonableness of the defendant's conduct as measured by clearly established law. In this case, plaintiff's excessive-force claim was premised upon a clearly established right of which the defendant should have known, namely the right to be free from unreasonable search and seizure as guaranteed by the 4th Amendment of the U.S. Constitution." The Appeals Court ruled, therefore, that Officer X's use of force was a violation of Lady X's civil rights under 42 U.S.C. §1983 and remanded the case to the trial court where, at trial, Lady X was awarded substantial damages.

SANDRA LEMAY, ETC., APPELLANT,
v. MICHAEL KONDRK AND TAYLOR DOUGLAS, ETC., APPELLEE.
CASE NO. 5D02-1468
COURT OF APPEAL OF FLORIDA, FIFTH DISTRICT
JUNE 20, 2003, FILED

Torts / Public Entity Liability / Qualified Immunity

An employee of a state subdivision enjoys qualified immunity from suit and liability, except in certain limited circumstances. The scope of that immunity, and the exceptions thereto, are found in Florida Statutes chapter 768.28(9)(a).

Torts / Public Entity Liability / Qualified Immunity

The purpose of the qualified immunity granted to state actors in Florida Statutes chapter 768.28(9) is to immunize public employees from liability for ordinary negligence, while providing injured claimants a remedy against governmental entities through the waiver of sovereign immunity. This promotes vigorous performance of duties by government employees, free from the fear of negligence actions, while at the same time providing redress through governmental assumption of liability to persons injured by the ordinary negligence of government employees.

Torts / Qualified Immunity

Granting public employees *qualified immunity* serves the public interest by allowing those employees to act with independence and without fear of consequences. Those consequences include both liability for money damages, and the general cost of subjecting officials to the risks of trial, distraction of officials from their governmental duties, inhibition of discretionary action, and deterrence of able people from public service. Even pretrial matters, such as discovery, are to be avoided, if possible, as inquiries of this kind can be peculiarly disruptive of effective government.

Torts / Negligence Generally

Wanton conduct, or willful and wanton conduct, have been described as lying somewhere between ordinary negligence and intentional conduct. Willful and wanton conduct is generally something more than ordinary negligence but less than deliberate conduct. Most definitions of willful or wanton conduct require that it appear that the defendant had knowledge of existing conditions, was conscious from such knowledge that injury would likely or probably result from his conduct, and, with reckless indifference to the consequences, consciously and intentionally does some wrongful act or omits to discharge some duty which produces the injurious result.

Torts / Negligence Generally

Willful, Wanton and Reckless is defined as lying between intent to do harm, which includes proceeding with knowledge that the harm is substantially certain to occur and the mere unreasonable risk of harm to another involved in ordinary negligence. There is a penumbra of what has been called "quasi-intent." To this area the words "willful," "wanton," or "reckless" are customarily applied; and sometimes, in a single sentence, all three. Although efforts have been made to distinguish them, in practice such distinctions have consistently been ignored, and the three terms have been treated as meaning the same thing or at least as coming out at the same legal exit. They have been grouped together as an aggravated form of negligence, differing in quality rather than in degree from ordinary lack of care. They apply to conduct which is still, at essence, negligent, rather than actually intended to do harm, but which is so far from a proper state of mind that it is treated in many respects as if it were so intended.

Torts / Negligence

The usual meaning assigned to "willful," "wanton," or "reckless," according to taste as to the word used, is that the actor has intentionally done an act of an unreasonable character in disregard of a known or obvious risk that was so great as to make it highly probable that harm would follow, and which thus is usually accompanied by a conscious indifference to the consequences. Since, however, it is almost never admitted, and can be proved only by the conduct and the circumstances, an objective standard must of necessity be applied in practice. The "willful" requirement, therefore, breaks down and receives at best lip service where it is clear from the facts that the defendant, whatever his state of mind, has proceeded in disregard of a high and excessive degree of danger either known to him or apparent to a reasonable person in his position.

PRIOR HISTORY: Appeal from the Circuit Court for Putnam County.
DISPOSITION: Reversed.
OPINION: Sandra Lemay ["Lemay"], as Personal Representative of the Estate of Roy Ault, appealed the dismissal of her wrongful death claim against Michael Kondrk ["Kondrk"], a Putnam County Deputy Sheriff. The trial court concluded that the amended complaint failed to allege any act on Kondrk's part that could be found to have been in bad faith or with malicious purpose or done in a manner exhibiting wanton and willful disregard of human rights, safety or property as is required to avoid the qualified immunity afforded Kondrk pursuant to section 768.28(9)(a), Florida Statutes (1998). The Appeals Court disagreed and reversed.

The amended complaint alleged that at about midnight on November 1, 1997, Roy Ault ["Ault"] drove to a Fast Track convenience store in rural Putnam County, purchased two twelve packs of beer and drove away. At approximately 3:00 a.m., Ault returned to the convenience store on foot because his car had broken down. Ault, who was obviously intoxicated, purchased food and another beer, and then went to the store's outside pay phone to call for a ride.

Shortly thereafter, the store clerk called 911, seeking assistance. As Ault was trying to call family members for assistance, Deputy Kondrk arrived. The exterior of the convenience store and its parking lot were lit. Ault was staggering, had urinated in his pants but had broken no laws. The store clerk had not asked Ault to leave the premises or requested that Kondrk order Ault to leave. Nonetheless, Kondrk ordered Ault and his companion to leave the parking lot. Ault, who was wearing dark clothing, complied, and began walking down Highway 20, a two-lane unlit highway with no sidewalks or paved shoulders. A short time later, however, Ault returned to the Fast Track parking lot. Kondrk again ordered him to leave, and Ault again walked away down the dark highway. About forty minutes later, Ault was struck and fatally injured by a pickup truck as he was walking in the traffic lane of Highway 20. Postmortem tests showed that Ault had a blood alcohol level of 0.158.

Lemay instituted a wrongful death complaint against Kondrk individually. The complaint alleged that Kondrk's actions demonstrated a wanton and willful disregard for Ault's rights and safety. Lemay alleged that Kondrk owed a duty not to place Ault in greater peril than he found him, not to create a substantial zone of risk, and not to subject Ault to an unreasonable risk of harm by creating and placing Ault in a dangerous and life threatening situation. On Kondrk's motion, the trial court dismissed the complaint, finding that Lemay "failed to identify any action or conduct of Michael Kondrk which could be said to have been in bad faith and with malicious purpose or in a manner exhibiting wanton and willful disregard of Mr. Ault's rights."

As an employee of a state subdivision, (sheriff's department) Kondrk enjoyed qualified immunity from suit and liability, except in certain limited circumstances. The scope of that immunity, and the exceptions thereto, are found in section 768.28(9)(a), Florida Statutes, which, in pertinent part, provides:

> No officer, employee, or agent of the state or of any of its subdivisions shall be held personally liable in tort or named as a party defendant in any action for any injury or damage suffered as a result of any act, event, or omission of action in the scope of his or her employment or function unless such officer, employee, or agent acted in bad faith or with malicious purpose or in a manner exhibiting wanton and willful disregard of human rights, safety, or property.

The purpose of the qualified immunity granted to state actors in section 768.28(9), Florida Statutes, is to "immunize public employees from liability for ordinary negligence while providing injured claimants a remedy against governmental entities through the waiver of sovereign immunity. This promotes vigorous performance of duties by government employees, free from the fear of negligence actions while at the same time providing redress through governmental assumption of liability to persons injured by the ordinary negligence of government employees," *Rupp v. Bryant*, 417 So. 2d 658, (Fla. 1982). Granting public employees qualified immunity serves the public interest by allowing those employees to act with independence and without fear of consequences. *Harlow v. Fitzgerald*, 457 U.S. 800, 819, (1982). Those consequences include both liability for money damages, and "the general cost of subjecting officials to the risks of trial, distraction of officials from their governmental duties, inhibition of discretionary action, and deterrence of able people from public service." Even pretrial matters, such as discovery, are to be avoided if possible as "inquiries of this kind can be peculiarly disruptive of effective government."

In her amended complaint, Lemay contended that Kondrk's actions exhibited a wanton and willful disregard for Ault's rights and safety. While Lemay did not contend that Kondrk intended Ault to be harmed when he ordered Ault to leave the convenience store parking lot, she did contend that a jury could find the risk to Ault's safety (and that of passing motorists) was obvious and foreseeable to any reasonable person, particularly a trained law enforcement officer, and that despite that obvious risk, Kondrk forced Ault out into the darkness, disregarding the consequences of doing so.

The threshold question was whether Lemay's factual allegations, assumed to be true, could be reasonably found to constitute conduct "exhibiting wanton and willful disregard of human rights, safety or property." In *Ingram v. Pettit*, 340 So. 2d 922, 924 (Fla. 1976), the Supreme Court of Florida explained the difficulty in dividing negligence into degrees:

> Our jurisprudence has a history of difficulty in dividing negligence into degrees. The distinctions articulated in labeling particular conduct as "simple negligence," "gross negligence," and "willful and wanton misconduct" are best viewed as statements of public policy. These semantic refinements also serve a useful purpose in advising jurors of the factors to be considered in those situations where the lines are indistinct. We would deceive ourselves, however, if we viewed these distinctions as finite legal categories and permitted the characterization alone to cloud the policies they were created to foster.

> As Ingram recognized, courts have encountered great difficulty in attempting to draw clear and distinct lines between the various grades of negligence, concluding that perhaps no rule can ever be devised which will definitively separate one from the other. Different degrees of negligence are easier to demonstrate than to define. The same conduct, in different settings, could and does result in different degrees of liability.

> Wanton conduct, or willful and wanton conduct, have been described as lying somewhere between ordinary negligence and intentional conduct. Willful and wanton conduct is generally something more than ordinary negligence but less than deliberate conduct. Most definitions of willful or wanton conduct require that it appear that the defendant had knowledge of existing conditions, was conscious from such knowledge that injury would likely or probably result from his conduct, and with reckless indifference to the consequences consciously and intentionally does some wrongful act or omits to discharge some duty which produces the injurious result.

> Perhaps Prosser and Keeton best defined willful and wanton conduct: "Willful, Wanton and Reckless. A different approach, at least in theory, looks to the actor"s real or supposed state of mind. Lying between intent to do harm, which, as we have seen, includes proceeding with knowledge that the harm is substantially certain to occur, and the mere unreasonable risk of harm to another involved in ordinary negligence, there is a penumbra of what has been called quasi-intent." To this area the words "willful," "wanton," or "reckless," are customarily applied; and sometimes, in a single sentence, all three. Although efforts have been made to distinguish them, in practice such distinctions have consistently been ignored, and the three terms have been treated as meaning the same thing, or at least as coming out at the same legal exit. They have been grouped together as an aggravated form of negligence, differing in quality rather than in degree from ordinary lack of care. They apply to conduct which is still, at essence, negligent, rather than actually intended to do harm, but which is so far from a proper state of mind that it is treated in many respects as if it were so intended.

> The usual meaning assigned to "willful," "wanton," or "reckless," according to taste as to the word used, is that the actor has intentionally done an act of

an unreasonable character in disregard of a known or obvious risk that was so great as to make it highly probable that harm would follow, and which thus is usually accompanied by a conscious indifference to the consequences. Since, however, it is almost never admitted, and can be proved only by the conduct and the circumstances, an objective standard must of necessity be applied in practice. The "willful" requirement, therefore, breaks down and receives at best lip service, where it is clear from the facts that the defendant, whatever his state of mind, has proceeded in disregard of a high and excessive degree of danger, either known to him or apparent to a reasonable person in his position.

The result is that "willful," "wanton," or "reckless" conduct tends to take on the aspect of highly unreasonable conduct, involving an extreme departure from ordinary care in a situation where a high degree of danger is apparent. It is at least clear, however, that such aggravated negligence must be more than any mere mistake resulting from inexperience, excitement, or confusion, and more than mere thoughtlessness or inadvertence, or simple inattention.

In other words, the actor"s conduct is in reckless disregard of the safety of another when he does an act or intentionally fails to do an act which it is his duty to the other to do, knowing or having reason to know of facts which would lead a reasonable man to realize, not only that his conduct creates an unreasonable risk of physical harm to another, but also that such risk is substantially greater than that which is necessary to make his conduct negligent.

The Appeals Court concluded that a reasonable jury hearing all the facts contained in the complaint and observing the demeanor of the witness could conclude that Kondrk's conduct rose to the level of willful and wanton negligence which resulted in Ault's death. The plaintiff had pled enough facts to survive a motion to dismiss and to allow the facts to be fleshed out.

Considering the facts in the light most favorable to the plaintiff, the Appeals Court held that Kondrk forced Ault, who was so intoxicated he could not even control his bladder, to leave a lighted public location at 3 a.m., where he was safe and was trying to use the public telephone to obtain family assistance, and made him walk out into the darkness of an unlighted two-lane rural road with no shoulder. He apparently did this even though the operator of the convenience store had not asked that Ault be removed. Kondrk was able to compel Ault to walk out, down this dark road, precisely because of his authority as a law enforcement officer. There is as yet nothing in this record to explain why Kondrk did this to Ault other than the allegation that Ault had annoyed him. The Appeals Court could not say that the alleged conduct failed, as a matter of law, to meet the description of "willful and wanton" conduct.

REVERSED.

CHAPTER 17. THE LAST-CLEAR-CHANCE DOCTRINE

The doctrine of last clear chance raises the question in negligence law as to who had *the last clear chance* to avoid sustaining or inflicting an injury. A recurring theme in *last-clear-chance* litigation involves pedestrians and automobiles. The doctrine of *last clear chance* can be construed as an affirmative defense.

Fox hunts are still legal in some Southern states in this country. Some fox hunters have given up the use of horses and have gone to the use of ATVs as a means of following the hounds. In one Southern state recently, a pack of forty-odd hounds were set afield with a couple of ATVs bringing up the rear. The problem was that if Brer Fox went in a certain direction, he would lead the dogs across an interstate arterial and it would be necessary for the hunters to see that the dogs got across the roadway safely. To this end, four hunters were dispatched to where it was thought the hounds would cross to see that all went well.

When the hunters got to that place where it was thought the dogs would cross, and parked their vehicles in the northbound breakdown lane, the dogs were already crossing and it was necessary for the hunters to take up positions across the four lanes of the North-South thoroughfare and median strip in order to guide the dogs safely across. As the dogs continued to cross, a vehicle appeared some 1500 feet away from over a rise in the road. The vehicle maintained its speed as it approached the hunters in the roadway and slowed down only when it got near the parked ATVs, at which time it swung wide into the left-hand lane to give the vehicles a wide birth. The driver of the approaching vehicle testified at trial that he did not see the hunter he hit, standing in the left lane frantically waiving his arms, as the hunter testified at trial. Fortunately, the hunter was not killed, although he was seriously injured. Once healed, the hunter sued the vehicle operator for negligence and the vehicle operator put forth on a *last-clear-chance* affirmative defense. (An affirmative defense is a defense that, if proven, disposes of the action.)

Well, it did not go well for the hunter at trial. The trial court ruled that for a plaintiff to defeat a last-clear-chance affirmative defense he must show that he (1) placed himself in a position of peril from which he could not escape by the exercise of reasonable care; (2) That the motorist knew the plaintiff's perilous position and his incapacity to escape from it before injury or could have discovered it by the exercise of reasonable care; (3) that the motorist had the time and means to avoid injuring the plaintiff; and (4) that the motorist negligently failed to use the time and means available to him to avoid injuring the plaintiff.

The Trial court went on to say that cases discussing the first element have consistently distinguished between situations in which the injured pedestrian was either facing oncoming traffic or had his back turned to traffic. The court said that those who could not see the oncoming danger could not reasonably be expected to avoid it. Those who could see, however, were expected to avoid it. The court said, "Where the injured party is at all times in control of the danger of the situation and simply chooses to ignore it, a defendant's *last-clear-chance* affirmative defense will be upheld. Case Dismissed!"

PRESTON CARTER V. SENATE MASONRY, INCORPORATED
COURT OF SPECIAL APPEALS OF MARYLAND
846 A.2D 50
APRIL 6, 2004

LEGAL CONSIDERATIONS

Torts / Doctrine of Last Clear Chance

The doctrine of last clear chance permits a contributorily negligent plaintiff to recover damages from a negligent defendant.

Civil Procedure / Judgment as Matter of Law

An appellate court presents the facts in the light most favorable to a party who prevailed at trial and lost below on a judgment notwithstanding the jury's verdict (JNOV) (When a judge overrules a jury verdict, he issues a judgment notwithstanding the verdict, a JNOV). That also means that, in the appellate court's analysis, it will reverse the grant of the JNOV if there is any evidence from which the jury could have reached the conclusion that it reached.

PRIOR HISTORY: Appeal from the Circuit Court for Prince George's County.

DISPOSITION: Reversed with instructions to reinstate the jury's verdict.

OPINION: This appeal concerns the legal doctrine of *"last clear chance."* Preston Carter accused an employee of Senate Masonry, Incorporated ("Senate") of negligently harming him at a construction site. A jury in the Trial Court for Prince George's County accepted that accusation, but found Carter negligent as well. Nonetheless, it awarded Carter damages with the apparent belief that the Senate employee had the *last clear chance* to avoid injuring Carter, and his failure to do so warranted compensation for Carter. The trial judge disagreed and granted Senate's post-trial motion for judgment notwithstanding the jury's verdict ("JNOV"). The Appeals Court disagreed with the trial judge and reinstated the jury's verdict.

I

It is critical to note at the outset that the Appeals Court presented the facts in the light most favorable to Preston Carter because he prevailed with the jury at trial but lost on the judges judgment notwithstanding the verdict award (JNOV). That meant that, in the Court's analysis, the Court reversed the grant of the JNOV if there was any evidence from which the jury could have reached the conclusion that it reached.

The evidence at trial consisted of three primary witnesses: two fact witnesses presented by Carter and an expert witness presented by Senate. Carter was a commercial plumber with twenty years' experience. He testified that on August 15, 1997, he was working in Columbia, Maryland, at the construction site for a new Safeway supermarket. While installing some rudimentary plumbing, Carter walked over to the nearby scaffolding to locate certain pipe fittings. He noticed a forklift that was situated about a hundred feet away from him. The forklift operator was delivering a cube of cinder blocks to the scaffold.

As Carter knelt on the ground searching for parts, he perceived the forklift to move in behind him, coming as close as six to ten feet from him and then stop in front of the scaffolding. The operator of the forklift then maneuvered the machine to place a pan of mortar upon the cube of cinder blocks that had just been delivered to the scaffold. His action caused several of the blocks to fall, striking Carter in the head, neck, shoulder, and back. It was Carter's testimony that he would have been clearly visible to the forklift operator all the time that he knelt near the scaffold.

Hervan Montiel, the Senate employee who operated the forklift, testified as plaintiff's witness and recounted the series of events as follows:

"I remember the day of the accident. My tractor was parked. I tried to move the arm of the tractor towards the scaffold. On my right side a person was coming by, and since he didn't stop, I stopped the arm of my tractor. He went underneath and he went to my left side. I waited for him to go away at least some eight or ten feet. When he was no longer in front of me, I continued my concentration on the job I was doing. I remember that when I placed the box of mortar and was taking out the forks, I heard someone scream or yell. When I saw what happened, the man was on the ground. That's all I remember."

At that the trial court noted that Carter and Montiel differed in their description of the sequence of events. Carter said that the forklift began its operation once he had already stopped near the scaffold. According to Montiel, however, he began the operation, stopped to let Carter pass, then continued his work.

Both Carter and Montiel denied having said anything to one another as they proceeded with their respective tasks. Carter explained, "When you're working construction you don't think to ask a guy to stop laying brick while you look for fittings." He did not believe his actions were unsafe. Montiel acknowledged that he thought the placement of block on the scaffold created a dangerous situation.

Senate Masonry put forth the testimony of Stephen Fournier, an expert in civil engineering, who investigated "the circumstances" of Carter's injuries in order "to determine if anybody associated with the work acted in an unsafe or inappropriate manner." The exclusive source of his eyewitness information was other Senate employees. Fournier testified that Carter put "himself in a position of danger," but also that Montiel increased the risk of injury by operating the forklift without a pallet. He was equivocal in his opinion as to whether Montiel had a duty to warn Carter of danger. Fournier stated that, if Montiel knew Carter was in a position of danger, he had a duty to warn; but, then, in response to questions posed by Senate's counsel, he remarked that Montiel "acted reasonably" in continuing with his work, without communicating with Carter.

At the close of the evidence, Senate moved for judgment upon the assertions that Carter acted negligently, but Montiel did not. Carter responded that Montiel breached a duty to warn and a duty to stop the forklift operation once he saw Carter kneeling by the scaffold. He raised the specter of the last-clear- chance doctrine. The trial court reserved ruling on the motion, stating, "There are facts that would sustain a finding of negligence and facts that would find there was no contributory negligence." The judge also noted his uncertainty as to whether the last-clear-chance doctrine applied. Accordingly, the court denied Carter's motion for judgment, which he premised on the last-clear-chance doctrine.

Preparing the case for deliberation, the trial court instructed the jury on negligence and contributory negligence, saying:

> The plaintiff has alleged that the Defendant had the last clear chance to avoid the injuries sustained by the Plaintiff. Before you can determine the issue of last clear chance, you must (1) determine that the Defendant was negligent, (2) that the Plaintiff was contributorily negligent, and, (3) that the Defendant had an opportunity to prevent the injury sustained by Carter.

The jury returned a verdict in favor of Carter, finding that Senate Masonry was negligent through the actions of its employee Montiel, that Carter was contributorily negligent, and that Senate had the last clear chance to avoid the accident. It awarded Carter about $66,000.00 in economic damages and $150,000.00 in non-economic damages.

Senate Masonry then moved for Judgment Notwithstanding the Verdict (JNOV) with the principal assertion that Carter and Montiel committed their respective negligence simultaneously, so Senate could not be held to have squandered the final opportunity to avoid the accident. Also, Senate argued that Montiel did not have "superior knowledge" over Carter as to the risk inherent in his actions.

Carter rebutted both of those assertions. He attributed greater knowledge to Montiel, who surveyed the scene from the height of the forklift cab and who worked with cinder blocks on a regular basis. Moreover, Carter chronicled the events as follows: (1) He, Carter, negligently stooped near the scaffold; (2) Montiel negligently failed to warn him to leave the area; and (3) Montiel negligently continued with the forklift operation. With this sequence of events, Montiel was the final bearer of the accident and injury, or so Carter argued.

The trial judge engaged counsel in lengthy discussions about the facts of the case and the plethora of cases on point, but he was confident that, no matter how he ruled, the case would be appealed. Ultimately, the court granted Senate's JNOV, without much explanation.

II

Both Senate and Carter conceded, for purposes of the incident appeal, that there were sufficient facts from which the jury could find that each of them acted negligently. That leaves them debating only whether Montiel could have avoided the accident, i.e., whether he held the last clear chance to transform the unfortunate hit to a near miss.

The Appeals Court explained that "The doctrine of last clear chance permits a contributorily negligent plaintiff to recover damages from a negligent defendant if each of the following elements is satisfied: (1) the defendant is negligent; (2) the plaintiff is contributorily negligent; and (3) the plaintiff makes 'a showing of something new or sequential which affords the defendant a fresh opportunity to avert the consequences of his original negligence.'"

The theory behind the doctrine of *last clear chance* is that "if the defendant has the last clear opportunity to avoid the inflicting of harm, the plaintiff's negligence is not the 'responsible cause' of the result. 'A fresh opportunity' is the operative phrase, for the doctrine will apply only if 'the acts of the respective parties were sequential and not concurrent.' In other words, the defendant must have had a chance to avoid the injury after plaintiff's negligent action was put in motion. The doctrine 'assumes' that, after the primary negligence of the plaintiff and defendant, 'the defendant could, and the plaintiff could not avert the accident.' In this way, the defendant should have recognized and responded to the plaintiff's position of 'helpless peril.'"

The Appeals Court's research revealed more than four dozen reported Maryland cases discussing the *last-clear-chance doctrine*. Its history in Maryland dates back to 1868 and traces its roots to English common law. The doctrine is more often described than applied because of the requirement that plaintiffs show a new act of negligence following their own actions.

In *Sears v. Baltimore and Ohio Railroad Co.*, 148 A.2d 366 (1959), for example, the Court of Appeals declined to extend the doctrine to a plaintiff/appellant whose truck collided with a train as it crossed a set of tracks. The Court wrote:

There was no evidence sufficient to go to the jury to support a finding that, assuming the appellant's negligence, there was a time after such negligence when the appellee, the defendant, could have averted the accident and the appellant could not have. Both the train and the truck were moving at the time of the impact, and it is clear that if the appellee (the train) was negligent, its negligence was concurrent and not sequential. We have said that in order for the last-clear-chance doctrine to be applicable "something new, or independent, must be shown, which gave the defendant a fresh opportunity to avert the consequences of his original negligence and the plaintiff's contributory negligence." Even though the operator of the appellee's locomotive saw the appellant's truck standing or moving slowly at a point close to the tracks, he had the right to assume that the appellant would stop before he reached the track upon which the train was proceeding. The appellant did not present any evidence to support an inference that the appellee had a "fresh opportunity" to avert the consequences of his own contributory negligence in driving onto the tracks.

In contrast, the premier example of the last clear chance doctrine at work is *Ritter v. Portera*, 474 A.2d 556 (1984), which involved a group of young people and a moving car. One of the teenagers perched on the hood of the car, and, as the driver sped up and drove away, she fell off the car, grabbed hold of the bumper, and was dragged at least twenty feet. Clearly, the driver was negligent in inviting people to sit on the hood of his car, but the injured person was also negligent in accepting the invitation. For the trial court, the contributory negligence barred the teenager's claim against the driver.

The Appeals Court reversed, however, reasoning that the injured teenager was not a "responsible cause of the accident." Instead, the driver "could have, and indeed should have, refused to move the vehicle while the teenager sat on the hood of his car." Because the driver's negligence was so clearly sequential to whatever negligence preceded it, the injured teenager was entitled to pursue a claim for recovery.

III

Carter faced the same hurdle as the plaintiffs in the cases discussed above. He could not recover if the facts showed only that he and Montiel both acted unreasonably, which would create only a concurrent negligence. Rather, Carter had to show that the jury could have read the facts to mean that Montiel was negligent, Carter was negligent, and then Montiel had a new opportunity to change the course of events.

The Appeals Court concluded that the facts could have been read to show the sequential course of events that Carter needs to defeat the grant of JNOV. The jury could have found from the testimony that Montiel negligently first placed the cube of cinder blocks on the forklift without using a pallet and placed them on the scaffold, possibly breaking some; that later, with the pan of mortar on the forklift, he saw Carter kneeling by the scaffold in harm's way and failed to warn him of the danger; and that, following a pause in his operations, he negligently proceeded to place the mortar on the scaffold, causing the cinder blocks to fall. There are various points along this continuum of negligent conduct where the jury might have interjected Carter's negligence, but the bottom line is that the jury could have concluded that Montiel held the final opportunity to avoid the accident.

Beyond the doctrinal phrases of "last clear chance," "fresh opportunity," and "helpless peril," the jury could have found from the evidence in this case an account of two men acting dangerously on a construction site, but with one man having superior knowledge of the impending danger as well as the superior ability, and thus the last clear chance to avert it. Montiel was not like the train conductor in Sears, who could only watch the truck impede on the railroad tracks. Montiel controlled the final force that brought about this accident, the forklift. Like the young driver in Ritter, Montiel had a "fresh opportunity" to avoid the accident. He could have refused to move his vehicle as long as Carter remained in danger. Because the jury could have lawfully found in favor of Carter, the trial court should have respected the jury's decision.

Judgment of the trial court for Prince George's County was reversed, with instructions to reinstate the jury's verdict.

Chapter 18. The Open and Obvious Danger Doctrine

When the owner of commercial property makes his premises available to the public, he suggests to the public that his property is safe and void of hazard. If an invitee to a landowner's property is injured in some way and the injury sustained is not the result of an *open-and-obvious* hazard, then the landowner, shop owner, restaurateur, salon operator, etc., is liable in negligence. If, on the other hand, the hazard is obvious, i.e., *open and obvious*, then there is no liability that accrues to the property owner.

Assume for a moment that you are going into the office of a motel and a sprinkler is getting the sidewalk to the entrance wet enough to create a slippery condition that could lead to a fall. You fall, and damage your hip. Your hip requires medical attention and the effects linger on for six months. Thinking the motel owner was negligent, you engage an attorney and bring a lawsuit. Your case gets underway and after three or four months the motel owner's lawyer brings a motion for summary judgment claiming that there is no genuine issue of material fact because your claim is barred by the doctrine of *Open-and-Obvious Danger*, a danger you could have easily avoided by walking on the grass for a few feet. The trial-court judge agrees and grants summary judgment as a matter of law, and it's all over.

Assume on the other hand, that you check into a motel at the end of winter. The accumulation of snow has been substantial, but it has warmed up considerably the last few days and winter is clearly on the ebb. You stay up late that night to watch some TV-special or other with the result that you sleep late the next morning and don't issue forth until after ten or so. As you are stepping out from under the overhanging roof the next morning, POW! You get hit in the head by what seems like a ton of snow and ice that has fallen from the roof.

Well, what a headache! But the headache doesn't go away. It persists for days. Finally, you go to the E.R. at your local hospital when you get home and, sure enough, you've sustained a cervical fracture. Things seem to go from bad to worse and you wind up with migraines and a lot of serious physical discomfort and a hefty medical bill. You get in touch with a lawyer who lives in the community you were visiting when the accident occurred and he brings a suit in negligence against the motel owner on your behalf. Three or four months into the proceedings, the motel's lawyer files a motion for summary judgment, citing the doctrine of *open-and-obvious danger*. In this situation the trial court denies the grant of summary judgment on the ground that your injury was not the result of an *open-and-obvious danger* and that, therefore, your case will proceed to trial. At trial, the jury agrees that the situation resulting in your injury was not an *open-and obvious danger*, and they award you meaningful damages. In the following case, *Lugo v. Ameritech Corporation*, 629 N.W.2d 384, (2001 Mich.) the same doctrine of law comes into play.

ODIS LUGO, PLAINTIFF-APPELLEE,
v. AMERITECH CORPORATION, INC., DEFENDANT-APPELLANT.
SUPREME COURT OF MICHIGAN
629 N.W.2D 384
JULY 3, 2001

DISPOSITION: Judgment of the Court of Appeals reversed and judgment of the trial court is reinstated.

LEGAL CONSIDERATIONS

Torts / General Premises Liability / Open and Obvious Danger

Only those special aspects that give rise to a uniquely high likelihood of harm will serve to remove a condition from the *open-and-obvious-danger doctrine*.

Torts / General Premises Liability / Open and Obvious Danger

The *open-and-obvious-danger doctrine* should not be viewed as some type of "exception" to the duty generally owed to invitees to a business property, but rather should be viewed as an integral part of the definition of that duty.

Torts / Real Property Torts / General Premises Liability / Open and Obvious Danger

If the particular activity or condition creates a risk of harm only because the invitee does not discover the condition or realize its danger, then the *open-and-obvious-danger doctrine* will cut off liability if the invitee should have discovered the condition and realized its danger. On the other hand, if the risk of harm remains unreasonable, despite its obviousness or despite knowledge of it by the invitee, then the circumstances may be such that the invitor is required to undertake reasonable precautions.

Torts / General Premises Liability / Open and Obvious Danger

The general rule is that a premises possessor is not required to protect an invitee from *open-and-obvious dangers*, but, if special aspects of a condition make even an open-and-obvious risk unreasonably dangerous, the premises possessor has a duty to undertake reasonable precautions to protect invitees from that risk.

Torts / General Premises Liability

In general, a premises possessor owes a duty to an invitee to exercise reasonable care to protect the invitee from an unreasonable risk of harm caused by a dangerous condition on the land. However, this duty does not generally encompass removal of open and obvious dangers.

Torts / General Premises Liability

Where the dangers are known to the invitee or are so obvious that the invitee might reasonably be expected to discover them, an invitor owes no duty to protect or warn the invitee.

Torts / General Premises Liability

With the axiom being that the duty is to protect invitees from unreasonable risks of harm, the underlying principle is that even though invitors have a duty to exercise reasonable care in protecting their invitees, they are not absolute insurers of the safety of their invitees.

Civil Procedure / Summary Judgment

The party opposing a motion for summary disposition is required by Michigan Court Rule 2.116(G)(4) to set forth specific facts showing that there is a genuine issue for trial with regard to the issues raised in the summary disposition motion.

OPINION: This premises liability action arose from a fall in a parking lot owned by the defendant. Plaintiff apparently fell after stepping in a pothole in the parking lot. The trial court granted summary judgment in favor of the defendant, but the Court of Appeals reversed, rejecting defendant's position that plaintiff's claim was barred by the "open-and-obvious-danger" doctrine. The Supreme Court reversed the judgment of the Court of Appeals and reinstated the judgment of the trial court. The pothole was open and obvious, and plaintiff had not provided evidence of any special aspects of the condition of the parking lot to justify imposing liability on defendant.

I

Plaintiff was walking through a parking lot toward defendant's building to pay a telephone bill when she apparently stepped in a pothole and fell. Plaintiff testified at her deposition that she was not watching the ground and that she was concentrating on a truck in the parking lot at the time. However, she also testified that nothing would have prevented her from seeing the pothole. Defendant moved for summary judgment, claiming that the pothole constituted an open-and-obvious danger from which it had no duty to protect plaintiff. The trial court granted the motion, stating:

> This court takes the position that there is no material question of fact here. It is quite clear that the plaintiff was walking along without paying proper attention to the circumstances of where she was walking, and there is a legal duty to look where you are walking. This court cannot be anymore precise than that.

The Court of Appeals reversed the grant of summary disposition in a two-to-one decision. The Court of Appeals majority concluded that the circuit court erred in holding that plaintiff's legal duty to look where she was walking barred her claim. The Appeals Court stated that, under principles of comparative negligence, a plaintiff's negligence can only reduce the amount of recovery, not eliminate altogether a defendant's liability. The Court also determined that the open-and-obvious-danger rule did not apply because there was a genuine issue of material fact regarding whether defendant should have expected that a pedestrian might be distracted by the need to avoid a moving vehicle, or might even reasonably step into the pothole to avoid such a vehicle.

The Supreme Court of the State of Michigan, disagreed with the holding of the Court of Appeals. Further, while it did not embrace the reasoning of the trial court, it agreed with its result.

II

The proper focus in this case was the extent of the open-and-obvious-danger doctrine in premises liability cases. In general, a premises possessor owes a duty to an invitee to exercise reasonable care to protect the invitee from an unreasonable risk of harm caused by a dangerous condition on his land. However, this duty does not generally encompass removal of open-and-obvious dangers: Where the dangers are known to the invitee or are so obvious that the invitee might reasonably be expected to discover them, an invitor owes no duty to protect or warn the invitee unless the invitor should anticipate the harm.

Accordingly, the *open-and-obvious-danger doctrine* should not be viewed as some type of exception to the duty generally owed invitees, but rather as an integral part of the definition of that duty. The Supreme Court stated that if a particular activity or condition creates a risk of harm only because the invitee does not discover the condition or realize its danger, then the *open-and-obvious doctrine* will cut off liability if the invitee should have discovered the condition and realized its danger. On the other hand, if the risk of harm remains unreasonable, despite its obviousness of the danger or despite knowledge of it by the invitee, then the circumstances may be such that the invitor is required to undertake reasonable precautions.

In sum, the Court held that the general rule is that a premises owner is not required to protect an invitee from *open-and-obvious* dangers, but, if special aspects of a condition make even an *open-and-obvious risk* unreasonably dangerous, the premises possessor has a duty to undertake reasonable precautions to protect invitees from that risk. In other words, the axiom is that the duty is to protect invitees from unreasonable risks of harm, the underlying principle is that even though invitors have a duty to exercise reasonable care in protecting their invitees, they are not absolute insurers of the safety of their invitees. Consequently, because the danger of tripping and falling on a step is generally open and obvious, the failure-to-warn theory does not establish liability. However, there may be special aspects of a given step structure that make the risk of harm unreasonable, and, accordingly, a failure to remedy the dangerous condition may be found to have breached the duty to keep the premises reasonably safe.

Consistent with the above, the Supreme Court concluded that, with regard to *open-and-obvious dangers*, the critical question is whether there is evidence that creates a genuine issue of material fact regarding whether there are truly special aspects of the *open-and-obvious condition* that differentiate the risk from typical *open-and-obvious* risks so as to create an unreasonable risk of harm.

An illustration of such a situation might involve, for example, a commercial building with only one exit for the general public where the floor is covered with standing water. While the condition is *open and obvious*, a customer wishing to exit the store must leave the store through the water. In other words, the *open-and-obvious* condition is effectively unavoidable. Similarly, an *open-and-obvious* condition might be unreasonably dangerous because of special aspects that impose an unreasonably high risk of severe harm. To use another example, consider an unguarded thirty foot deep pit in the middle of a parking lot. The condition might well be *open and obvious*, and a person would likely be capable of avoiding the danger. Nevertheless, this situation would present such a substantial risk of death or severe injury to one who fell in the pit that it would be unreasonably dangerous to allow the condition, at least absent reasonable warnings or other remedial measures being taken. In sum, only those special aspects that give rise to a uniquely high likelihood of harm or severity of harm if the risk is not avoided will serve to remove that condition from the *open-and-obvious danger doctrine*.

Finally, it appeared obvious to the Court that the degree of potential harm from an *open-and-obvious condition* may, in some unusual circumstances, be the key factor that makes such a condition unreasonably dangerous. While it is reasonable to expect invitees to avoid common potholes, that does not mean it is reasonable to leave a gaping hole in a parking lot even though the difference in the degree of harm likely to follow from an invitee's failure to avoid the hazard is the only material difference between the two situations.

III

Applying these general principles to the incident case, the Supreme Court concluded the defendant was entitled to summary judgment which provides for summary disposition when there is no genuine issue as to any material fact and the moving party is entitled to judgment or partial judgment as a matter of law. Further, the party opposing a motion for summary disposition (in this case the plaintiff) is required to set forth specific facts showing that there is a genuine issue for trial with regard to the issues raised in the summary disposition motion. In this case, the disputed issue was whether plaintiff's claim was barred by the open-and-obvious-danger doctrine.

The evidence submitted to the trial court allowed for no genuine issue of material fact with respect to whether plaintiff's claim was barred by the open-and-obvious-danger doctrine. This case simply involved a common pothole in a parking lot. While the plaintiff argued that the pothole was filled with debris, the evidence presented to the trial court simply did not allow a reasonable inference that the pothole was obscured by debris at the time of plaintiff's fall. Indeed, plaintiff's testimony at her deposition was that she did not see the pothole because she "wasn't looking down," not because of any debris obscuring the pothole.

Potholes in pavement are an everyday occurrence that ordinarily should be observed by a reasonably prudent person. Accordingly, in light of plaintiff's failure to show special aspects of the pothole at issue, it did not pose an unreasonable risk to her.

While the Supreme Court agreed with the result reached by the trial court, it considered it important to disapprove part of that court's apparent rationale. The trial court's remarks indicated that it may have granted summary disposition in favor of defendant because the plaintiff "was walking along without paying proper attention to where she was walking." However, in resolving an issue regarding the open-and-obvious doctrine, the question is whether the condition of the premises at issue was open and obvious and, if so, whether there were special aspects of the situation that nevertheless made it unreasonably dangerous. In a situation where a plaintiff was injured as a result of a risk that was truly outside the open-and-obvious danger doctrine and that posed an unreasonable risk of harm, the fact that the plaintiff was also negligent would not bar a cause of action. This is because Michigan follows the rule of comparative negligence. Under comparative negligence, where both the plaintiff and the defendant are blameworthy of negligence with regard to the plaintiff's injury, the amount of damages the plaintiff may recover is reduced but not precluded altogether. That is to say that a defendant may present evidence of a plaintiff's negligence in order to reduce a defendant's liability.

Accordingly, it is important for courts in deciding summary disposition motions by premises possessors in open-and-obvious-danger cases to focus on the objective nature of the condition of the premises at issue, not on the subjective degree of care used by the plaintiff. In the present case, there was no evidence of special aspects that made the open-and obvious pothole unreasonably dangerous.

IV

The Supreme Court agreed that a premises possessor is not generally required to protect an invitee from open-and-obvious dangers. It also agreed that circumstances may arise in which an open-and-obvious condition is nevertheless unreasonably dangerous so as to give rise to a duty upon a premises owner to in some manner remove or otherwise appropriately protect invitees against the danger. The Court further agreed that any comparative negligence by an invitee is irrelevant to whether a premises possessor has breached its duty to that invitee in connection with an open-and-obvious danger because an invitee's comparative negligence can only serve to reduce, not eliminate, the extent of liability.

Simply put, there must be something out of the ordinary, in other words, special, about a particular open-and-obvious danger in order for a premises owner to be expected to anticipate harm from that condition. Indeed, it seems obvious to us that if an open-and-obvious condition lacks some type of special aspect regarding the likelihood of harm, it is not unreasonably dangerous. The Court could not imagine an open-and-obvious condition that is unreasonably dangerous but lacks special aspects making it so. In other words, the duty to exercise reasonable care is not breached in cases involving ordinary steps. In the incident case, the plaintiff established nothing more than the existence of a common, ordinary pothole. Because of the great variety of circumstances in which premises liability claims may be raised, it may be practically impossible to demarcate the extent of a premises possessor's duties with great precision. Nevertheless, the Court believed that its approach, focusing on the existence or absence of special aspects of an open-and-obvious danger, would guide trial courts of the future in considering whether particular open-and-obvious conditions pose an unreasonable risk of harm better than would be the case without this further exposition of the open-and- obvious doctrine.

Finally, this opinion does not require a premises owner or possessor to be an "insurer of the safety of invitees." Indeed, the Court's resolution of the present case in favor of defendant would belie any such claim. However, a premises possessor does have a duty to undertake reasonable efforts to make its premises reasonably safe for its invitees.

For the above reasons, the Supreme Court reversed the judgment of the Court of Appeals and reinstated the judgment of the trial court.

CHAPTER 19. THE ASSUMPTION OF RISK DOCTRINE

The *Doctrine of Assumption of Risk* has four facets: (1) express *assumption of risk*, (2) implied primary *assumption of risk*, (3) implied reasonable *assumption of risk*, and (4) implied unreasonable *assumption of risk*. The basic tenet of this doctrine is that a party may not receive damages for the injurious consequences of a risk he knowingly undertakes. That is to say that a party may not recover in damages for an injury received when he voluntarily exposed himself to a known and obvious danger. The requirements for a defendant claiming *assumption of risk* as a legal, affirmative defense, are that: (1) *express assumption of risk*, a plaintiff has knowledge of the danger; (2) *implied primary assumption of risk*, the plaintiff knows the condition is dangerous; (3) *implied reasonable assumption of risk*, the plaintiff appreciates the nature or the extent of the danger, *and (4) implied unreasonable assumption of risk*, the plaintiff voluntary exposes himself to the danger, .

A golfer was hit in the head by an errant golf ball as he was returning his golf cart to the cart-return area. He fell off his cart and hit his head on the pavement and took some serious damage with loss of memory and physical debilitation. Once his impairments had been clearly delineated, he brought a lawsuit against the owner of the golf course alleging negligence of the willful and wanton variety because the owner had failed to adequately guard against such a possibility despite the fact that the owner had constructed a high wire fence sectioning off the area.

At trial the owner claimed *primary implied assumption of risk* as an affirmative defense and the lower court concurred dismissing the case whereupon the plaintiff appealed. On appeal, the appeals court reversed the trial court saying: "A golf course is not usually considered a dangerous place, nor the playing of golf a hazardous undertaking. It is a matter of common knowledge that players are expected not to drive their balls without giving warning when within hitting distance of persons in the field of play. Countless persons traverse golf courses the world over in reliance on that very expectation. *Primary implied assumption* of risk is not applicable here because golf is simply not the type of game in which participants are inherently, inevitably or customarily struck by the ball. Case remanded!"

At trial the plaintiff was awarded a sizable judgment, the jury reasoning the fact of the fence to be indicative of the owners awareness of a foreseeable injury. The cart-return area, after all, could have been moved.

SHAWNA BARBER V. EASTERN KARTING CO., ET AL.
COURT OF SPECIAL APPEALS OF MARYLAND
673 A.2D 744 (1996 MD.)
MARCH 28, 1996

LEGAL CONSIDERATIONS

Negligence / Defenses / Assumption of Risk

West Virginia adopted what is known as comparative *assumption of risk*. Comparative *assumption of risk* consists of two distinct principles. First, *assumption-of-risk doctrine* requires actual knowledge of the dangerous condition. Second, a plaintiff is not barred from recovery by the doctrine of *assumption of risk* unless his degree of fault arising therefrom equals or exceeds the combined fault or negligence of the other parties to the accident.

Civil Procedure / Summary Judgment

Maryland Rule of Civil Procedure, Cir. Ct. 2-501(a), permits a party to file at any time a motion for summary judgment on all or part of an action on the ground that there is no genuine dispute as to any material fact and that the party is entitled to judgment as a matter of law.

Civil Procedure / Summary Judgment

A material fact is a fact the resolution of which will somehow affect the outcome of a case. If the facts are susceptible to multiple inferences, all inferences must be resolved in favor of the non-moving party. In addition, the inferences drawn must be reasonable.

Negligence / Exculpatory Clauses

When a statute imposes a standard of care, a clause in an agreement structured to exempt a party from tort liability is unenforceable. Therefore, to the extent a release in the present case intends to exempt the defendant from tort liability to the plaintiff for the failure of the defendant to conform to the standard of care expected of members of his occupation, the clause is unenforceable.

Torts / Negligence / Exculpatory Clauses

A general clause in a pre-injury agreement exempting a defendant from all liability for any future loss or damage will not be interpreted to include the loss or damage resulting from the defendant's intentional or reckless misconduct or gross negligence unless the language of the agreement clearly indicates that the plaintiff specifically accepted such a risk.

Civil Procedure / Summary Judgment

A motion for summary judgment should be granted only when it is clear that there is no genuine issue of fact to be tried and inquiry concerning the facts is not necessary to clarify the application of the law.

PRIOR HISTORY: APPEAL FROM the Circuit Court for Anne Arundel County.

DISPOSITION: Judgment of the Circuit Court for Anne Arundel County affirmed in part and reversed in part and remanded for further proceedings consistent with this opinion.

PROCEDURAL POSTURE: The appellant was an amateur racer and was injured on a racetrack and filed an action against appellees, racetrack and manufacturer and seller of go-carts. The Trial Court for Anne Arundel County (Maryland) granted summary judgment in favor of all of the appellees, and the appellant appealed.

OVERVIEW: The racer suffered an extremely serious injury when her hair became entangled in the rear axle of a high-performance go-kart that she was driving during a go-cart racing event organized and sponsored by the racetrack. There were no seatbelts or shoulder harnesses, and the rear axle, which was also very close to the driver's head, was exposed and was not equipped with any type of shield or guard. The racer had signed a release prior to her race. After her injury, the racer filed an action against the racetrack, manufacturer, and the seller of the go-cart. The trial court granted summary judgment in favor of all the appellees (defendants in this case). On appeal, the Appeals Court reversed the grant of summary judgment on the grounds that the grant of summary judgment did not apply to the strict product liability and negligence claims against the manufacturer and seller of the go-carts. The Court found that summary judgment should not have been granted based upon a claim of the racer's contributory negligence and *assumption of risk*.

OUTCOME: The Appeals Court affirmed the grant of summary judgment to the racetrack citing that the complaint alleged only negligence and not reckless conduct. The Court reversed the grant of summary judgment to the manufacturer and seller of the go-carts on the grounds that that summary judgment did not apply to the strict product liability and negligence claims against the manufacturer and seller of the go-karts. The Court found that the action should not have been dismissed based upon racer's *assumption of the risk* and contributory negligence, both of which were lacking.

OPINION: Shawna Barber appealed from two orders of the Circuit Court for Anne Arundel County granting summary judgment in favor of appellees Woodbridge Karters, Inc. (Woodbridge), Margay Racing Products, Inc. (Margay), and Eastern Karting Company (Eastern). Several questions were presented in this appeal; the Court restated them as follows:

I. Did the trial court err in granting summary judgment in favor of Margay and Eastern on the ground that the anticipatory release fully excused Margay and Eastern from appellant's strict product liability claims?

II. Did the trial court err in granting summary judgment in favor of Woodbridge, Margay, and Eastern based on their release-from-liability clause, because: (1) the release clause allegedly was not intended to apply to claims for injuries not ordinarily associated with go-kart racing; and (2) the terms of the release clause were allegedly not made clear to appellant Barber?

III. Did the trial court err in granting summary judgment in favor of Woodbridge based on the anticipatory release because the evidence on the record purportedly established a genuine dispute as to whether appellant fully intended to release Woodbridge from liability based on Woodbridge's allegedly reckless conduct?

IV. Did the trial court err in granting summary judgment in favor of Margay and Eastern on the ground that appellant Barber assumed the risk of her injury?

V. Did the trial court err in granting summary judgment in favor of Margay and Eastern on the ground that appellant Barber was contributorily negligent?

To all but the third question, the Court responded in the affirmative. As a result of its exception of the third question, it remanded this case to the circuit court for further proceedings consistent with its opinion.

FACTS

On September 18, 1993, appellant suffered an extremely serious injury when her hair became entangled in the rear axle of a high-performance go-kart that she was driving during a go-kart racing event organized and sponsored by Woodbridge. Woodbridge, a not-for-profit corporation, operates a go-kart racing club that organizes and sanctions go-kart racing competitions.

Appellant was driving an "Enduro" go-kart manufactured by Margay and sold by Eastern to Cort Kane, an experienced go-kart racer. Kane was appellant's boyfriend at the time, and is now appellant's husband. This go-kart is not the ordinary type one would expect to find at amusement parks or at Ocean City, Maryland. Rather, it is a high-performance racing go-kart capable of reaching speeds in excess of 100 m.p.h., is between six and seven feet long, and rides only inches above the track surface. When in the reclined driving position, the driver's head rests against a headrest in the rear of the vehicle. In this position, according to appellant's estimation, the driver's head is approximately four inches from the rear-mounted engine and rear axle. There are no seatbelts or shoulder harnesses, and the rear axle is exposed and is not equipped with any type of shield or guard.

The racing event, in which appellant suffered her tragic injuries, was held at the Summit Point Raceway (raceway) in Summit Point, West Virginia. The race-way is Woodbridge's "home" track. Both Margay and Eastern are identified in Woodbridge's 1993 Driver Information Packet and on the 1993 Pit Pass as spon-sors of the event. Appellant attended the event with Kane. Prior to the Summit Point event, appellant had never raced in a go-kart race. Indeed, she had never previously operated a racing go-kart. Appellant was not a member of Wood-bridge or of any other go-kart club and her only experience with go-kart racing was when she accompanied Kane to a go-kart racing event in Charlotte, North Carolina in late August 1993. During the Charlotte event, in which Kane raced the go-kart, appellant assisted Kane, changing certain go-kart parts and making various adjustments to the go-kart in preparation for the races. She also helped Kane start the go-kart's motor with a special starter unit and she timed Kane's laps.

When the couple arrived for the Summit Point event, a raceway attendant handed them a clipboard with a form on it that they were required to sign in order to enter the raceway. The form, entitled "Release and Waiver of Liability, Assumption of Risk and Indemnity Agreement" reads as follows:

> IN CONSIDERATION of being permitted to compete, officiate, observe, work for, or participate in any way in the EVENT(S) or being permitted to enter for any purpose any RESTRICTED AREA (defined as any area requiring special authorization, credentials, or permission to enter to which admission by the general public is restricted or prohibited), EACH OF THE UNDERSIGNED, for himself, his personal representatives, heirs, and next of kin agrees to absolve the racetrack and its promoters of all liability contingent or otherwise to the parties participation in the events and activities accommodated and facilitated by the venue.

> I HAVE READ THIS RELEASE AND WAIVER OF LIABILITY, ASSUMP-TION OF RISK AND INDEMNITY AGREEMENT, AND FULLY UNDER-STAND ITS TERMS, UNDERSTANDING THAT I HAVE GIVEN UP SUB-STANTIAL RIGHTS BY SIGNING IT AND HAVE SIGNED IT FREELY AND VOLUNTARILY WITHOUT ANY INDUCEMENT, ASSURANCE OR GUAR-ANTEE BEING MADE TO ME AND INTEND MY SIGNATURE TO BE A COMPLETE AND UNCONDITIONAL RELEASE OF ALL LIABILITY TO THE GREATEST EXTENT ALLOWED BY LAW.

According to appellant, she did not read the Release because she did not be-lieve there was sufficient time to do so with several cars behind them waiting to enter the raceway. In any event, appellant stated that she felt that she had no choice but to sign the Release if she wanted to enter the raceway. Appellant further alleged that she was never given a copy of the Release, nor did anyone at the event discuss the Release with her, explain its terms and scope, or discuss the risks of injury associated with the racing event.

Upon her arrival at the raceway for the Summit Point event, appellant planned to attend a course for novice drivers, but Woodbridge cancelled the course due to morning rain. Woodbridge's policy regarding novice drivers attending the novice class is reflected in its 1993 Driver Information Packet, as follows: "All novices (persons who have competed in less than three (3) races) must attend novice school, if the novice school is offered, before being allowed to race or practice. It is recommended that first time drivers to the track also attend the novice school." Indeed, prior to appellant's participation, no one from Woodbridge (1) asked appellant whether she had ever driven in a go-kart race before or had go-kart racing experience; (2) told appellant that she could not drive in a race without participating in a training session for first-time drivers; (3) gave appellant an information packet or any other materials containing safety instructions or warnings; or (4) asked appellant whether she was a member of Woodbridge.

Rather, appellant simply paid an entry fee and obtained a go-kart tag number. A Woodbridge official checked the go-kart to confirm that it met racing specifications and to make sure that it was not improperly modified. The race official also inspected appellant's racing helmet to make sure that it was a regulation helmet. No one, however, asked appellant to put the helmet on to see whether it fit properly.

Before the race, appellant drove the go-kart three times around the track during a practice run. Prior to the practice run, appellant put her shoulder length hair in a ponytail with a rubber band, folded it up onto the top of her head so that the ponytail would be inside the helmet, and tucked a few loose hairs into the collar of her racing suit. During the practice run, appellant's hair did not fall down or come out of her helmet.

After the practice run, but before the race, appellant attended a brief driver's meeting conducted by a Woodbridge official. During this meeting, track conditions, flag positions, and safety rules relating to driving the go-karts were discussed. According to appellant, at no time during the meeting, or otherwise, did anyone ever warn her that loose clothing or hair could be dangerous while driving the go-kart. Specifically, no one instructed appellant to use a hair net or stocking to keep her hair in place inside the helmet so that it would not get caught in the go-kart's moving parts.

Shortly after the meeting, the race in which appellant would drive started. About twenty-minutes into her race, with more than seven laps completed, appellant's hair got caught in the rear axle of the go-kart. This caused appellant's scalp to be torn literally from her head. Appellant was taken by ambulance to a local hospital, but, due to the nature of her injury, she had to be flown by helicopter to the Washington Hospital Center in Washington D.C. At the Washington Hospital Center, surgeons attempted to re-attach her scalp, which was lacerated into five pieces. Unfortunately, appellant's scalp could not be saved, and skin grafts from her leg and buttocks were necessary. Over the course of the next several weeks, appellant underwent multiple operations (totaling many hours) and vigorous physical therapy. Her injuries range from the permanent loss of her scalp, hair, and eyebrows, to muscle and nerve damage preventing her eyelids from properly closing. Appellant states that she suffers from severe emotional problems associated with the accident and the loss of her hair and scalp.

Although understanding that go-kart racing involved certain dangers (e.g., collisions with other go-karts, overturning go-karts, etc.), appellant alleges that she never thought about, considered, understood, or contemplated the possible danger of her hair getting caught in the go-kart's moving parts and her scalp being torn from her head. Nonetheless, appellant stated in pre-trial discovery that she arranged her hair in the above-described fashion "because I had a definitely instinctive fear of my hair dangling in the air, whether it be getting in my face keeping me from seeing or whether it be getting caught in moving parts. Getting caught in moving parts did not occur to me then but I just thought that it would be dangerous." Additionally, prior to her accident, appellant was aware of the go-kart's moving parts behind the headrest, and was at least familiar with the general setup of the go-kart.

On July 8, 1994, appellant filed a four-count complaint against Woodbridge, Margay, and Eastern in the Circuit Court for Anne Arundel County. In the first count, appellant sued Margay and Eastern for strict product liability, alleging that the go-kart was defectively designed. In the second count, she sued Margay and Eastern for strict product liability, alleging that Margay and Eastern should have warned appellant of the design defects and latent dangers associated with the exposed rear axle. In the third count, appellant sued Margay and Eastern for negligently designing the go-kart. In the fourth count, appellant sued Woodbridge for negligently failing to warn her that loose hair or clothing could get caught in the go-kart's moving parts and cause her injury.

Woodbridge filed a motion for summary judgment arguing, among other things, that there was no evidence of negligence on its part, and that, in any event, appellant's claim was barred by operation of the Release she had signed. A hearing on the motion was held on March 28, 1995. The trial court ruled from the bench, stating that "it is clear from the language of this release that appellant has fully released Woodbridge from all liability." Accordingly, the trial judge granted summary judgment in favor of Woodbridge. A written order to the same effect followed.

Margay and Eastern also filed motions for summary judgment. On April 24, 1995, the circuit court heard argument on the motions. Following the hearing, on May 12, 1995, the trial court issued a written Memorandum of Opinion and Order granting summary judgment in favor of Margay and Eastern. Therein, the trial court determined that the Release barred all of appellant's claims, including the strict product liability claims, against Margay and Eastern since both were "sponsors," and therefore "releasees," under the Release. Additionally, the trial court ruled that appellant assumed the risk of her injuries and was contributorily negligent.

From these orders, appellant appealed to the Appeals Court.

LEGAL ANALYSIS

Standard of Review and Choice of Law

Preliminarily, it was necessary to set forth the principles governing the standard of review for the appeal. The governing principles permitted a party to "file at any time a motion for summary judgment on all or part of an action on the ground that there is no genuine dispute as to any material fact and that the party is entitled to judgment as a matter of law." In response to a motion for summary judgment, the opposing party "shall identify with particularity the material facts that are disputed." The summary judgment proceeding was not a substitute for a trial on the merits, but was a proceeding to determine whether a trial was needed to resolve a factual dispute.

A material fact is a fact the resolution of which will somehow affect the outcome of a case. If the facts are susceptible to multiple inferences, all inferences must be resolved in favor of the non-moving party (the appellant in this case, was the party appealing from the trial court). In addition, the inferences drawn must be reasonable. Where several inferences may be drawn, summary judgment must be denied and the dispute submitted to the trier of fact. Conclusory denials or bald allegations will not defeat a motion for summary judgment. Similarly, a mere scintilla of evidence in support of the non-moving party's claim is insufficient to avoid the grant of summary judgment.

Additionally, it was critical to note that, although suit was filed in a Maryland court, the case was governed by West Virginia law. Specifically, as the parties conceded and as the trial court recognized, under the doctrine of *lex loci contractus* (the law of the place where the contract was formed), the meaning and enforceability of the Release from Liability, signed by the plaintiff, was governed by West Virginia law, and under the doctrine of *lex loci delicti* (the law of the place where the injury occurred), the substantive tort law principles of the accident were those of West Virginia not Maryland.

The Legal Principles of West Virginia are such that before turning to the merits of this appeal, the Appeals Court needed to present an overview of the West Virginia legal principles germane to the case. At the onset, the Court noted that both parties had diligently and thoroughly presented the Court (the Maryland appeals court) with many cases from West Virginia and other jurisdictions in support of their respective positions. After considering the issues and examining the authorities presented, the Appeals Court was convinced that the outcome of the appeal devolved, in large part, on a proper understanding and application of one case: *Murphy v. North Am. River Runners, Inc.,* 412 S.E.2d 504 (W. Va. 1991), a West Virginia case. Because *Murphy* was of utmost importance to the disposition of the appeal, it was necessary to examine *Murphy* in detail.

The issue in Murphy was as follows:

> Whether the trial court . . . properly granted a summary judgment to the defendant on the ground that the anticipatory release (disclaimer) executed by the plaintiff was a complete bar to any action by the plaintiff against the defendant

for injuries sustained by the plaintiff during a whitewater rafting expedition conducted by the defendant.

In *Murphy*, the plaintiff went whitewater rafting as a paying passenger in a raft owned and operated by a defendant party. The guide of the raft in which Murphy was a passenger attempted a rescue operation of another raft that had become stuck among the rocks in the rapids of the river being rafted. In an attempt to dislodge the encumbered raft, the guide intentionally bumped the plaintiff's raft into the stranded raft. As a result, the plaintiff was thrown about the raft, causing a serious knee and ankle injury.

Prior to the rafting trip, the plaintiff had signed a document which the defendant had drafted entitled "Raft Trip Release, Assumption of Risk & Permission." The pertinent provisions of the release as set forth in Murphy were as follows:

> . . . during the raft trip . . . certain risks and dangers exist or may occur, including, but not limited to, hazards of traveling on a rubber raft in rough river conditions using paddles or oars and other raft equipment, hiking in rugged terrain, being injured by animals, reptiles or insects, becoming ill in remote places without medical facilities available, and being subject to the forces of nature.

> In consideration of the right to participate in such river trip, . . . I UNDERSTAND AND DO HEREBY AGREE TO ASSUME ALL OF THE ABOVE RISKS AND OTHER RELATED RISKS WHICH MAY BE ENCOUNTERED ON SAID RAFT TRIP, INCLUDING ACTIVITIES PRELIMINARY AND SUBSEQUENT THERETO. I do hereby agree to hold [defendant] harmless from any and all liability, actions, causes of actions, claims, expenses, and damages on account of injury to my person or property, even injury resulting in death or injuries which may arise in the future as a result of my trip or as a result of my participation in any other activities associated with my trip.

> I expressly agree that this release, waiver and indemnity agreement is intended to be as broad and inclusive as permitted by the law of the State of West Virginia and that if any portion thereof is held invalid, it is agreed that the balance shall, notwithstanding, continue in full legal force and effect. This release contains the entire agreement between the parties hereto and the terms of this release are contractual and not merely recital.

> I further state that I HAVE CAREFULLY READ THE FOREGOING RELEASE AND KNOW THE CONTENTS THEREOF AND I SIGN THIS RELEASE AS MY OWN FREE ACT. This is a legally binding document which I have read and understood.

After the injury in the West Virginia case, in MURPHY, the plaintiff filed suit against the rafting company, alleging that the defendant's guide negligently, carelessly, and recklessly caused her injuries. The defendant moved for summary judgment based on the terms of the raft release, the disclaimer. In opposition to the motion, the plaintiff filed an affidavit of an experienced river guide who testified that there existed reasonable alternatives to the above-described rescue operation that would have posed no risk of harm to the passengers of the plaintiff's raft. The plaintiff also filed her own affidavit stating that she was not informed in advance of the possibility that her raft might be involved in the rescue of a stranded raft by the "bumping" of her raft into a stranded raft. The plaintiff's affidavit further stated that she never contemplated that the raft release covered such intentional acts, but only applied to ordinary negligence in the form of piloting errors associated with an ordinary rafting trip. The trial court granted summary judgment to the defendant based on the Plaintiff's release.

On appeal, the Supreme Court of Appeals of West Virginia explained the law as follows:

> Generally, in the absence of an applicable safety statute, a plaintiff who expressly and, under the circumstances, clearly agrees to accept a risk of harm arising from a defendant's negligent or reckless conduct may not recover for such harm unless the agreement is invalid as contrary to public policy. When such an express agreement is freely and fairly made between parties who are in an equal bargaining position, and there is no public interest with which the agreement interferes, the disclaimer agreement, the release from liability, will generally be upheld. (That is to say that the public has no interest in the terms of a contract freely bargained between parties so long as the terms of agreement are legal.)

> A clause in an agreement exempting a party from tort liability is, however, unenforceable on grounds of public policy if the agreement exempts a party charged with a duty of care from tort liability to a party to whom a duty of care is owed. In order for an express agreement assuming risk to be effective, it must appear that the plaintiff has given his or her assent to the terms of the agreement. Particularly where the agreement is prepared by the defendant, it must appear that the terms were in fact brought home to, and understood by the plaintiff before it may be found that the plaintiff has agreed to those terms. Stated another way, to relieve a party from liability for his or her own negligence by contract, the language of the contract to that effect must be clear and definite.

> Moreover, in order for the express agreement to assume the risk to be effective, it must also appear that its terms were intended by both parties to apply to the particular conduct of the defendant which has caused the harm. To determine whether there was such intent, when the agreement is prepared by the defendant, its terms will be construed strictly against the defendant.

> In particular, a general clause in a pre-injury exculpatory agreement or anticipatory release purporting to exempt a defendant from all liability from any future loss or damage will not be construed to include the loss or damage resulting from the defendant's intentional or reckless misconduct or gross negligence unless the circumstances clearly indicate that such was the plaintiff's intention. Similarly, a general clause in an exculpatory agreement or anticipatory release exempting a defendant from all liability for any future negligence will not be construed to include intentional or reckless misconduct or gross negligence, unless such intention clearly appears from the circumstances.

> These specific rules of anticipatory release construction are related to the general rule that a release ordinarily covers only such matters as may fairly be said to have been within the intention of the parties at the time the agreement was formed.

After reciting these principles of law, the Murphy court observed that the West Virginia Whitewater Responsibility Act (Act) applied. According to the court, the Act's purpose was to define those areas of responsibility for which commercial whitewater guides are liable for injury in light of the fact that it is impossible to eliminate the inherent risks involved in whitewater rafting. The Murphy court further stated that the Act imposed certain duties on whitewater guides that immunized guides from liability for injuries resulting from the inherent risks of the activities which are essentially impossible to eliminate regardless of all feasible safety measures.

One such statutorily imposed duty requires guides to conform to the standard of care expected from members of the profession. Accordingly, the Murphy court held as follows:

> As stated previously, when a statute imposes a standard of care, a clause in an agreement purporting to exempt a party from tort liability to a member of a protected class for failure to conform to that statutory standard is unenforceable. Therefore, to the extent that the anticipatory release in the present case purports to exempt the defendant from tort liability to the plaintiff for the failure of the defendant's guide to conform to the standard of care expected of members of his occupation, the disclaimer is unenforceable.

Thus, because the testimony of the plaintiff's experienced guide essentially stated in his affidavit that the defendant's guide failed to observe the standard of care expected of members of his occupation during a rescue operation, a genuine issue of material fact was raised and the trial court should not have granted summary judgment to the defendant.

Next, and more significantly, the Appeals Court observed that the plaintiff's complaint explicitly alleged that the defendant's conduct was reckless, as well as negligent. As a result, the Murphy court stated:

> As stated previously, a general clause in a pre-injury exculpatory agreement or anticipatory release purporting to exempt a defendant from all liability for any future loss or damage will not be interpreted to include the loss or damage resulting from the defendant's intentional or reckless misconduct or gross negligence unless the circumstances clearly indicate that such was the plaintiff's intention. This rule parallels the rule that a release is construed from the standpoint of the parties at the time of its execution. Extrinsic evidence is admissible to show both the relation of the parties and the circumstances which surrounded the transaction.

The *Murphy* court then recognized that contract interpretation is a matter for the court. Where the meaning of a contract is uncertain and ambiguous, parol evidence is admissible to demonstrate the intent of the parties underlying the formation of the contract (parol evidence is oral evidence, evidence that is germane to a contract but which exists outside the written terms of the contract). Where parol evidence is not in conflict with the terms of the contract, the court will interpret the meaning of the written terms of the contract. Where, however, there is a conflict on a material point necessary to the interpretation of the contract, the meaning of the contract is a matter for the jury, and parol evidence is admissible.

After reciting these principles, the *Murphy* court held as follows:

> In light of the inquiry needed here concerning the relation of the parties and the circumstances surrounding the execution of the anticipatory release in order to determine the parties' intent with respect to the reckless conduct of the defendant, the trial court improperly granted the defendant's motion for summary judgment. A motion for summary judgment should be granted only when it is clear that there is no genuine issue of material fact to be tried, and inquiry concerning the facts is not necessary to clarify the application of the law.

It is relatively clear that the West Virginia high court, the Murphy court, held that summary judgment was inappropriate because the plaintiff generated a genuine issue of material fact by her affidavit, which stated that she never contemplated that the raft release covered intentional acts, but only covered ordinary acts of negligence such as piloting errors associated with an ordinary ride on the river. In other words, despite the defendant's obvious attempt to draft the disclaimer in a very broad and all-inclusive manner, recklessness was not covered because the plaintiff, by her affidavit, successfully raised a genuine issue of fact regarding whether such conduct was contemplated by her release from liability. Accordingly, the Murphy court reversed and vacated the summary judgment entered in favor of the defendant and remanded the case for further proceedings consistent with their opinion. THAT IS TO SAY:

I

First, appellant Shawna Barber argues that the trial court erred in granting summary judgment in favor of Margay and Eastern on the ground that the disclaimer Release she signed fully absolved Margay and Eastern of appellant's strict liability claims. We agree with Barber. (Strict Liability is a concept applied by the court that holds a manufacturer of a product, or provider of a service in which there are inherent hazards to be strictly liable for injuries sustained unless the individual using the product or availing himself/herself of the service releases the seller of all liability accruing from damages or injury).

Construing the facts in the light most favorable to appellant Barber, the Court held that, under the Murphy decision, the plaintiff-appellant had generated a genuine issue of material fact sufficient to overcome Margay's and Eastern's motions for summary judgment on the strict liability claims. Preliminarily, the Court recognized that the trial court was correct in determining that Margay and Eastern were "sponsors" under the Release, and therefore were "releasees" under the terms of the disclaimer. This, however, was insufficient to shield Margay and Eastern from appellant Shawna Barber's strict product liability claims. The Court explained:.

> Appellant's affidavit in opposition to Margay's and Eastern's motions for summary judgment unequivocally states that she never contemplated or intended that her disclaimer would bar such claims as hers, and that nobody ever informed her that this might be the case. To be sure, her release purports to cover all claims 'caused by the NEGLIGENCE OF PROVIDERS or otherwise,' and 'is

intended to be as broad and inclusive as is permitted by the laws of West Virginia. Additionally, appellant's signature was intended 'TO BE A COMPLETE AND UNCONDITIONAL RELEASE OF ALL LIABILITY TO THE GREATEST EXTENT ALLOWED BY LAW.' As explained above, however, the disclaimer in the Murphy case employed similarly broad and all-inclusive language, yet the plaintiff generated a genuine dispute of fact regarding whether she meant to release her claims against the defendant for reckless conduct.

In the same way that there is a factual dispute regarding whether the plaintiff in Murphy intended the release to bar claims for the defendant's reckless conduct, there is a factual dispute regarding whether appellant in the present case intended her disclaimer to bar claims of strict liability. Strictly construing the Release against Margay and Eastern, we can safely say that a reasonable person in appellant's position would not contemplate or intend that her release would eliminate strict product liability claims against the manufacturer and seller of the go-kart. Indeed, while a driver might expect to be releasing claims for ordinary injuries associated with racing a go-kart, e.g., 'spin-outs,' collisions, etc., it is entirely reasonable to conclude that surrendering claims for product liability against the manufacturer and seller of the go-kart would be the farthest thing from a driver's mind upon signing a disclaimer at the entrance of a raceway. This is what appellant has stated in affidavits and discovery, and her statements are undisputed fact for purposes of summary judgment. Applying Murphy, therefore, we hold that summary judgment was improperly granted in this regard.

Furthermore, appellant's sworn statements, taken in the light most favorable to her, were sufficient to demonstrate that there was 'an unequal bargaining position' with respect to the disclaimer. Appellant points out that her affidavit stated, 'No one discussed this Release with me, explained its terms or made clear to me its scope, or discussed with me any of the risks of injury associated with the racing event purportedly covered by the release.' She further stated that there was pressure to sign the release and that there was insufficient time for a meaningful reading of the document because cars were behind her waiting to enter the raceway. In addition, if she wanted to enter the raceway, she had no choice but to sign the disclaimer as presented. Moreover, she did not arrive at the raceway by herself, but rather accompanied by her companion Kane. These facts undeniably generate, at a minimum, a genuine dispute of material fact.

Additionally, as Murphy requires, 'it must appear that the terms of the Release were in fact brought home to, and understood by, the plaintiff, before it may be found that the plaintiff has agreed to them.' Alternatively stated, to relieve contractually a party from liability for its negligence, language to that effect must be clear and definite. In light of Murphy's strict construction of the disclaimer against the defendant in that case, we are satisfied that the document in the instant case is not sufficiently clear and definite to enable us to conclude, as a matter of law, that appellant must have understood her release to cover the strict product liability claims.

II

Based on the foregoing, the Appeals Court held that the trial court erred in granting summary judgment in favor of Margay and Eastern on appellant's strict product liability claims. Despite the fact that both Margay and Eastern are absolved of liability under the terms of plaintiff Barber's release, plaintiff has presented sufficient facts to generate a jury question regarding whether the release in fact extinguishes those claims. Appellant Barber next asserted that the trial court erred in granting summary judgment in favor of Woodbridge, Margay, and Eastern because: (1) the disclaimer document allegedly was not intended to release claims for injuries not ordinarily associated with go-kart racing; and (2) the terms of the release were allegedly not made clear to appellant. the Court's focus at this juncture was only on the propriety of summary judgment on appellant's negligence claim against Woodbridge for negligently failing to warn her that loose hair or clothing could get caught in the go-kart's moving parts and cause her injury, and her additional negligence claim against Margay and Eastern for negligently designing the go-kart.

Addressing the propriety of summary judgment on appellant's negligence claim against Woodbridge, as previously noted, the trial court granted summary judgment for Woodbridge on the ground that the Plaintiff's release exculpated Woodbridge for any alleged negligence on its part. For the reasons stated above, that a genuine dispute of material fact existed with regard to whether there was an unequal bargaining position between the parties, the Court reversed the trial court's grant of summary judgment. The Court reiterated that the appellant presented sufficient facts to generate a jury issue regarding whether the release was ineffective for a lack of an equal bargaining position. Accordingly, the case was be remanded to the trial court on that basis.

In addition, the Appeals Court determined that summary judgment in favor of Woodbridge was improper because appellant raised a genuine dispute of material fact in two further respects. First, appellant presented sufficient facts to demonstrate that her disclaimer was not intended to cover her claim against Woodbridge. As the Court explained, the Murphy court held that in order for an anticipatory release to be effective, it must "appear that its terms were intended by both parties to apply to the particular conduct of the defendant which caused the harm. Appellant stated she never contemplated assuming the risk of getting her hair caught in the go-kart's rear axle, but rather only assumed the ordinary risks of go-kart racing. For that reason, the Court held that the Murphy decision required the Court to reverse the grant of summary judgment because appellant had generated a genuine issue of material fact that she never intended to absolve Woodbridge of the duty to warn her of the danger of her hair getting caught in the go-kart's rear axle.

Second, construing matters most favorably to appellant, appellant demonstrated that she was not barred from proceeding in her claim against Woodbridge because the terms of the release were not brought home to her in their entirety. In other words, according to Murphy, to relieve contractually a party from liability for its negligence, language to that effect must be clear and definite. Under the holding in Murphy as applied to the present case, the language of the release was not sufficiently clear and definite enough that the appellant could have understood the terms of the disclaimer to excuse Woodbridge of the duty to warn the plaintiff appellant of the risks and dangers of her hair getting caught in the go-kart's exposed rear axle.

Lastly, the Court addressed the issue of whether summary judgment in favor of Margay and Eastern was proper on appellant's negligence claim against Margay and Eastern for negligently designing the go-kart. The Court held that, consistent with its reasoning above, summary judgment was improper. First, appellant had raised a genuine dispute of material fact regarding unequal bargaining positions. Second, appellant's sworn statements sufficiently demonstrated that her release was not intended to cover her claim against Margay and Eastern for negligently designing the go-kart. Her allegations that she only assumed the ordinary risks associated with go-kart racing, and not risks associated with a poorly designed go-kart, were sufficient under the Murphy decision for her to avoid a grant of summary judgment against her on this claim. Finally, the terms of the release were not sufficiently clear and definite under Murphy to enable the Court to conclude that appellant understood her disclaimer to cover claims against Margay and Eastern for negligent design of the go-kart.

III

As the Court noted in Part II above, the circuit court erred in granting summary judgment in Woodbridge's favor. In other words, in addition to those arguments in Part II above, appellant argued that Woodbridge was not entitled to summary judgment because the record, viewed in appellant's favor, contained evidence of reckless conduct on Woodbridge's part, and that, therefore, under Murphy, appellant's release did not exculpate Woodbridge from liability for such conduct.

The Court further held that the circuit court erred in granting summary judgment to Woodbridge for only those reasons expressed in Part II above. The circuit court did not err in granting Woodbridge summary judgment on the basis of the alleged reckless conduct because appellant failed to plead that cause of action. Thus, the Appeals Court agreed with Woodbridge. Without regard to whether appellant had raised a genuine dispute of fact that Woodbridge somehow acted recklessly, the Court observed that appellant's complaint did not contain a claim against Woodbridge for liability based on reckless behavior. Rather, appellant's complaint (which was the only count against Woodbridge) alleged a cause of action against Woodbridge strictly for ordinary negligence. In this regard, the complaint alleged that Woodbridge failed "to exercise ordinary and reasonable care and prudence" in "wholly failing and neglecting to warn, notify or instruct" appellant of the dangers of hair becoming caught in the go-kart's moving parts.

Because appellant had not sued Woodbridge based on reckless conduct, the circuit court did not err, as appellant suggested, in granting summary judgment on the issue of reckless conduct. In other words, that the Release may not exculpate Woodbridge for reckless conduct under Murphy did not matter because appellant was not legally entitled to recover from Woodbridge for such conduct under her complaint as filed below. Each cause of action must be set forth in the complaint in separately numbered counts. The Court held that the appellant should have made the allegation in a separately numbered count, and that a claimant cannot recover on a cause of action not contained in its complaint. The trial court, therefore, did not err in the manner in which appellant argued.

IV and V

As the remaining two questions were closely related, the Court addressed them together. The Appeals Court had to determine whether the circuit court erred in granting summary judgment in favor of Margay and Eastern on the ground that the appellant assumed the risk of her injury, and, on that ground, that the appellant was contributorily negligent. The final part of the trial court's written Memorandum of Opinion and Order granting summary judgment in favor of Margay and Eastern read as follows: (1) "Did the Appellant Barber assume the danger and risk of possible injury by participating in a high-speed competitive race held at the Raceway on 19 September 1993, and did she know her Go-Kart had exposed, fast moving parts, within inches of her head, and that dangling hair posed a danger in racing sports.?" (2)."Was the appellant contributorily negligent in reference to the events that took place on September 19, 1993, at the racing event in which she participated?"

West Virginia has chosen to call its form of contributory negligence "comparative contributory negligence." This form of contributory negligence holds that a party is not barred from recovering damages in a tort action so long as his negligence or fault does not equal or exceed the combined negligence or fault of the other parties against whom negligence is claimed. There is no question that the appellant was contributorily negligent in that she did not secure her hair properly.

The Appeals Court determined that the trial court erred in granting summary judgment on those two grounds.

1. The Court began with an examination of West Virginia law concerning the defense of assumption of risk. West Virginia has adopted what is known as "comparative assumption of risk." Comparative assumption of risk consists of two distinct principles. First, "assumption of risk doctrine requires actual knowledge of the dangerous condition." Thus, the plaintiff will be deemed to have assumed the risk where he "has full knowledge and appreciation of the dangerous condition and voluntarily exposes himself to it." According to the West Virginia Supreme Court of Appeals, this is a "high standard," and, in several cases, the court has held that, as a matter of law, an assumption-of-risk jury instruction should not have been given. Second, a "plaintiff is not barred from recovery by the doctrine of assumption of risk unless his degree of fault arising therefrom equals or exceeds the combined fault or negligence of the other parties to the accident." Thus, "the plaintiff's degree of fault arising from the assumption of risk is determined by the jury, and the total award of damages is then diminished accordingly." The Court held that the defense of comparative assumption of risk was available against a plaintiff in a product liability case where it can be shown that the plaintiff had actual knowledge of the defective or dangerous condition, fully appreciated the risks involved, and continued to use the product.

Under those principles, it was clear that the trial court erred in granting summary judgment on the ground that appellant assumed the risk of the accident. The trial court was wrong in two regards. First, the trial judge failed to view the facts in the light most favorable to appellant. To be sure, there was evidence that appellant voluntarily drove the go-kart when she "knew the Go-Kart had exposed, fast moving parts, within inches of a driver's head," and "knew that dangling hair posed a danger in racing sports." Appellant, however, generated evidence demonstrating just the opposite. For example, in her affidavit, she stated as follows:

> Before the race in which I drove, I placed my hair up inside my helmet in the same manner that I had done for the practice run. I did this to keep my hair out of my face and out of the way, which is something I had always done when engaging in sports activities, such as horseback riding or bicycle riding. I wasn't concerned about any particular danger relating to the Kart. The possibility that my hair might get caught in the Kart's axle never occurred to me and certainly was not obvious to me, and no one warned me or even suggested there was a risk that this might happen. I did not know about or appreciate this danger, and surely did not appreciate how extremely serious an injury could result from this danger, such as the injury that I suffered when my hair got caught and my scalp was torn from my head.

Clearly, in light of the above, appellant Barber had raised a genuine dispute of material fact regarding whether she assumed the risk of her injury. The Court recognized that the record contained statements by appellant contradicting the above affidavit excerpt. This factual conflict, however, was not one that could be properly resolved on summary judgment, but needed to be left for a jury.

Second, the trial judge should not have granted summary judgment in Margay's and Eastern's favor based on appellant's assumption of risk because the trial judge wholly ignored the "comparative" part of West Virginia's "comparative assumption of risk" doctrine. As the Appeals Court explained, an appellant cannot be barred from recovery under the doctrine of assumption of risk unless the degree of fault arising therefrom equals or exceeds the combined fault or negligence of the other parties to the accident. Thus, even if it had been correct (which it would not have been in this case) for the trial court to hold that appellant assumed the risk as a matter of law, given the evidence that appellant presented of Margay's and Eastern's culpability, a jury would be needed to make the requisite comparability determination.

In sum, therefore, the trial court should not have granted summary judgment in Margay's and Eastern's favor on the ground that appellant assumed the risk of her injuries. In light of the evidence presented, this was a matter that the jury had to resolve consistent with the West Virginia doctrine of comparative assumption of risk as delineated in West Virginia law.

2. For similar reasons, The Appeals Court held that the trial judge erred in granting summary judgment in favor of Margay and Eastern on the ground that appellant was contributorily negligent. Under West Virginia law, "a party is not barred from recovering damages in a tort action so long as his negligence or fault does not equal or exceed the combined negligence or fault of the other parties involved in the accident." In addition, "it will be the jury's obligation to assign the proportion or degree of this total negligence among the various parties, beginning with the plaintiff."

First, the circuit court erred because it again failed to view the facts in the light most favorable to appellant. In this regard, the circuit court held that "there is no question that appellant was contributorily negligent, namely, she did not secure her hair properly." When viewed in the light least favorable to appellant, the simple fact that appellant's hair came down might indicate that she was negligent in the manner in which she secured her hair. There are other facts that indicate just the opposite. For example, appellant described methodically putting her hair in a ponytail with a rubber band, folding it up onto the top of her head so that the ponytail would be inside the helmet, and tucking a few loose hairs into the collar of her racing suit. She also stated that "during the practice run, she did not have any problem with her hair falling down or coming out of her helmet." Viewed in the light most favorable to appellant, this indicated that appellant secured her hair in a non-negligent manner.

Furthermore, the trial court's determination presumes that appellant had a duty to secure her hair in the first place. Indeed, this may be the case. Viewing the evidence in appellant's favor, however, it is conceivable that a jury might very well have concluded that it would not be negligent for appellant, a first-time go-kart racer, to fail to take special steps beyond those actually taken to secure her hair in the absence of instructions to do so from raceway officials or some prior knowledge of danger on her part. In other words, a jury could have concluded that securing one's hair would not be something that would occur to a reasonable person.

Second, as the Court discussed previously with respect to the comparative assumption of risk defense, the trial court neglected to consider the "comparability" aspect of West Virginia's contributory negligence defense. Even if the Court assumed for the sake of argument that appellant was negligent in the manner in which she secured her hair, a jury would be needed to determine whether her degree of negligence equaled or exceeded the combined negligence or fault of Margay and Eastern.

For the reasons stated, the circuit court erred in granting summary judgment in Margay's and Eastern's favor based on appellant's alleged contributory negligence.

CONCLUSION

Based on the foregoing, the Appeals Court affirmed in part and reversed and remanded in part the judgment of the trial court.

Chapter 20. The Public Duty Doctrine

The Public Duty Doctrine has its origins in an 1855 case in which an individual was kidnapped and held for ransom. When the plaintiff had been released, he sued the county sheriff alleging that despite his request for protection, the sheriff refused to protect him. The case went to the United States Supreme Court where in the decision of *South v. Maryland*, 59 U.S. 396, (1855), the Supreme Court held that the sheriff's duty to preserve the peace was a public duty for which he was responsible to the public and not to any given individual, meaning that he could be prosecuted by the state but not sued by an individual. Thus was born the *public duty doctrine*, i.e., A DUTY OWED TO ALL IS A DUTY OWED TO NONE.

In 1988 the Xs began constructing a two-story addition to their home. The City issued them a building permit listing them as the "Contractor," and Mr. X performed much of the construction work by himself, including forming and pouring the foundation. During the approximately two-year period it took to complete the house, the City's building inspectors visited and inspected the house more than 40 times for compliance with the building code. In June of 1990, the City issued the Xs a certificate of occupancy, certifying that the building met applicable building codes

Later, the Ys purchased the house from the Xs. As time passed, the Ys noticed problems with the home's construction. Experts inspected the home and determined it did not comply with the City's building code in several respects. The natural gas piping did not meet code requirements. Windows and roof vents were installed without proper flashing, siding had not been installed and sealed properly, and no vapor barrier existed in most of the interior walls causing water leaks and condensation to form. The structural supports in the house were significantly overloaded and the house foundation did not have adequate frost-depth footings. The structure was also built on uncontrolled fill, causing the house to heave and settle in different directions and damaging the structure. A structural engineer advised the Ys to either fix the foundation of the house immediately or vacate the residence.

The Ys brought an action against the Xs and the City. The Ys asserted the City owed a duty to ensure that all buildings are constructed according to relevant building codes and to properly inspect buildings under construction to ensure the builder is following all relevant building codes, and that the City breached its duty by negligently inspecting and approving the construction of the foundation of the residence, as said foundation did not meet the required building code. The Ys asserted the Xs had committed constructive and actual fraud, breach of warranty, negligence, and consumer fraud. The Ys sought equitable rescission (the return of their money) and punitive damages from the Xs. (Equitable rescission is the unmaking of a contract, in this case the contract that resulted in the purchase of the home.)

During the trial, the Ys maintained that the City owed a duty to them to properly inspect the construction of houses and to enforce the building codes in force at the time a particular house was constructed. Because the City can only act through its employees, they maintained the City was liable for the negligence of its employees. The Ys averred that the City was liable for all damages proximately caused by its employees' negligent inspection and approval of the construction of the house they purchased as being in compliance with applicable building codes.

During closing arguments to the jury, the attorney for the City conceded the City was negligent but argued its negligence was not the proximate cause of the Ys' damages. The jury found in favor of the Ys on all claims. The jury found the Xs and the City each 50 percent at fault in causing the Ys' damages in the amount of $214,000. The appeals court upheld the trial court finding in effect negating the public-duty doctrine as a bar to individuals suing municipalities. The case of Beaudrie expands on the doctrine of Public Duty.

NICOLE M. BEAUDRIE, PLAINTIFF-APPELLANT,
v. PAULINE HENDERSON, DEFENDANT-APPELLEE, AND CITY OF
DEARBORN, AND DEARBORN POLICE DEPARTMENT, DEFENDANTS.
SUPREME COURT OF MICHIGAN
631 N.W.2D 308, (2001 MICH.)
JULY 27, 2001, FILED

LEGAL CONSIDERATIONS

Public Entity Liability / Public-Duty Doctrine

The Legislature has expressed its intent to subject lower-level government employees to potential liability for performing their jobs in a grossly negligent manner. This is so even though the governmental agency itself would be exempt from liability. Thus, expanding the common-law *public-duty doctrine* to shield all government employees from tort liability is at least arguably inconsistent with this statutory scheme.

Torts / Public Entity Liability / Immunity / Public-Duty Doctrine

The fact that Michigan's governmental immunity statute makes public employees immune from liability for conduct that does not amount to gross negligence and is not the proximate cause of injury certainly undermines the need for the common-law immunity granted by the *public-duty doctrine*.

Civil Procedure / De Novo Review

The appellate court reviews the decision of the trial court in granting summary disposition *de novo*.

Civil Procedure / Summary Judgment Standard

A motion for summary disposition tests the legal sufficiency of the complaint on the basis of the pleadings alone. The purpose of such a motion is to determine whether the plaintiff has stated a claim upon which relief can be granted. The motion should be granted if no factual development could possibly justify recovery.

Torts / Duty Generally

Summary disposition of a plaintiff's gross negligence claim is proper if the plaintiff fails to establish a duty owed. Whether a defendant owes a plaintiff a duty of care is a question of law for the court.

Torts / Public Entity Liability

The liability of government employees, other than those who have allegedly failed to provide police protection, should be determined using traditional tort principles without regard to the defendant's status as a government employee.

Public Entity Liability

The fact that a public employee owes general duties to the public at large does not logically preclude the imposition of a private, individual duty. (There is a legal theory that holds that a duty to all is a duty to none. The meaning of the theory is that a duty to all, the public, when breached, is a matter for criminal prosecution not civil prosecution. Civil prosecution is between individuals, criminal prosecution is between the state and an individual.) These duties are not mutually exclusive. Consequently, any attempt to draw a distinction between a government employee's public duty and private duty has proven to be confusing and prone to arbitrary and inconsistent application.

Public Entity Liability

A traditional common-law duty analysis provides a far more familiar and workable framework for determining whether a public employee owes a tort-enforceable duty in a given case to a given individual. Moreover, the need for an expanded application of the public duty doctrine has been undermined by the protections afforded governmental employees by Michigan's broad governmental immunity statute.

DISPOSITION: The decision of the Court of Appeals was reversed, and this case was remanded to the trial court for further proceedings.

OVERVIEW: A dispatcher argued that the *public-duty doctrine* shielded her from liability, and was granted summary disposition. The Michigan Supreme Court held that the liability of government employees, other than those who have allegedly failed to provide police protection, should be determined using traditional tort principles without regard to the defendant's status as a government employee. The fact that a public employee owed general duties to the public at large did not logically preclude the imposition of a duty to private individuals. The Governmental Immunity Act signified that a defendant's status as a government employee alone did not preclude liability. For purposes of determining the liability of public employees other than police officers, determining a government employee's duty would be done by using the same traditional common-law duty analysis applicable to private individuals.

OUTCOME: The judgment of the lower court was reversed.

OPINION: Plaintiff was abducted, assaulted, and raped by her ex-boyfriend. This case pertains to the actions of defendant Pauline Henderson, a police dispatcher and friend of the assailant's mother. Defendant Henderson allegedly was contacted at her place of employment by the assailant's mother while plaintiff was being held captive. Plaintiff alleged that defendant was grossly negligent and engaged in active misconduct when she failed to notify the police of the whereabouts of plaintiff's assailant and acted in concert with the assailant's mother in withholding information from authorities. Defendant argued that the *public-duty doctrine* shielded her from liability, and moved for summary disposition. The trial court denied defendant's motion, but, on appeal, the Court of Appeals reversed.

On appeal from the Appeals Court, the Michigan Supreme Court, the Court, granted leave to consider whether the public-duty doctrine, first recognized by this Court in *White v Beasley*, 552 N.W.2d 1 (1996), should be extended to protect governmental employees other than police officers who are alleged to have failed to provide protection from the criminal acts of third parties. The Supreme Court concluded that, given the comprehensive governmental immunity statute, this judicially created doctrine (the public-duty doctrine) should not be so extended. Thus, the Supreme Court reversed the decision of the Court of Appeals and remanded the case to the trial court for further proceedings.

Michigan law provides, in relevant part:

> (1) Except as otherwise provided in Michigan law, a governmental agency is immune from tort liability if the governmental agency is engaged in the exercise or discharge of a governmental function. Except as otherwise provided, the law does not modify or restrict the immunity of the state from tort liability as it existed before July 1, 1965.

(2) Except as otherwise provided in Michigan law, and without regard to the discretionary or ministerial nature of the conduct in question, each officer and employee of a governmental agency, each volunteer acting on behalf of a governmental agency, and each member of a board, council, commission, or statutorily created task force of a governmental agency is immune from tort liability for an injury to a person or damage to property caused by the officer, employee, or member while in the course of employment or service or caused by the volunteer while acting on behalf of a governmental agency if all of the following are met:

(a) The officer, employee, member, or volunteer is acting or reasonably believes he or she is acting within the scope of his or her authority.

(b) The governmental agency is engaged in the exercise or discharge of a governmental function.

(c) The officer's, employee's, member's, or volunteer's conduct does not amount to gross negligence that is the proximate cause of injury or damage. As used in this subdivision, 'gross negligence' means conduct so reckless as to demonstrate a substantial lack of concern for whether an injury results.

Factual and Procedural Background

Because this appeal arose under Michigan Rule of Civil Procedure 2.116(C)(8), the Supreme Court took all material facts from plaintiff's first amended complaint. According to her complaint, plaintiff was abducted by her ex-boyfriend, David Wilke, on April 6, 1994. Earlier that day, plaintiff had given preliminary examination testimony against Wilke in a case that developed out of a series of prior assaults committed by Wilke against her, including criminal sexual conduct. Wilke was released on bond.

At approximately 1:21 a.m. on April 7, 1994, the Dearborn Police Department issued an all points bulletin (APB) regarding a suspected abduction, including a description of Wilke and the vehicle that was believed to be involved. The police knew the plaintiff had parked her own vehicle in her driveway, but never made it inside her home. The police also knew that Wilke had criminal charges pending against him involving plaintiff, that he had been released on bond, that he had threatened to kill plaintiff in the past, and that he had access to handguns. Plaintiff's amended complaint specifically quoted the following portion of the APB:

> The victim parked her vehicle in the driveway and never made it inside her home in the south end of our city. The victim has pending charges out against the suspect, and he was freed on bond today. He has threatened to kill her in the past and he does have access to handguns.

Around 9:30 a.m., defendant, who was working as a dispatcher at the Dearborn Police Department, received a call from Wilke's mother, who was defendant's personal friend. Wilke's mother informed defendant that Wilke was missing, that she believed him to be armed and dangerous, and that it appeared he had taken plaintiff with him.

Plaintiff's first amended complaint further alleged that defendant suspected that Wilke had taken plaintiff to a family-owned trailer at Camp Dearborn. Plaintiff alleged that defendant contacted Camp Dearborn, represented herself as a Dearborn police dispatcher, and requested that Camp Dearborn employees verify whether the suspect vehicle was there. She gave the employees a description of the vehicle, its license plate number, and warned them not to approach the vehicle.

Approximately fifteen minutes later, defendant received notification that Wilke and the vehicle were indeed at Camp Dearborn. At that point, defendant contacted Wilke's mother. Plaintiff alleged that the two women agreed to withhold information from the police until Wilke's mother could contact Wilke's attorney. Wilke's mother, having spoken with Wilke's attorney, allegedly contacted the defendant again at approximately 11:45 a.m., at which time they agreed to withhold information about Wilke's whereabouts. At approximately noon, defendant left Dearborn Police Dispatch, picked up Wilke's mother and sister, and drove to Camp Dearborn.

According to plaintiff's first amended complaint, "as a direct and proximate result of these acts and/or omissions by Defendant Pauline Henderson, the brutal rape, beating and abduction of Plaintiff Nicole Beaudrie was allowed to continue, and the suspect, David James Wilke, was allowed the opportunity to escape the fenced perimeter of Camp Dearborn with his victim." Plaintiff subsequently filed suit against defendant, alleging that defendant's conduct amounted to "intentional misconduct, active malfeasance, and gross negligence," and that plaintiff's continued victimization was "a direct and proximate result" of defendant's actions.

Defendant moved for summary disposition under Michigan Rule of Civil Procedure, 2.116(C)(8) on the ground that, under the public-duty doctrine, she did not owe any duty to plaintiff. The trial court denied the motion. On appeal, the Court of Appeals then reversed in a split decision.

The Appeals Court reviewed the trial court's decision *de novo*. *Maiden v. Rozwood*, 597 N.W.2d 817 (1999). A motion for summary disposition brought under Michigan law tests the legal sufficiency of the complaint on the basis of the pleadings alone. The purpose of such a motion is to determine whether the plaintiff had stated a claim upon which relief could be granted. The motion should be granted if no factual development could possibly justify recovery. *Spiek v. Dept. of Transportation*, 572 N.W.2d 201 (1998).

Summary disposition of a plaintiff's gross negligence claim was proper if the plaintiff failed to establish a duty owed in tort. Whether the defendant owed the plaintiff a duty of care was a question of law for the court.

It appears that the origins of the common-law public-duty doctrine can be traced to *South v Maryland*, 59 United States Supreme Court 396, (1855). There, the plaintiff was kidnapped and held for ransom. Upon his release, the plaintiff sued the county sheriff, alleging that, despite the plaintiff's request for protection, the sheriff neglected and refused to protect him or to otherwise keep the peace. In rejecting the plaintiff's claim, the United States Supreme Court held that the sheriff's duty to preserve the public peace was "a public duty, for neglect of which he is amenable to the public, and punishable by indictment only."

Before the Michigan Supreme Court's 1996 decision in *White, supra*, the Court had not recognized the *public-duty doctrine*. However, the lead opinion in *White* noted that the Court of Appeals had consistently relied on the doctrine as early as 1970. A majority of the Appeals Court has agreed that the *public-duty doctrine* serves a useful purpose and should apply in Michigan.

The Scope of the Public Duty Doctrine under White, 552 N.W.2d 1 (1996).

Before the Supreme Court could determine the future of the public-duty doctrine in Michigan, it was necessary to examine its current state. At issue in White was whether the defendant police officer who failed to assist and protect the plaintiff from a criminal assault by a third party was liable in tort. The Court invoked the public duty doctrine and found no liability.

Chief Justice Brickley's lead opinion in *White* adopted the following articulation of the public-duty doctrine from Justice Cooley's leading 19th century treatise on torts:

> If the duty which the official authority imposes upon an officer is a duty to the public, a failure to perform it, or an inadequate or erroneous performance, must be a public, not an individual injury, and must be redressed, if at all, in some form of public prosecution (criminal not civil prosecution). On the other hand, if the duty is a duty to the individual, then a neglect to perform it, or to perform it properly, is an individual wrong (a civil issue), and may support an individual action for damages.

However, it was not entirely clear from the Supreme Court's fractured decision in *White* whether application of the public-duty doctrine was intended to apply to all government employees or only to police officers who are alleged to have failed to provide police protection. The lead opinion suggested an expansive application of the doctrine:

> In conclusion, we find that the public-duty doctrine still serves useful purposes. Government employees should enjoy personal protection from tort liability based on their action in conformity with, or failure to conform to, statutes or ordinances not intended to create tort liability. The job titles of government employees alone should not create a duty to specific members of the public.

Fairly read, nothing in the lead opinion indicated an intent to limit application of the *public-duty doctrine* to any particular class of governmental employees.

Justice Boyle agreed with the statement in the lead opinion that "applied to police officers, the public-duty doctrine insulates officers from tort liability for the negligent failure to provide police protection." The justice noted that "a contrary result could lead to officers arresting (and detaining) all persons who might conceivably jeopardize a foreseeable plaintiff." However, Justice Boyle argued that, even when limited to police officers, the doctrine should only apply to cases involving nonfeasance, i.e., "'passive inaction or the failure to actively protect others from harm.'"

Justice Cavanagh would have limited the decision "to only those cases in which liability is alleged on the basis of the police officer's failure to protect an individual from the actions of a third party." He opined that the case "should have no bearing in a case involving an injury caused by the police officer's own actions." Justice Cavanagh noted that "the public-duty doctrine recognizes that police officers and their departments must make discretionary or policy decisions in order to carry out the duties imposed on them." However, Justice Cavanagh also suggested that the public-duty doctrine should apply to "fire fighters, life guards, and similar governmental safety professionals."

Justice Levin dissented, arguing that the public-duty doctrine is inconsistent with the governmental immunity statute, which "holds that governmental officers and employees, except those at the highest levels, are subject to liability on the basis of gross negligence, which is defined as reckless conduct."

Clearly then, the various opinions in *White* offered relatively little guidance to lower courts regarding the scope of the doctrine recognized in that case. Since *White*, the Court of Appeals has not hesitated to broadly apply the public-duty doctrine outside the police protection context, e.g., *Elmadari v. Filiak*: a city maintenance worker owed no duty to a child injured by an allegedly dangerous slide; *McGoldrick v. Holiday Amusements, Inc.*, a state ski lift inspector owed no duty to an injured skier; *Koenig v. South Haven*, city officials owed no duty to decedent who was swept off a pier into a lake during inclement weather; *Reno v. Chung*, a medical examiner owed no duty to the plaintiff who was mistakenly convicted of murder in part because of the examiner's report.

The Future of the Public-Duty Doctrine in Michigan

The Supreme Court next addressed the issue left open in *White*: should the *public-duty doctrine* apply in cases other than those alleging a failure to provide police protection from the criminal acts of a third party? As illustrated by the Court's differing opinions in *White*, as well as the split decision in the Court of Appeals in the incident case, the doctrine has proven difficult to define and apply. Even more important, further expansion of the doctrine was unwarranted because the governmental immunity statute already provided government employees with significant protections from liability.

Thus, the Appeals Court rejected further expansion of the *public-duty doctrine*. The liability of government employees, other than those who have allegedly failed to provide police protection, should be determined using traditional tort principles without regard to the defendant's status as a government employee.

Shortcomings of the Public-Duty Doctrine

As stated, the *public-duty doctrine* is widely applied. The lead opinion in *White* set forth two commonly cited justifications for retaining the doctrine: "First, the doctrine protects governments from unreasonable interference with policy decisions, and, second, it protects government employees from unreasonable liability." However, as the Supreme Court of Colorado recognized in *Leake v. Cain*, 720 P.2d 152, 158 (Colo, 1986):

> A growing number of courts have concluded that the underlying purposes of the *public-duty rule* are better served by the application of conventional tort principles and the protection afforded by statutes governing sovereign immunity than by a rule that precludes a finding of an actionable duty on the basis of the defendant's status as a public employee.

However, application of the public-duty doctrine has not been so limited. In our view, application of the doctrine has been reduced to a conclusory statement that where there is a duty to all, there is a duty to none. Such a "reformulation" of the doctrine is tantamount to a grant of common-law governmental immunity, an area already dealt with by statute in many jurisdictions, including Michigan. The Supreme Court of Alaska was one of the first courts to reject the doctrine on precisely that basis. In *Adams v. State*, 555 P.2d 235 (Alas, 1976), the plaintiffs were injured in a hotel fire. The hotel had been inspected eight months earlier by the state fire marshal's office. It was alleged that the state inspectors had failed to abate several hazards that they had discovered. Rejecting the argument that the state owed a duty only to the public generally, the Supreme Court of Alaska noted that an application of the public-duty doctrine in that case would have resulted in a finding of no duty even though "a private defendant would have owed such a duty." In the absence of statutory immunity, the court declined to make it more difficult to establish a duty when the state is the defendant.

Other courts have also recognized that routine application of the public-duty doctrine has resulted in an artificial distinction between so-called "public" and "private" duties. In *Commercial Carrier Corp v. Indian River Co.*, 371 So. 2d 1010, 1015 (Fla, 1979), the Florida Supreme Court explained that it is circuitous reasoning to conclude that no cause of action exists for a negligent act or omission by an agent of the state or its political subdivision where the duty breached is said to be owed to the public at large but not to any particular person.

The Michigan Supreme Court agreed with these sentiments. The fact that a public employee owes general duties to the public at large does not logically preclude the imposition of a private, individual duty. These duties are not mutually exclusive. Consequently, any attempt to draw a distinction between a government employee's "public duty" and "private duty" has proven to be confusing and prone to arbitrary and inconsistent application

Relationship Between the Public Duty Doctrine and the Governmental Immunity Act

A government employee is immune from civil (Tort) liability under the governmental immunity statute if all the following conditions are met: (a) The officer is acting or reasonably believes he or she is acting within the scope of his or her authority. (b) The governmental agency is engaged in the exercise or discharge of a governmental function. (c) The officer's conduct does not amount to gross negligence that is the proximate cause of injury or damage. As used in this subdivision, "gross negligence" means conduct so reckless as to demonstrate a substantial lack of concern for whether an injury results.

In the Court's view, the Legislature had expressed, through the provisions mentioned, its intent to subject lower-level government employees to potential liability for performing their jobs in a grossly negligent manner. Judges, legislators, and the elective or highest appointive executive officials of all levels of government are, of course, absolutely immune from liability for their policy-making decisions. This is so even though the governmental agency itself would be exempt from liability. Thus, expanding the common-law public-duty doctrine to shield all government employees from tort liability is at least arguably inconsistent with statutory scheme.

Even if that were not the case, the fact that the governmental immunity statute makes public employees immune from liability for conduct that does not amount to "gross negligence" and is not "the proximate cause" of injury certainly undermines the need for the common-law "immunity" granted by the public-duty doctrine.

The Supreme Court of Vermont employed similar reasoning in *Hudson v. East Montpelier*, 638 A.2d 561 (1993), where it "declined to adopt the confusing and inconsistent public-duty doctrine as a means of limiting liability of government employees who are already protected to some extent by statutory immunity."

The Supreme Court recognized that public employees often are required to perform various tasks by virtue of their position. However, "private persons also have affirmative duties arising from their employment responsibilities that others do not have." Again, the governmental immunity act contemplates that government employees may be held liable for performing their jobs in a grossly negligent manner. Indeed, the Legislature has expressly authorized government agencies to defend and indemnify employees facing potential tort liability for injuries caused by the employee "while in the course of employment and while acting within the scope of his or her authority."

In sum, the Legislature, through the governmental immunity statute, has signified that a defendant's status as a government employee alone does not preclude liability. We choose not to undermine that public policy choice by expanding the application of the judicially created public-duty doctrine.

Consistent with its decision in *White*, the Supreme Court determined that it would continue to apply the public-duty doctrine, and its concomitant "special relationship" exception, in cases involving an alleged failure to provide police protection. Under the "special relationship" test adopted and applied by a majority of the Court in *White*, a police officer may be exposed to liability for failure to protect a plaintiff from the criminal acts of a third party only if the following elements are met: "(1) an assumption by the municipality, through promises or actions, of an affirmative duty to act on behalf of the party who was injured; (2) knowledge on the part of the municipality's agent that inaction could lead to harm; (3) some form of direct contact between the municipality's agents and the injured party; and (4) that party's justifiable reliance on the municipality's affirmative undertaking ."

The Supreme Court agreed with Chief Justice Brickley's statement in *White* that "police officers must work in unusual circumstances. They deserve unusual protection. "Moreover," the Court held, "the public-duty doctrine as applied in *White* is consistent with the general common-law rule that no individual has a duty to protect another who is endangered by a third person's conduct absent a 'special relationship' either between the defendant and the victim, or the defendant and the third party who caused the injury." Under the "special relationship" test adopted and applied by a majority of the Court in *White*, a police officer could be exposed to liability for failure to protect a plaintiff from the criminal acts of a third party only if the following elements were met: "(1) an assumption by the municipality, through promises or actions, of an affirmative duty to act on behalf of a party who was injured; (2) knowledge on the part of the municipality's agent that inaction could lead to harm; (3) some form of direct contact between the municipality's agents and the injured party; and (4) that party's justifiable reliance on the municipality's affirmative undertaking."

Application

The Court of Appeals (the second court to which this case was taken) relied solely on the *public- duty doctrine* in ordering that summary disposition be entered in defendant's favor. As stated, application of the *public-duty doctrine* is limited to cases like *White* involving an alleged failure of a police officer to protect a plaintiff from the criminal acts of a third party. We agree with plaintiff that this case clearly does not fall within the circumstances presented in *White*. Accordingly, the Court of Appeals erred in relying on the *public-duty doctrine* to dismiss plaintiff's case.

CONCLUSION

Distinguishing between a government employee's "public" and "private" duties proved to be an unwieldy exercise. Moreover, the need for expanding the public-duty doctrine outside the police protection context was undermined by the comprehensive protections from liability provided to government employees by the governmental immunity statute. Therefore, the Michigan Supreme Court declined to expand the doctrine.

The decision of the Court of Appeals was reversed, and the case was remanded to the trial court for further proceedings consistent with the Supreme Court's ruling.

Chapter 21. The Doctrine of the Statute of Limitations

The *Doctrine of the Statute of Limitations* governs the time in which an action may be initiated. While there are some generalities with respect to limitation's periods, there is variation for some causes of action and a party is well advised to check specifically for the limitation of the action that is anticipated. If a party believes it has a cause of action and wishes to determine the limitation's factor, a telephone call or letter to one's state law library may prove helpful.

The sticking points for *statutes of limitations* is how much time is allowed in which to bring an action, and when does the clock commence to tick and under what conditions does it stop ticking (toll). Medical malpractice lawsuits have probably been most instrumental in expanding the concept of the *statutes of limitations* in that they have mitigated the harsh application of the statutes. If a statue of limitation governing legal malpractice says a party must bring an action within three years of first comprehending malpractice, is there no leeway?

Well, at one time there was none. As a result of decisional law regarding medical malpractice, however, the once procrustean contours of the doctrine have loosened. The continuous-representation doctrine is a lineal descendant of the continuous-treatment doctrine which directly derives from medical malpractice lawsuits. There had to be some way with regard to medical malpractice to bring a lawsuit after an initial medical faux pas in situations where the health-care provider continued to treat a patient and the medical error was not discovered until long after its occurrence. In other words, there had to be some way to stay the time in which an action could be brought when a course of treatment included wrongful acts or omissions running continuously from some related original condition or complaint. Once the continuous- treatment doctrine was promulgated, over time it was deemed to be analogous to other situations beyond medicine: it was deemed related to business situations where continuing fraud was involved with the result that the statute did not begin to run until the fraud was discovered, and it was deemed related to legal malpractice situations as well.

A recent legal-malpractice case serves as an example. This was a 2003 case in which a plaintiff brought an action for misrepresentation against his lawyer, a small-town attorney. The plaintiff was being represented in a divorce action in which the plaintiff's counsel had agreed, unbeknownst to the plaintiff, that his client would not be allowed unsupervised visitation rights with his two young children. The unaware plaintiff continued on with the same counselor. When the plaintiff realized he had been seriously misrepresented, he severed his ties with counsel, hired another lawyer and brought a legal malpractice action. His former attorney moved for a summary judgment in the trial court claiming the *statute of limitations* had run since the time he had committed his client to the no-visitation agreement, and the trial court granted the motion and dismissed the malpractice action. The plaintiff appealed and the appellate court reversed and remanded, holding that the continuous-treatment doctrine, as applied in medical malpractice cases, had prevented the statute of limitations from beginning to run at the time the malpractice event had occurred and, as a result, forestalled the running of the statute until the lawyer's concealment was discovered.

On remand, the plaintiff prevailed and was awarded damages. The following case is illustrative of the doctrine.

HARRISON ENTERPRISES, INC. D/B/A PAULDING CABLE COMPANY, A
MISSISSIPPI CORPORATION AND ELVIN LEE HARRISON, JR.
V. TRILOGY COMMUNICATIONS, INC., A DELAWARE CORPORATION
SUPREME COURT OF MISSISSIPPI
818 SO. 2D 1088, 2002 MISS.
FEBRUARY 14, 2002

LEGAL CONSIDERATIONS

Governments / Statutes of Limitations / Statute of Limitations

The rule in Mississippi is that a partial payment does not take a case out of the operation of the running of the statute of limitations unless such partial payment is accompanied by (1) an express acknowledgement of a further indebtedness, and (2) an express promise to pay. This rule on partial payment applies to a simple debit and credit open account. Still, it has never been held in Mississippi that parol evidence (parol evidence is verbal evidence) is inadmissible to apply to what debt is at issue.

Civil Procedure / Summary Judgment Standard

An appellate court conducts de novo review of an order granting or denying summary judgment and examines all the evidentiary matters before it, i.e., admissions in pleadings, answers to interrogatories, depositions, affidavits, etc. The evidence is viewed in the light most favorable to the party against whom the motion has been made. Consequently, summary judgment should be granted if the pleadings, discovery materials, and affidavits show that there is no genuine issue of material fact, and that the moving party is entitled to summary judgment as a matter of law.

Governments / Causes of Action

An acknowledgment of indebtedness and a renewed promise to pay is not sufficient to toll the statute of limitations under Mississippi Code Annotated §15-1-73 (1995) if it is vague and indefinite. Instead, an acknowledgment must state when the balance is due, to whom the balance is due, and for what the balance is due. It must be both a specification of the debt referred to and a promise to pay a fixed amount in order to support a new promise. Further, the acknowledgment of the debt and the promise to pay must be definite and unequivocal.

DISPOSITION: Summary judgment affirmed.

PROCEDURAL POSTURE: Defendant buyer sought review of the judgment of the Rankin County Circuit Court (Mississippi) granting summary judgment in favor of plaintiff seller, where the seller sought payment of the buyer's account.

OVERVIEW: The seller, Harrison, sold goods to the buyer on an open account. The seller did business with the buyer until August 1996, at which time the buyer owed the seller over $71,000. After several unsuccessful attempts to collect the debt, in March 1997, the seller offered to renegotiate the payment schedule, but the buyer failed to satisfy the new payment schedule. After the seller granted multiple extensions of time, the buyer failed to pay the account. The buyer wrote a letter to the seller admitting that its account was overdue and promising to pay by August 1997. The appellate court found that this letter was sufficient to toll the statute of limitations under Mississippi. Code Annotated § 15-1-73 (1995) because the letter's acknowledgement of the debt and promise to pay were definite and unequivocal. The buyer's promise to pay induced the seller into not filing suit.

OUTCOME: The judgment was affirmed.

OPINION: Trilogy Communications, Inc. (Trilogy) manufactured, sold, and delivered goods and merchandise to Harrison Enterprises, Inc. (Harrison Enterprises) on an open account status by invoices dated May, June, and July of 1995, and August of 1996. When Harrison Enterprises failed to pay, Trilogy made demand for payment, triggering discussions and negotiations regarding payment of the account. These discussions and negotiations failed to resolve the issue.

On October 28, 1998, Trilogy filed a complaint in the Rankin County Circuit Court, seeking payment of the open account naming Harrison Enterprises and Elvin Lee Harrison, Jr. (Harrison) as defendants. After discovery, Harrison Enterprises and Harrison filed a motion for judgment on the pleadings, or in the alternative summary judgment. In response, Trilogy filed its own motion for summary judgment. After a hearing on the motions, the circuit court granted summary judgment in favor of Trilogy, and denied the motion of Harrison Enterprises and Harrison for dismissal.

Harrison Enterprises and Harrison timely filed this appeal with the Mississippi Supreme Court, raising the following question:

DID THE TRIAL COURT ERR IN AWARDING SUMMARY JUDGMENT TO THE PLAINTIFF, TRILOGY COMMUNICATIONS, INC.?

"Viewing the evidence in the light most favorable to Harrison Enterprises and Harrison, we conclude that Trilogy is entitled to a judgment as a matter of law, and we affirm the judgment of the circuit court."

FACTS:

Trilogy began to manufacture, sell, and deliver goods to Harrison Enterprises, on an open account, in August of 1994. At the beginning of this relationship, Harrison signed a personal guarantee agreeing to be liable for the debts of Harrison Enterprises in its dealings with Trilogy. Trilogy continued doing business with Harrison Enterprises until August of 1996, at which time Harrison Enterprises owed Trilogy $ 71,453.75. Trilogy made several attempts to collect this outstanding debt to no avail.

In March of 1997, Trilogy offered to work with Harrison Enterprises by renegotiating their payment schedule, requesting them to pay $2,000 a week until the debt was paid. Trilogy warned that failure to do so could result in Trilogy taking legal action.

In May of 1997, Trilogy sent a letter to Harrison Enterprises stating:

Dear Mr. Harrison,

Your account with Trilogy Communications is **SERIOUSLY DELINQUENT!!!**

We have made arrangements for you to pay a set amount per month, and you have not followed through with your payments, nor have you returned the signed promissory note. We have extended your terms in order to help you out when you needed an additional 30 days. Yet we have not received any type of payment from you.

At this point, unfortunately, it is out of my hands. I have been instructed to give you an additional 15 days to make payment in FULL and if you do not send payment in full, you will receive a final demand letter from our attorney whereupon you will be given 30 days to pay the entire balance or he will file suit immediately.

Thirteen days later, on June 10, 1997, Harrison responded to this communication with a letter that acknowledged the account was overdue and asked Trilogy to give them until the middle of August and they would pay their account in full.

After receiving the letter, Trilogy again gave Harrison Enterprises additional time to pay. However, again Harrison Enterprises failed to live up to its promise.

In early September of 1997, Harrison Enterprises' attorney contacted Trilogy's attorney and requested that Trilogy withhold filing the lawsuit as they were trying to obtain the funds to pay the account. Harrison Enterprises' attorney made a similar request in October, stating that the payment would be made by October 31, 1997.

In spite of these continuing assurances, the account was never paid, forcing Trilogy to file a complaint against Harrison Enterprises and Harrison in October of 1998, seeking collection of the balance of the account, accrued interest and attorney fees. After discovery, both sides filed motions for summary judgment. After a hearing on the motions, the trial court granted Trilogy's motion for summary judgment holding that: the statute of limitations had not run, that Harrison Enterprises and Harrison had failed to assert a viable defense to the action, that there was no material issue of fact, and that Trilogy was entitled to a judgment as a matter of law. Later, the circuit court assessed attorney fees of $17,000, bringing the total judgment against Harrison Enterprises and Harrison to $ 88,453, jointly and severally. Aggrieved, Harrison Enterprises and Harrison now appeal to the Mississippi Supreme Court.

STANDARD OF REVIEW

The Supreme Court of Mississippi conducts de novo review of an order granting or denying summary judgment and examines all the evidentiary matters before it, admissions in pleadings, answers to interrogatories, depositions, affidavits, etc. *Gant v. Maness*, 786 So. 2d 401, 403 (Miss. 2001). The evidence is viewed in the light most favorable to the party against whom the motion has been made. Consequently, summary judgment should be granted if the pleadings, discovery materials and affidavits show that there is no genuine issue of material fact, and that the moving party is entitled to summary judgment as a matter of law. *Ainsworth v. Stroud*, 765 So. 2d 598, 601 (Miss. Ct. App. 2000).

ANALYSIS:

WAS THE 6/10/97 LETTER SUFFICIENT TO TOLL THE STATUTE OF LIMITATIONS?

All parties agreed that this case dealt with an open account, and thus, the three-year statute of limitation of Mississippi Code Annotated §15-1-29 (1995) was applicable. However, the parties differed as to whether the June 10, 1997, letter sent by Harrison to Trilogy was an acknowledgment of debt and a renewed promise to pay that was sufficient to toll the statute of limitations as allowed by Mississippi Code Annotated §15-1-73 (1995).

The Supreme Court of Mississippi has long held that such acknowledgment is not sufficient if it is "vague and indefinite." *United States Fid. & Guar. Co. v. Krebs*, 190 So. 2d 857, 861 (Miss. 1966) (citing *Trustees of Canton Female Acad. v. Gilman*, 55 Miss. 148 (1877)). Instead, such an acknowledgment must "state when the balance is due, to whom the balance is due, and for what the balance is due." It must "be both a specification of the debt referred to and a promise to pay a fixed amount in order to support a new promise." (citing *Fletcher v. Gillan*, 62 Miss. 8 (1884)). Further, "the acknowledgment of the debt and the promise to pay must be definite and unequivocal." (citing *Philp v. Hicks*, 112 Miss. 581, 589, 73 So. 610, 612 (1917)).

However, the Court has also held that "superficial uncertainties as to exact amounts due, resolvable by explanation, are not sufficient to impair identification of the indebtedness." *Dyer v. Lowe*, 201 Miss. 516, 521, 29 So. 2d 324, 325 (1947). Also, the requirement "when the balance is due," does not necessarily require a specific date. For example, the Court has held that a letter, which had been either lost or destroyed, that reportedly said, "Enclosed I hand you $25.00, which you will credit on my note in the county treasury. I will come down some time soon, and pay you the balance of the note," was sufficient proof of a new promise to toll the statute of limitations. *Heflin v. Kinard*, 67 Miss. 522, 524, 7 So. 493, 493 (1890).

However, a "simple acknowledgment of a debt on account, even in writing, is not sufficient to toll the statute." *McArthur v. Acme Mech. Contractors, Inc.*, 336 So. 2d 1306, 1308 (Miss. 1976).

The rule in Mississippi is that a partial payment does not take a case out of the operation of the running of the statute of limitations unless such partial payment is accompanied by (1) an express acknowledgement of a further indebtedness, and (2) an express promise to pay.

The Court, therefore, applied the rule adopted in *Krebs*, 190 So. 2d 857, on "partial payment" to attach to a simple debit and credit open account. This being done here, there is no uncertainty as to what specific debt was meant by the writer.

At issue here was the letter addressed to Trilogy, dated June 10, 1997, on Harrison Enterprises official stationery, and signed by Harrison in his official capacity as president of Harrison Enterprises. That letter read:

"WE REALIZE OUR ACCOUNT IS OVER DUE. IF YOU WILL GIVE US UNTIL THE MIDDLE OF AUGUST WE WILL BE ABLE TO PAY OUR ACCOUNT IN FULL."

Harrison Enterprises and Harrison contended that this letter falls short of the legal requirements of an acknowledgment of indebtedness and a promise to pay necessary to toll the running of the statute (Remember, Harrison wants the statute of limitations to run out so that he can escape paying his bill). They claimed the letter did not state the amount of the balance, or when, to whom, or for what it was due. They, Harrison, et al, claimed the letter did not contain a specification of the debt, nor did it promise to pay anything at all; therefore, it was not definite and unequivocal.

Trilogy contended that the letter was not vague and indefinite. According to Trilogy, the letter stated that the debt was overdue to Trilogy and would be paid in full in August, answering the "to whom, when, and for what" requirement. The letter promised to pay a specified amount-in full. It was specific as to which debt it reaffirmed, the only debt Harrison Enterprises owed to Trilogy. Further, Trilogy quoted Harrison where Harrison admitted that the letter was an acknowledgment of debt and a promise to pay.

The Court agreed with Trilogy. The letter was not vague or indefinite. The letter's acknowledgment of the debt and promise to pay was definite and unequivocal. The letter was addressed to Trilogy on Harrison Enterprises stationary and signed by Harrison-satisfying the "to whom" requirement. It stated that the debt was overdue and would be paid in August, satisfying the "when" requirement. It said OUR ACCOUNT, satisfying the "for what" requirement. Further, it was a promise to pay and was specific in the amount that would be paid: "WE WILL BE ABLE TO PAY OUR ACCOUNT IN FULL." In his deposition, Harrison, the president of Harrison Enterprises, admitted that the letter was an acknowledgment and reaffirmation of the debt. To argue now that it was not so intended is disingenuous. The letter was sufficient to toll the statute of limitations; therefore, this issue was without merit.

Harrison Enterprises and Harrison claim that all of their actions were sincere, honest and with the intention of resolving the matter. They claim that Trilogy was negligent, and in fact had received the letter six months before the statute had run, but waited ten months before filing the complaint. Conversely, Trilogy argues that Harrison Enterprises repeatedly expressed a willingness, desire, and interest to pay. Further, Harrison Enterprises had repeatedly promised to pay and had on several occasions requested that Trilogy postpone filing suit in order to give them time to pay. Trilogy claims that allowing Harrison to hide behind the statute of limitations now would set a bad precedent and encourage others in the future to lie in order to escape their obligations.

The Supreme Court agreed with Trilogy. The stated purpose behind the limitation's statute was to discourage lawsuits. Furthermore, it was to reward the vigilant, not the negligent. It was to prevent false and stale claims. Trilogy was trying to solve the problem without resorting to a lawsuit. Trilogy was vigilant in pursuing this debt, relying on the continual reassurances by Harrison Enterprises. The claim was neither false nor stale. Evidence has not been lost, memories have not faded, witnesses are available and the facts are readily capable of production.

The record clearly showed that the only reason Trilogy did not file its complaint earlier was that it was induced to delay by Harrison Enterprises' promises of payment. If the letter had not effectively tolled the statute, Trilogy's cause of action would have been procedurally barred. Further, Harrison Enterprises had reason to know such consequences would follow. Thus, the Court held that Trilogy had satisfied its burden of proof.

CONCLUSION

The judgment was affirmed in favor of Trilogy.

Chapter 22. The Doctrine of Equitable Estoppel

"Estoppe," says Lord Coke of the old English bench, "cometh from the French word *estoupe*, from whence the English word stopped cometh, and it is called an estoppel or conclusion because a man's own act or acceptance stoppeth or closeth up his mouth to allege or plead otherwise."

The *Doctrine of Equitable Estoppel* comes into play when a party, through its own chicanery, has barred a lawsuit against itself by manipulating the statute of limitations time frame so as to obstruct an adverse party's cause of action. As a rule, all causes of action, except murder, have specific limitation's time frames. While the specific period for bringing an action may vary from cause of action to cause of action, a well represented party may successfully avoid civil action by beating around the bush until the limitation's period has run out, creating the impression that the statute has tolled for some reason or other when it has not. (Tolled means stopped ticking temporarily). The effect of the statute of limitations can, however, be deflected by invoking the *doctrine of equitable estoppel*.

If a defendant can forestall a plaintiff from bringing his action until the statute of limitations has run, then that party can move for summary judgment as a matter of law and the court must, under normal circumstances, grant a motion ending the action. If a plaintiff can cite equitable estoppel as a defense against a defendant's motion for summary judgment that turns on a statute of limitations violation, and the plaintiff can support its defense by showing that the defendant intentionally, through chicanery, forestalled the plaintiff's action, then equitable estoppel can be invoked. A trial court will normally uphold the defense because tolling operates on the statute of limitations and equitable estoppel acts on the individual.

The prime purpose of equitable estoppel, then, is to prevent a party from benefiting from his wrongdoing. Logic dictates that a late filing of an action against a defendant should not come as a surprise to the defendant when the tardiness of the filing comes about as a result of the defendant's own machinations. The concepts of the statute of limitations and equitable estoppel work in tandem, then, to prevent injustice.

Fixed limitations on actions at law are based on public-policy considerations and are, as a result, the progeny of legislative enactment. Statutes of limitations come about as a result of a legislative intent to protect defendants from stale claims and unfair surprise. As limitations, they provide parties with reasonable safeguards against the need to defend themselves against dusty lawsuits. In short, as we have learned previously, statutes of limitation protect against lazy antagonists and their lawsuits, missing or deceased witnesses, faded memories, misplaced or lost records, etc.!

There was a case where a young women discovered a picture of her semi-nude body in a California skin magazine. The picture had been taken seven years earlier by her boyfriend in a private moment. The young lady brought a civil action against the magazine's publisher and the publisher claimed the lawsuit was barred by the four-year-statute of limitations. The trial court ruled in the publisher's favor and the young lady appealed. The appeals court ruled that the doctrine of equitable estoppel was controlling and remanded the case for jury trial, denying the publisher the statute of limitations defense. The appeals court held that because the publisher had not given the young lady notice that her picture was being published, the limitations period did not commence to run until she discovered the magazine's use of her revealing photograph, and that her lawsuit, therefore, represented a valid claim. At trial, the young lady received ample consideration for her embarrassment.

D. ROBINSON, APPELLANT,
v. NASREEN B. SHAH, M.D.
COURT OF APPEALS OF KANSAS
936 P.2D 784 (1997)
APRIL 18, 1997

LEGAL CONSIDERATIONS

Governments / Statutes of Limitations

Where a person has a cause of action against an adversary and is duped through misrepresentation of fact, he can maintain an action for deceit against the wrongdoer.

Torts / Deceit & Fraud

A fraudulent act generally is comprised of anything calculated to deceive, including all acts, omissions, and concealments involving a breach of legal or equitable duty, trust, or confidence justly reposed, resulting in damage to another.

Torts / Deceit & Fraud

The broad outlines of fraud are said to include any cunning, deception, or artifice used in violation of legal or equitable duty, to circumvent, cheat, or deceive another. The forms it may assume and the means by which it may be practiced are as multifarious as human ingenuity can devise, and the courts consider it unwise or impossible to formulate an exact, definite, and all-inclusive definition of the action.

Torts / Deceit & Fraud

A suppression or concealment of the truth is not at all times such fraud or deceit as will be relieved against. There must be a concealment of facts which the party is under a legal or equitable duty to communicate and in respect of which he could not be innocently silent.

Torts / Deceit & Fraud

Actionable fraud includes an untrue statement of fact, known to be untrue by the party making it, which is made with the intent to deceive or recklessly made with disregard for the truth where another party justifiably relies on the statement and acts to his or her detriment.

Torts / Deceit & Fraud

In order to prove fraud, the following facts must be shown: (1) an untrue statement known to be untrue by the party making it and made with the intent to deceive; (2) justifiable reliance by the victim on the truth of the statement; (3) damages as a result of that reliance.

Torts / Actions Against Healthcare Workers

This does not mean that a doctor can never be liable for fraud or breach of contract. Instead, a fraud or breach of contract cause of action can only be based upon a physician's misconduct if that misconduct is a breach of the legal duty which every doctor has the obligation to uphold.

Torts / Actions Against Healthcare Workers

If the cause of action is really one for malpractice, just calling it a cause of action for fraud does not change its true nature. The nature of a claim, whether it sounds in tort or contract, is determined from the pleadings and from the real nature and substance of the facts alleged therein.

Torts / Healthcare Law

A physician is obligated to his patient under the law to use reasonable and ordinary care and diligence in the treatment of the cases he undertakes, to use his best judgment, and to exercise his learning.

PRIOR HISTORY: Appeal from Pawnee District Court.

DISPOSITION: Reversed and remanded.

OPINION: The plaintiff appealed from a ruling by the trial court that her fraud and medical malpractice causes of action against the defendant were barred by the statute of limitations. The trial court's ruling was accompanied by the realization of all concerned that this case required the attention of the appellate court. The facts in this action were particularly egregious and call into question the relationship between fraud and the statute of limitations. Procedurally, the plaintiff's lawsuit was dismissed as barred by the statute of limitations prior to a trial on the merits. Under those circumstances, all of the parties agreed that the Appeals Court would accept the facts as presented by the plaintiff as true. Those facts were set out in the trial court's journal entry and were adopted by the Appeals Court as true and correct for the purposes of the incident appeal. It was possible, however, that the actual facts proven at trial might not be precisely as the Court assumed them to be at the inception of review. Nevertheless, for the purposes of the appeal, the plaintiff's version of the facts was assumed to be true and correct.

The plaintiff was a longtime patient of Dr. Nasreen B. Shah, M.D., hereinafter referred to as the defendant, and placed her physical well-being in the hands of that physician from 1975 to 1986. During that period of time, the defendant treated the plaintiff for various gynecological disorders.

On November 9, 1983, the defendant performed a total abdominal hysterectomy and bilateral salpingo-oophorectomy on the plaintiff. Approximately 1 week after the surgery, the plaintiff was discharged from the hospital and was assured that there were no complications or potential problems which might arise as a result of the surgery.

On the day after the plaintiff was discharged from the hospital, she began to experience abdominal distress. She consulted the defendant about these symptoms, and the defendant ordered x-rays to be taken of the plaintiff's kidneys, ureter, and bladder in an effort to explain her discomfort.

The x-rays were taken at St. Joseph's Memorial Hospital and were read and interpreted by Dr. C. J. Cavanaugh, a radiologist associated with that facility. Dr. Cavanaugh was of the opinion, after reading the x-rays, that they showed the presence of surgical sponges which had been left in the plaintiff's abdomen after surgery. Dr. Cavanaugh called the defendant and reported the findings of the x-rays and, in addition, sent to the defendant a copy of a written report reflecting those findings.

Incredibly and shamefully, the defendant fraudulently concealed the findings of these x-rays from the plaintiff. Instead of being truthful, the defendant deliberately lied to the plaintiff and told her the x-rays were negative and that there were no apparent or unusual complications from the recent abdominal surgery, and she assured the plaintiff that she did not require further treatment. At no time did the defendant reveal to the plaintiff the fact that she had left surgical sponges in the plaintiff's abdomen after her most recent surgery.

Over the next several years, the plaintiff continued to see the defendant for gynecological check-ups. She continued to experience abdominal pain and discomfort. The defendant, however, continued to conceal from the plaintiff the existence of the surgical sponges left in the plaintiff's abdomen.

The plaintiff ceased seeing the defendant as her physician in 1986. However, she consulted other physicians and continued to experience frequent pain and discomfort in her abdomen as well as intestinal, urological, and gynecological problems. Although the plaintiff brought her complaints to the attention of other physicians, no one was able to diagnose the source of her problems.

In 1993, one of the physicians attending to the plaintiff's problems diagnosed a pelvic mass, which he felt could be causing some discomfort. On August 11, 1993, the plaintiff underwent pelvic sonograms and x-rays, which revealed the existence of retained surgical sponges.

The plaintiff contends that the defendant, from November 18, 1983 onward, had actual knowledge of the presence of the retained surgical sponges in the plaintiff's abdomen and knew very well the potential for future complications which could arise from their presence. Despite this knowledge, the plaintiff contended, the defendant fraudulently concealed the existence of this condition from her.

The trial court found that the plaintiff was unable to discover the fact that the defendant had negligently left surgical sponges in her abdomen, that fact being fraudulently concealed from her and not discovered until August 11, 1993.

This action was filed on August 16, 1994.

The plaintiff's legal problems are obvious. According to her factual contentions, in 1983, the defendant left surgical sponges in the plaintiff's abdomen and knew she had done so no later than November 18, 1983. Despite such knowledge, the defendant fraudulently concealed the existence of the retained sponges from the plaintiff and lied to her about the nature of her condition. It was not until August 11, 1993, that the plaintiff knew or could have known what the defendant had done. This is a passage of nearly 10 years. All of the related statutes of limitations and statutes of repose had expired. The plaintiff was without a remedy, and the defendant was home free unless an exception exists to preserve her causes of action against the defendant. If no such exception exists, the defendant will be rewarded for her fraud in concealing from the plaintiff that surgical sponges were left in her abdomen. Over 10 years passed since the defendant's act of fraudulent concealment. The trial court held that all of the plaintiff's potential legal remedies against the defendant were outlawed by the statute of limitations. That decision was a direct result of the defendant's fraudulent concealment of the plaintiff's condition. The defendant sought to use the statute of limitations as a shield from the consequences of her negligence and her fraud. The Appeals

Court did not believe the law was powerless to correct such an injustice and had to decide whether the defendant was to be rewarded for her fraudulent conduct or not.

STATUTES OF LIMITATION

As the Court viewed this lawsuit, the following statutes of limitation and statutes of repose were relevant under Kansas law:

"The statute holds that following actions shall be brought within two years:

"An action arising out of the rendering of or failure to render professional services by a health-care provider not arising as a result of contract. A cause of action arising out of the rendering of or the failure to render professional services by a health-care provider shall be deemed to have accrued at the time of the occurrence of the act giving rise to the cause of action unless the fact of injury is not reasonably ascertainable until some time after the initial act, then the period of limitation shall not commence until the fact of injury becomes reasonably ascertainable to the injured party, but in no event shall such an action be commenced more than four years beyond the time of the act giving rise to the cause of action.

"In an action for relief on the ground of fraud, the cause of action shall not be deemed to have accrued until the fraud is discovered.

"Except as provided elsewhere, causes of action shall not be deemed to have accrued until the act giving rise to the cause of action first causes substantial injury, or, if the fact of injury is not reasonably ascertainable until some time after the initial act, then the period of limitation shall not commence until the fact of injury becomes reasonably ascertainable to the injured party, but in no event shall an action be commenced more than 10 years beyond the time of the act giving rise to the cause of action."

The plaintiff's causes of action against the defendant were based on medical malpractice and fraud. It was perfectly obvious from a reading of the statutes that each cause of action must be brought within 2 years of its accrual and that the medical malpractice statute of repose is 4 years, whereas the fraud statute of repose was 10 years. It does not require great legal insight to realize that the plaintiff was dead in the water unless the fraudulent conduct on the part of the defendant either tolled or somehow extended the periods of limitations.

IS THERE A CAUSE OF ACTION FOR FRAUD?

The relevant portions of count II of the plaintiff's petition read as follows:

"2. That defendant Shah fraudulently concealed the finding of sponges in the plaintiff's November 18th, 1983, x-ray, breached her fiduciary duty of full disclosure and made misrepresentations to plaintiff that there were no complications or potential complications resulting from the November 9, 1983 surgery, when, in fact, defendant Shah had actual knowledge of the presence of surgical sponges in the plainttiff's abdomen and of the potential of future complications that would result from this condition.

"3. That the above referenced tortious conduct of the defendant deprived plaintiff of her right to prompt medical treatment thereby causing her prolonged and severe pain, suffering, physical disabilities, and related loss of time, income and enjoyment of life. Furthermore, defendant's tortious conduct deprived plaintiff of her right to timely seek and recover legal damages for the defendant's medical negligence causing her the loss in opportunity to utilize and invest such damages."

The Court saw no reason why the defendant should not be held responsible for a fraud which caused a patient to allow his or her malpractice cause of action to become barred by the statute of limitations. The Court further saw no reason why a defendant should not be held responsible for fraudulently causing a patient not to seek prompt medical treatment for his or her condition which subsequently resulted in his or her suffering needless years of prolonged, severe, and unnecessary pain and discomfort. The plaintiff's petition alleged that the defendant's fraud caused her those damages.

In its opinion, for obvious reasons, the Court focused on the fact that the defendant fraudulently caused the plaintiff to lose her malpractice cause of action.

The law in Kansas has long permitted a party who has lost a cause of action by virtue of the fraud of another to maintain an action for fraud against the perpetrator for the loss of a cause of action. In Clark v. Amos, 58 P.2d 81 (1936), the Kansas Supreme Court dealt with such a cause of action. The court commented as follows:

"It is the law that where a person has a cause of action against an adversary and is duped through misrepresentation of fact by the latter whereby the injured party permits the statute of limitations to bar his action, he can maintain an action for deceit (fraud)* against the wrongdoer under some circumstances, not on account of the original negligence but on account of the subsequent wrongdoing, the misrepresentation of fact which deceived the injured party with the consequence that the time bar ran against the original action."*

The plaintiff sought to prosecute the above type of cause of action. If she was not permitted to do so, the Court believed a gross injustice would result. Public policy should, and the Court thought it did, prevent such an injustice.

As the Court perceived it, the question was why a physician could not be sued for defrauding a patient out of a cause of action. In count II of the plaintiff's cause of action, she sought recovery not for the original negligence or malpractice by the physician but for the fraud of the physician who deceived her "with the consequence that the time bar ran against the original action." As the Court viewed it, the fraudulent concealment was not malpractice, it was fraud, pure and simple. For that reason and the reasons which follow, the Court concluded the trial court erred in dismissing the plaintiff's lawsuit as untimely as to the cause of action for fraud, and the Appeals Court reversed that decision and remanded the matter for a trial on the merits.

In Umbehr v. Board of Wabaunsee County Commissioners, P 4, 843 P.2d 176 (1992), fraud was defined as follows: "A fraudulent act generally is comprised of anything calculated to deceive, including all acts, omissions, and concealments involving a breach of legal or equitable duty, trust, or confidence justly reposed, resulting in damage to another."

In Moore v. State Bank of Burden, 729 P.2d 1205 (1986), the Court found the following:

"The broad outlines of fraud are said to include any cunning deception, or artifice used in violation of a legal or equitable duty not to cheat or deceive another. The forms it may assume and the means by which it may be practiced are as multifarious as human ingenuity can devise, and the courts consider it unwise or impossible to formulate an exact, definite, and all-inclusive definition of the action. It is synonymous with, or closely allied to, other terms indicating positive and intentional wrongdoing, but is distinguishable from mistake and negligence.

"Actual fraud is an intentional fraud, and the intent to deceive is an essential element of the action. Constructive fraud, however, is a breach of a legal or equitable duty which, irrespective of moral guilt, the law declares fraudulent because of its tendency to deceive others or violate a confidence, and neither actual dishonesty of purpose or intent to deceive is necessary. A suppression or concealment of the truth is not at all times a fraud or deceit that will be open to suit: There must be a concealment of facts which the party is under a legal or equitable duty to communicate and in respect of which he could not be innocently silent.

"Actionable fraud includes an untrue statement of fact, known to be untrue by the party making it, which is made with the intent to deceive or recklessly made with disregard for the truth where another party justifiably relies on the statement and acts to his or her injury and damage.*

The Court believed that the allegations set forth in count II of the plaintiff's petition set forth a classic cause of action for fraud. It was beyond question that the defendant's lies to the plaintiff were made to deceive her and conceal the defendant's negligence. It cannot be seriously argued that the defendant did not have a legal and an equitable duty to tell the plaintiff the truth. That duty was breached. The breach of that duty by the defendant caused, the plaintiff alleges, the plaintiff to lose a valuable cause of action and suffer 10 years of needless pain and discomfort.

The Court thought it important to note that the defendant in this case was not alleged to either have been mistaken or negligent in her failure to disclose the truth to her patient. She was accused of deceit and lies amounting to intentional wrongdoing. As pointed out above, "not every concealment of the truth is actionable. However, when such concealment violates a legal or equitable duty, it becomes actionable and fraudulent."

The Court pointed out that in order to prove fraud, the following facts had to be shown: (1) an untrue statement known to be untrue by the party making it with an intent to deceive; (2) justifiable reliance by the victim on the truth of the statement; (3) damages as a result of that reliance. The plaintiff's petition set forth sufficient allegations to state a cause of action for actual fraud against the defendant.

The defendant argued, however, that one cannot have a fraud cause of action against a physician. The premise for this argument was that when a physician defrauds a patient out of a cause of action for malpractice, it is not fraud, it is simply more malpractice. Thus, according to the defendant, the physician may hide behind his or her fraudulent conduct and enjoy the benefits of that fraud because it is not fraud, it is malpractice.

The Court did not concede that the law was so unjustly weighted on the side of the wrongdoer. It seemed senseless for the defendant to argue that the "gravamen" of the plaintiff's cause of action was malpractice when that action, according to the defendant, had been eliminated by the lies and fraud of the defendant herself.

This Court held that a physician is obligated to his patient under the law to use reasonable and ordinary care and diligence in the treatment of the cases he undertakes, to use his best judgment and to exercise that reasonable degree of learning, skill and experience which is ordinarily possessed by other physicians in the same or similar locations. A physician also has the duty to make a reasonable disclosure to the patient of pertinent facts within his knowledge relating to proposed treatment in order that the patient may intelligently consent or refuse the treatment. Fraud is fraud, and we reject the notion that physicians are not answerable for it as are the other members of our society.

STATUTE OF LIMITATIONS AS TO FRAUD

Having held that the plaintiff had set forth a valid cause of action for fraud against the defendant, the next question was whether the cause of action was timely filed.

Kansas law has established a limitation of 2 years within which to bring an action for relief on the ground of fraud. It goes on to provide that such a cause of action shall not be "deemed to have accrued until the fraud is discovered."* In this case, the cause of action was filed within 2 years of the discovery of the fraud. However, state law goes on to provide that "in no event shall an action be commenced more than 10 years beyond the time of the act giving rise to the cause of action." The action in this case was filed more than 10 years after the fraud was perpetrated. The question is whether the statute of repose was also tolled by the defendant's concealment of the cause of action.

The Court held that it was not the 2-year statute of limitations that gave it concern but the 10-year statute of repose. The incident action was begun within 2 years of the discovery of the fraud but more than 10 years after the fraud was perpetrated. The effect of a statute of limitations and a statute of repose are exactly the same. Both statutes operate to extinguish a cause of action after a certain period of time has expired. However, the Kansas Supreme Court defined and distinguished the two statutes:

"A statute of limitations extinguishes the right to prosecute an accrued cause of action after a period of time. It cuts off the remedy. It is remedial and procedural. A statute of repose limits the time during which a cause of action can arise and usually runs from an act of a defendant. It abolishes the cause of action after the passage of time even though the cause of action may not have yet accrued. It is substantive."*

In this case, the Court concluded that the fraudulent concealment by the defendant tolled not only the statute of limitations but the statute of repose as well.

The Court's decision was based on common sense and logic. There is no reason grounded in logic to presume that the fraudulent concealment of a defendant will toll a statute of limitations but not a statute of repose. If the basis of the fraudulent concealment doctrine is to deprive a defendant of the benefit of his fraud, then it must apply to a statute of repose with the same vigor it applies to a statute of limitations. In this case, the reason neither statute was complied with was the fraud of the defendant. It is illogical and nonsensical to say that the defendant's fraud tolls the statute of limitations but not the 10-year statute of repose.

"Unfortunately," the Court said, "Kansas law remains governed by decisions made over 60 years ago which refuse to recognize the doctrine of fraudulent concealment in malpractice cases. It appears that in Kansas the only tort which is not tolled by fraudulent concealment is one involving medical malpractice. For reasons which, in our judgment, defy logic, the Supreme Court of Kansas has continued throughout years past to refuse to apply the doctrine of fraudulent concealment to medical malpractice actions. In McCoy v. Wesley Hospital & Nurse Training School, the court said: 'Our statutes do not make concealment one of the grounds for tolling the statute of limitations in medical malpractice suits. Perhaps that should be done, but it is the function of the legislature and not of the courts to do it.'*

"That philosophy is not recognized by most courts in the United States. The doctrine of fraudulent concealment is a doctrine applied by the courts exercising their equitable powers, and those powers do not spring from the legislature.* Howeverso, we conclude that the refusal to recognize fraudulent concealment as tolling a medical malpractice cause of action continues in this state. We think, philosophically, that the law currently enforced in Kansas is wrong and ill-advised. Our research indicates that the issue has not been squarely faced for 60 years.

"Despite our feelings in this matter, however, we recognize that we are not empowered to reverse or alter prior decisions of our Supreme Court. This is particularly true where the court shows no signs of being ready to abandon its prior decisions even though we may consider those decisions to be ill-advised. While we strongly believe that the doctrine of fraudulent concealment in tolling a malpractice statute of limitations and statute of repose should be employed in this state, we are not at liberty to do so.

"Even so, we believe that a more focused rule should be employed in this case to prevent the law from being successfully used as a vehicle for fraud. We refer to the doctrine of equitable estoppel. The New Mexico High Court has expressed sentiments with which we agree in discussing a case involving fraudulent concealment:

"The doctrine of equitable estoppel is based not upon an interpretation of a statute but rather upon a legal theory.* The theory is premised on the notion that the one who has prevented a plaintiff from bringing suit within the statutory period should be estopped from asserting the statute of limitations as a defense.

"Our Supreme Court appears to be convinced that the tolling of the statute of limitations is a legislative prerogative. While that may be true, it provides no obstacle to the employment of the doctrine of equitable estoppel under the circumstances in the instant case. Equitable estoppel does not depend upon legislative authority;* it is an inherent power of the courts used to punish unconscionable conduct and estop a guilty party from taking advantage of his or her fraudulent conduct. Equitable estoppel is a way of saying that the statute of limitations and the statute of repose are valid and would be absolute defenses to an action but, where fraudulent conduct is involved, a defendant will not be permitted to raise those defenses. The Kansas Supreme Court has implied that in a proper case, where the wrong was not discovered within the running of the statute of limitations, equitable estoppel would be an appropriate doctrine to be invoked on the part of the defrauded plaintiff. And the appellate courts of Kansas have long employed equitable estoppel to prevent litigants from benefiting from wrongful actions. In Bowen v. Westerhaus, 578 P.2d 1102 (1978), the court reviewed the law concerning equitable estoppel as follows:

"Equitable estoppel is the effect of the voluntary conduct of a person whereby he is precluded from asserting rights against another person when his own conduct has been fraudulent. A party asserting equitable estoppel must show that another party, by its acts, representations, admissions, or silence when it had a duty to speak, induced that party to believe that certain facts existed. It must also show it rightfully relied and acted upon such belief and would be adversely affected if the other party were permitted to deny the existence of such facts.

"It is a legal maxim, well understood, that nothing can interrupt the running of the statute of limitations. Courts, however, have grafted upon such statutes an exception based upon estoppel. Generally speaking, actual fraud in the technical sense, bad faith, or an attempt to mislead or deceive is not essential to create such an estoppel; to invoke the doctrine, the defendant must have done something that amounted to an inducement to plaintiff to delay bringing his action,* but the doctrine is not available for the protection of one who has suffered loss solely by reason of his own acts or omissions. The Court of Equity aids the vigilant and not those who slumber on their rights."

The Appeals Court, in Coffey v. Stephens, 599 P.2d 310 (1979), held that::

"One general statement of the doctrine of equitable estoppel which runs throughout the cases in which the doctrine is asserted is that a defendant, who has acted in such a fashion that his conduct is sufficient to lull his adversary into a false sense of security forestalling the filing of suit until after the statute has run, will be precluded from relying on the bar of the statute of limitations.

"If a defendant, electing to rely on the statute of limitations, has previously by deception or in violation of his duty toward plaintiff, caused the plaintiff to subject his claim to the statutory bar, defendant must be charged with having wrongfully obtained an advantage which the court will not allow him to hold. This can be done by the defendant's silence when under a duty to speak."

The Appeals Court concluded that the incident case was an appropriate case for application of the doctrine of equitable estoppel, holding that the defendant in a malpractice case cannot take advantage of a defense based on the statute of limitations or the statute of repose where the defendant's own fraudulent concealment has resulted in the delay in discovering the defendant's wrongful actions. Under such facts, a defendant is equitably estopped from raising the defenses of the statute of limitations and the statute of repose.

Accordingly, the Court held that in the event the plaintiff would be able to prove, during a trial on the merits, that she was prevented from discovering that she had a cause of action against the defendant for negligence, by the defendant's own fraudulent conduct and misrepresentation, then the defendant was to be equitably estopped from raising the defenses of the statutes of limitations or the statutes of repose, even though those may be, in fact, absolute defenses to the plaintiff's cause of action.

The decision of the trial court that the plaintiff's causes of action were barred by the statute of limitations and/or the statute of repose was reversed, and the matter was remanded for a trial on the merits.

CHAPTER 23. RES JUDICATA

INTEREST REIPUBLICAE UT SIT FINIS LITIUM: *The interest of the republic is that the quarrel be ended.* The term *Res judicata* ("race-jude-i-cata") is from the Latin and finds its way into the English Language in the year 1693. It means the matter (*Res*) has been *adjudicated* or decided (*Judicata* is the perfect passive participle of the Latin verb *Judico, judicare, judicavi, judicatus,* to decide).

A prior judgment can have preclusive effects in a subsequent action under the doctrine of *res judicata.* The doctrine of *res judicata* provides that a final judgment rendered by a court of competent jurisdiction is conclusive with respect to the rights of the parties and their associates, and, as to them, constitutes an absolute bar to any subsequent action involving a violation of the same rights arising from the same event or transaction. The adjudication in a prior suit will be conclusive in a later suit of any claim or issue arising from the same transaction and will act as a bar to the later suit if a single set of operative facts gives rise to the same assertion. For the doctrine of *res judicata* to accrue to a given situation, the following must apply:

1) There was a final judgment on the issue involved,

2) There is an identity of the issue involved, and,

3) There is an identity of the party or parties involved.

Let's say that you are taking one of your prize stallions to a horse show. On the way you are run into by Mr. X and your truck sustains heavy damage. You hire a lawyer and he gets an ample settlement from Mr. X's insurance company for the damage done to your truck.

Several months later you start having some physical problems and you go to an M.D., and the M.D. diagnoses an aneurysm. The doctor attributes your condition to your auto accident and commences therapy. As if that isn't enough, the front axle on your horse trailer collapses and your trailer takes some serious damage. Inspection reveals that the axle had apparently taken a hairline fracture in the accident with Mr. X. You go back to your lawyer and he attempts a settlement with the insurance company to no avail, and he initiates a law suit. The insurance company, arguing *res judicata*, motions for summary judgment on both counts of your claim: count I for damage to your trailer and count II for personal injury. The court grants summary disposition on the basis of *res judicata*. a matter already decided.

You appeal the lower court's grant of summary judgment. On appeal, the appeals court upholds the grant of summary disposition on the property damage to your trailer, property damage already having been adjudicated, but reverses on the personal injury since that issue was never addressed and *res judicata* does not apply. At trial you receive a damage award for the consequences of your aneurysm.

CHESTER DEMPSEY AND HELEN JANE DEMPSEY, APPELLANTS
v. THE CESSNA AIRCRAFT COMPANY, AND ALL, APPELLEES
SUPERIOR COURT OF PENNSYLVANIA
653 A.2D 679, (1995)
JANUARY 25, 1995

(The Dempseys lost their case at the lower-court level and appealed the appellate-court decision on issues of law, making them the appellants)*

LEGAL CONSIDERATIONS

Civil Procedure / Pleading / Res judicata

As a general rule, *res judicata* is an affirmative defense and should be pled as new matter in an answer to a plaintiff's complaint.

Civil Procedure / Res judicata

A final valid judgment upon the merits by a court of competent jurisdiction bars any future suit between the same parties or their privies on the same cause of action.

Civil Procedure / Res judicata

Regardless of whether the plaintiff effects a recovery in the first action, he may not re-litigate an action which has once been decided.

Civil Procedure / Res judicata

Application of the doctrine of *res judicata* requires that the two actions possess the following common elements: (1) identity of the thing sued upon; (2) identity of the cause of action; (3) identity of the parties; and (4) identity of the capacity of the parties.

Civil Procedure / Res judicata

A fundamental test applied for comparing causes of action, for the purpose of applying principles of *res judicata*, is whether the primary right and duty, and delict or wrong, are the same in each action. Under this test, there is but one cause of action where there is but one right in the plaintiff and one wrong on the part of the defendant involving that right. Thus, it has been said that the primary focus should be whether the ultimate and controlling issues have been decided.

Civil Procedure / Res judicata

Identity of two causes of action may be determined by considering the similarity in the acts complained of and the demand for recovery as well as the identity of the witnesses, documents and facts alleged. In determining whether *res judicata* should apply, a court may consider whether the factual allegations of both actions are the same, whether the same evidence is necessary to prove each action and whether both actions seek compensation for the same damages. If the acts or transactions giving rise to the causes of action are identical, there may be sufficient identity between the two actions for the summary judgment in the first action to be *res judicata* in the second.

Civil Procedure / Res judicata

A judgment upon the merits in one action bars a subsequent suit upon the same cause although brought in a different form of action, and a party therefore cannot, by varying the form of action or adopting a different method of presenting his case, escape the operation of the principle that one and the same cause of action shall not be twice litigated.

Civil Procedure / Res judicata

Where the damages suffered are a consequence of the same actions alleged in an earlier suit, a new cause of action is not present merely because the relief sought has changed. *Res judicata* may bar a second action based upon the same set of operative facts or transaction even if additional grounds for relief are presented. The fact that a different form or measure of relief is asked does not preclude the application of the judgment to prevent the maintenance of the second action. For application of the doctrine, it is not necessary that the two actions be identical with respect to the relief sought.

Civil Procedure / Contracts Law

If the procurement of a release was by fraud, when a party first discovers it, he may disaffirm the contract and offer to return the consideration or affirm the voidable contract and waive the fraud. The failure to tender back the consideration after a party discovers the alleged fraud constitutes a waiver of the fraud and an affirmance of the contract.

PRIOR HISTORY: Appeal from Order of the Court of Common Pleas, Civil Division, of Montgomery County

DISPOSITION: Affirmed. (The lower court decision in the Court of Common Pleas in favor of CESSNA was upheld.)

OVERVIEW: Appellant husband CHESTER DEMPSEY entered into an agreement to settle his personal injury action against appellee CESSNA. After the settlement had been completed and the consideration paid, appellant DEMPSEY learned that appellee CESSNA had failed to disclose certain information during discovery which could have strengthened the DEMPSEY'S claim. The DEMP-SEYS, husband and wife, filed an action in federal court against CESSNA, alleging that the settlement was induced by fraud. The federal court dismissed the action and ruled that the appellants, The DEMPSEYS, had waived any claim of fraud by accepting and not returning the $300.000 settlement money. Thereafter, having been rejected in federal court, the appellants, the DEMPSEYS, filed a petition in the state trial court to set aside the settlement on grounds of fraud. The trial court (the state lower court)dismissed the petition on grounds of *res judicata.* On the subsequent appeal to the state appeals court, that Court affirmed the order of the trial court. The state appeals court held that because the federal court action involved the same parties, issues, cause of action, and relief, the decision of the federal court was *res judicata* and barred any further action to rescind the $300,000 settlement and set it aside.

OUTCOME: The state appeals court affirmed the order of the trial court and dismissed the petition to set aside the $300,000 personal-injury settlement due to fraud because the issues had been litigated previously in the federal courts and so the doctrine of *res judicata* applied.

OPINION: Filed January 25, 1995

Chester Dempsey entered an agreement to settle a personal injury action pending against The Cessna Aircraft Company (Cessna) in Montgomery County for the sum of three hundred thousand dollars ($300,000.00). After the settlement had been completed and the consideration paid, however, Dempsey learned that Cessna had failed to disclose certain information during discovery which may have strengthened his claim. Therefore, he filed an action against Cessna in the United States District Court (federal court) for the Eastern District of Pennsylvania in which he alleged, inter alia (among other things), that he had been induced to settle his claim by fraud. The federal court dismissed the action, holding, that, under Pennsylvania law, Dempsey had agreed to the settlement contract and waived any claim of fraud by failing to disclaim the settlement and returning the $300,000 settlement consideration. This decision was affirmed by the Third Circuit Court of Appeals. See: *Dempsey v. Associated Aviation Underwriters,* 977 F.2d 567 (3rd Cir. 1992). Thereafter, Dempsey filed a petition in Montgomery County (state court) to set aside the settlement on grounds of fraud. The Montgomery County Court, in response to preliminary objections on the part of the defendants, dismissed the petition on grounds of *res judicata.* From this order, Dempsey filed the instant appeal. After careful review, we affirm the court's dismissal of Dempsey's petition. As a general rule, *res judicata* is an affirmative defense and should be argued as new matter in an answer to a plaintiff's claim or allegation. In the present case, however, the facts were not in dispute, and neither party objected to the procedure followed in the trial court. (An affirmative defense is one that, if proven, defeats a claim or allegation (a provable alibi is an example of an affirmative defense)).

As a matter of record and the basis of Dempsey's cause of action, Dempsey had been injured when a Cessna C-150 single engine aircraft crashed during take off. He filed an action against Cessna to recover for injuries sustained, alleging strict liability, negligence and breach of warranty (strict liability holds that a defendant, a manufacturer say, is responsible no matter what when a mechanical device of his manufacture malfunctions with catastrophic consequences to life or limb, such as when a plain falls out of the sky). The case was settled prior to trial for the sum of three hundred thousand ($300,000.00) dollars. Subsequently, Dempsey learned that Cessna had been aware of fuel tank problems with the aircraft and that this information had not been disclosed during discovery in response to Rule-26 discovery requests. Contending that he had been induced to settle by fraud, Dempsey filed the federal action and, after that action had been dismissed, a subsequent petition in Montgomery County to set aside the $300,000 settlement.

For example, in *Nocito v. Lanuitti*, 167 A.2d 262, (1961), where the plaintiff, Nocito, sought to recover damages for fraud which had induced him to execute a release in a trespass action, the Pennsylvania Supreme Court affirmed a judgment in favor of the defendant Lanuitti. The Court said: "If Lanuitti procured this release by fraud, when Nocito discovered it, he could have disaffirmed the settlement contract and returned the settlement money to Lanuitti. When he failed to return the monetary consideration he accepted for the release of his claim, he waived any future claim of fraud. Nocito's failure to tender back the monetary consideration after he discovered the alleged fraud constituted a waiver of any fraud and an affirmance of the settlement contract.

Was this decision *res judicata* when Dempsey subsequently filed a motion in the state court to set aside the settlement reached in the federal court action? The Superior Court held that it was:

> The doctrine of *res judicata* holds that [a] final valid judgment upon the merits by a court of competent jurisdiction bars any future suit between the same parties or their privies on the same cause of action. The purpose of the doctrine is to minimize the judicial energy devoted to individual cases, establish certainty and respect for court judgments, and protect the party relying on the prior adjudication from vexatious litigation. Where parties have been afforded an opportunity to litigate a claim before a court of competent jurisdiction, and where the court has finally decided the controversy, the interests of the state and of the parties require that the validity of the claim and any issue actually litigated in the action not be litigated again. It was held in *Ham v. Sulek*, 620 A.2d 5, 8 (1993) that: Regardless of whether a plaintiff effects a recovery in the first action, he may not re-litigate an action which has once been adjudicated.

Application of the doctrine of *res judicata* requires that the two actions involved possess the following common elements: (1) identity of the thing sued upon; (2) identity of the cause of action; (3) identity of the parties; (4) identity of the capacity of the parties. In the incident case, it was clear that the first, third and fourth elements were present, and the Court needed to focus only on the second element. The term "cause of action" is not easily defined, and the authorities have laid down no thoroughly satisfactory and all-embracing definition. (See 46 Am.Jur.2d, Judgments $406. (Am. Jur. is a legal encyclopedia: American Jurisprudence 2d.). "A fundamental test applied for comparing causes of action, for the purpose of applying principles of *res judicata*, is whether the primary right and duty, and delict or wrong, are the same in each action. Under this test, there is but one cause of action where there is but one right in the plaintiff and one wrong on the part of the defendant involving that right." (46 Am.Jur.2d, Judgments $406). Thus, it has been said that the primary focus should be whether the ultimate and controlling issues have been decided.

Identity of two causes of action may be determined by considering the similarity in the acts complained of and the demand for recovery as well as the identity of the witnesses, documents and facts alleged. In determining whether *res judicata* should apply, a court may consider whether the factual allegations of both actions are the same, whether the same evidence is necessary to prove each action and whether both actions seek compensation for the same damages. If the acts or transactions giving rise to the causes of action are identical, there may be sufficient identity between the two actions for the granting of summary judgment in the first action to be the basis for *res judicata* in the subsequent action.

In the federal action in this case, the issues were whether Cessna had withheld information which Dempsey had sought to discover and had thereby induced the appellant by fraud to settle his claim. In Dempsey's subsequent state court petition he raised the same issues. Thus, the complaint in the federal action and the complaint in the state action both relied upon and asserted the same conduct and transaction. Both actions also alleged the same injury, i.e., appellant's acceptance of an unfavorable settlement. Finally, both actions relied upon the same evidence: the discovery information which was allegedly withheld. In order to prevail in both actions, it was necessary to prove fraud. In both actions, moreover, the cause of action would be defeated by an affirmance of the settlement after the facts had become known (acceptance in that the settlement money was not returned thereby failing to negate the original settlement agreement).

It was of no consequence that the federal action was commenced by the complaint of fraud and the state action was commenced by petition to set aside the settlement agreement. The form in which two actions are commenced does not determine whether the causes of action are identical.

> The application of the doctrine of *res judicata* to identical causes of action does not depend upon the identity or differences in the forms of two separate actions. A judgment upon the merits bars a subsequent suit upon the same cause, though brought in a different form of action, and a party therefore cannot, by varying the form of action or adopting a different method of presenting his case,

escape the operation of the principle that one and the same cause of action shall not be twice litigated. (46 Am.Jur.2d, Judgments § 411).

Where the damages suffered were a consequence of the same actions alleged in an earlier suit, a new cause of action is not present merely because the relief sought has changed. *Res judicata* may bar a second action based upon the same set of operative facts or transaction even if additional grounds for relief are presented. The fact that a different form or measure of relief is asked does not preclude the application of the judgment to estop the maintenance of the second action. For application of the doctrine, it is not necessary that the two actions be identical with respect to the relief sought.

The Appellant Dempsey, when he discovered information which had not been supplied during discovery, asserted that he had been induced to settle his claim by fraud. He could then either have disaffirmed the settlement and offered to return the amount which he had been paid or he could have affirmed the set-tlement and waived his claim of fraud. In a federal action to recover additional damages the court held that Plaintiff had affirmed the settlement and waived the fraud. That decision is now *res judicata* and bars any subsequent action to rescind the settlement and set it aside. (If the truth be known, Dempsey had probably spent a sizable portion of the $300,000 settlement money and didn't have the full $300,000 to return).

The judgment of the lower court was affirmed.

Chapter 24. The Doctrine of Collateral Estoppel

Closely related to the doctrine of *Res judicata* is the doctrine of collateral Estoppel. The etymology of the term is not as clear as *res judicata* and can be regarded as a hybrid. The term comes into English in 1531. The estoppel part of the term is no doubt an alteration of the Anglo-French infinitive *estopere*, meaning simply, to stop. Estoppel, then, is a legal bar to denying a fact, i.e., an issue, previously asserted in another legal action when that action impinges on or comes together with a subsequent legal action. The term collateral is a term that clearly derives from the Latin verb *confero, conferre, contuli, collatus*, meaning to bring together. In other words, to be stopped from bringing together into a subsequent lawsuit a discredited issue from an earlier, collateral lawsuit.

Collateral estoppel bars re-litigation of issues. *Res judicata* bars re-litigation of claims. When an issue of ultimate fact has finally been determined, collateral estoppel bars re-litigation of that issue between the same parties in any subsequent action arising from the same transaction or occurrence or set of operative facts from which the issue derives.

In a case where an underage driver was driving a vehicle without consent of its owner, and a party who was injured in another vehicle when the vehicles collided brought suit, the insurance company was successful in avoiding damages because it was able to show the underage driver had virtually commandeered the vehicle and was driving the vehicle without the owner's consent. In dismissing the case, the court relied on the unambiguous status of the non-permissive driver and ruled that the insurance coverage applied only to drivers driving with permission of the owner..

Subsequently, the injured party brought a tort-claim lawsuit against the parents of the young driver, alleging negligence and claiming that the results of the first court action did not apply to the second court action because the fact that the driver was driving the vehicle without the permission of its owner was not at issue in the second lawsuit, that the owner's negligence was the issue instead. When the defendant parent's lawyer motioned for summary judgment, the court granted the motion on the ground that the action was barred by the doctrine of collateral estoppel in as much as the issue of parental negligence had already been decided indirectly when the court in the first lawsuit held that the young driver was driving without the permission of his parents and that, therefore, the owner, the parents, could not be found negligent. The injured party could not, in other words, rely on an isuue, the parent's negligence, nullified in a previous action. The plaintiff was collaterally estopped from doing so!

Consider the case of *McNeeley v. Spencer*.

WILLIAM MCNEELEY, APPELLANT

v. WILLIAM SPENCER, APPELLEE

COURT OF APPEALS OF KENTUCKY

2002 KY. APP.

SEPTEMBER 27, 2002

Civil Procedure / Collateral Estoppel

Although *collateral estoppel* and *res judicata* are cut from the same cloth, the effect of collateral estoppel is different from that of *res judicata*. Under the doctrine of *res judicata*, a judgment on the merits in a prior suit involving the same parties or their privies bars a second suit on the same cause of action, claim. Under the doctrine of *collateral estoppel*, on the other hand, such a judgment precludes re-litigation of issues actually litigated and determined in the prior suit, regardless of whether it was based on the same cause of action or claim as the second suit.

Civil Procedure / Collateral Estoppel

For the most part, the doctrine of collateral estoppel is applied in one or both of the following approaches toward barring a convict's legal malpractice claim against his defense attorney: (1) the plaintiff, who stands convicted, is precluded from re-litigating the issue of his admitted guilt in a collateral civil case and is thereby unable to establish his innocence, a prerequisite to proving causation or one of the elements of the alleged negligence; (2) post-conviction denial of relief based on ineffective assistance of counsel precludes a civil action for legal malpractice.

Civil Procedure / Collateral Estoppel

The standards to establish ineffective assistance of counsel and legal malpractice are sufficiently similar in substance to support the application of the defense of *collateral estoppel*. The first step of the standard for determining ineffective assistance of counsel, counsel's deficient performance under an objective standard of reasonableness, and the breach element of a claim of legal malpractice are the same, i.e., reasonableness, trial counsel must act reasonably. Further, the second step of the standard for determining ineffective assistance of counsel, prejudice, and the causation element of a claim of legal malpractice are also the same, i.e., a defendant must show that trial counsel's alleged deficiency affected the outcome of trial.

Torts / Collateral Estoppel

In order to establish a cause of action for legal malpractice, a plaintiff has the burden of establishing the following elements: (1) the existence of an attorney-client relationship (the duty); (2) negligence in the legal representation of the plaintiff (the breach); (3) that the negligence was a proximate cause of an injury (causation); and (4) the fact and extent of the injury alleged (damage). In order for a defendant in a criminal case to establish that he did not receive the effective assistance of counsel, he must show: (1) that counsel's performance was deficient and that, under an objective standard of reasonableness, counsel made an error so serious that counsel was not functioning as an attorney as guaranteed under the Sixth Amendment; and (2) that the deficiency was prejudicial to the defendant. There is ample authority to support the conclusion that, for purposes of collateral estoppel, the standards for establishing ineffective assistance of counsel in a criminal forum and legal malpractice in a civil suit are equivalent.

Civil Procedure / Summary Judgment Standard

Summary judgment is proper if the pleadings, depositions, answers to interrogatories, stipulations, and admissions on file, together with the affidavits, if any, show that there is no genuine issue as to any material fact and that the moving party is entitled to a judgment as a matter of law. Kentucky Rules of Civil Procedure 56.03. For summary judgment to be proper the movant must show that the adverse party cannot prevail under any circumstances. The proper function of summary judgment is to terminate litigation when, as a matter of law, it appears that it would be impossible for the respondent to produce evidence at trial warranting a judgment in his favor.

Civil Procedure / Standards of Review

The standard of review on appeal of a summary judgment is whether the trial court correctly found that there was no genuine issue as to any material fact and that the moving party was entitled to judgment as a matter of law. There is no requirement that the appellate court defer to the trial court since factual findings are not at issue. The record must be viewed in a light most favorable to the party opposing the motion for summary judgment and all doubts are to be resolved in his favor.

PRIOR HISTORY: APPEAL FROM JOHNSON CIRCUIT COURT.
DISPOSITION: Judgment of the lower court affirmed.
OPINION: AFFIRMED

William McNeeley, pro se, (PRO SE: representing himself) appealed from an order entered by the Johnson Circuit Court on November 16, 1999, which granted Lowell E. Spencer's motion for summary judgment and dismissed McNeeley's complaint for legal negligence. Having concluded that there was no genuine issue as to any material fact and that pursuant to the doctrine of *collateral estoppel*, (i.e., McNeely cannot change the facts as entered in his first trial and is bound by them), Spencer is entitled to summary judgment as a matter of law, the Appeals Court affirmed the trial court's finding..

McNeeley, who was represented by Spencer, was convicted of murder for the heinous killing of Sherman Newsome, the two-year-old son of Rebecca Newsome. McNeeley's jury trial was held in Johnson Circuit Court in 1992, and he received a sentence of life in prison. Evidence presented by the Commonwealth showed that McNeeley inflicted the fatal injuries on the toddler by stomping on his stomach and back. (McNeeley lived with his wife and their four children and with Rebecca Newsome and her six children.) McNeeley has unsuccessfully pursued post-conviction relief by direct appeal to the appellate court and by post-judgment motions he has filed.

McNeeley's conviction was first reviewed by the Kentucky Supreme Court in an opinion rendered on March 24, 1994. The Supreme Court noted some trial errors, but it affirmed McNeeley's conviction and sentence on the grounds that any errors in the trial-court proceedings were harmless due to the "compelling evidence of McNeeley's guilt." McNeeley then filed a motion claiming that Spencer had provided him with ineffective assistance of counsel, and that he was entitled to a new trial. The Johnson Circuit Court, without conducting an evidentiary hearing, denied McNeeley's motion. On September 26, 1997, the Kentucky Appeals Court affirmed that order, and concluded that McNeeley had failed to show that he had received ineffective assistance of counsel during his murder trial. McNeeley next attempted to have his conviction and sentence vacated in September 1998, by filing a subsequent motion in which he alleged that newly discovered evidence concerning a potassium level test performed on the child showed that the previously claimed time of death was incorrect. In denying the new motion, the Johnson Circuit Court concluded that even if the new evidence were considered, it would not change the guilty verdict with reasonable certainty. On April 5, 2002, the Appeals Court affirmed the denial of that motion.

The civil complaint that is the basis for the current appeal subsuming malpractice was filed in the Johnson Circuit Court on September 12, 1994, after the Supreme Court had affirmed McNeeley's conviction in his direct appeal. The complaint alleged that Spencer had committed legal malpractice during his representation of McNeeley on the murder charge, and it sought monetary damages. On November 16, 1999, the trial court granted Spencer's motion for summary judgment and dismissed McNeeley's complaint. This appeal followed.

McNeeley argued in his brief to the Appeals Court that the trial court erred by granting summary judgment, and he set forth several instances of alleged negligence by Spencer during his representation on the murder charge, including: (1) that Spencer failed to impeach (discredit) certain prosecution witnesses, (2) that Spencer failed to call certain witnesses who may have provided favorable testimony in his behalf; and (3) that Spencer failed to request a mistrial. McNeeley contended that these several instances of alleged negligence by Spencer presented genuine issues of material fact supporting his claim of malpractice. The flaw in McNeeley's argument was that the issue of whether Spencer provided him with reasonably competent representation at his murder trial had already been lititgated and decided unfavorably to him. Accordingly, the Appeals Court held that since McNeeley's claim of ineffective assistance of counsel had been found against him, the doctrine of collateral estoppel precluded the re-litigation of the issue of Spencer's effectiveness in the incident negligence action, and the trial court's granting of summary judgment in favor of Spencer was correct as a matter of law.

Summary judgment is proper if the pleadings, depositions, answers to interrogatories, stipulations, and admissions on file, together with the affidavits, if any, show that there is no genuine issue as to any material fact and that the moving party is entitled to a judgment as a matter of law. In *Paintsville Hospital Co. v. Rose*, the Supreme Court of Kentucky held that for summary judgment to be proper, the movant (the moving party) must show that the opposing party cannot prevail under any circumstances. The Court has also stated that "the proper function of summary judgment is to terminate litigation when, as a matter of law, it appears that it would be impossible for the respondent to produce evidence at the trial warranting a judgment in his favor." The standard of review on appeal of a summary judgment is whether the trial court correctly found that there was no genuine issue as to any material fact and that the moving party was entitled to judgment as a matter of law. There is no requirement that the appellate court defer to the trial court since factual findings are not at issue at the appellate level." (Issues of law are the subject matter of appeal.) The record must be viewed in a light most favorable to the party opposing the motion for summary judgment and all doubts are to be resolved in his favor."

In *Napier v. Jones By & Through Reynolds*, the Appeals Court discussed the application of the doctrine of collateral estoppel. Although collateral estoppel and *res judicata* are cut from the same cloth, the effect of collateral estoppel is different from that of *res judicata*:

> The basic distinction between the doctrines of *res judicata* and collateral estoppel has frequently been emphasized. Thus, under the doctrine of *res judicata*, a judgment 'on the merits' in a prior suit involving the same parties or their privies bars a second suit on the same cause of action, claim. Under the doctrine of collateral estoppel, on the other hand, such a judgment bars re-litigation of issues actually litigated and determined in a prior suit.

In McNeeley's subsequent motion alleging malpractice of counsel, he attempted to show that counsel's representation fell below an objective standard of reasonableness. In this negligence action, McNeeley was also alleging as one of the required elements for legal malpractice, "that the attorney neglected his duty to exercise the ordinary care of a reasonably competent attorney acting in the same or similar circumstances." Thus, since the doctrine of collateral estoppel barred McNeeley from re-litigating an issue in this legal malpractice action that had already been found adversely to him, the granting of summary judgment to Spencer was correct as a matter of law.

In *Ray v. Stone*, the Appeals Court discussed the applicability of the doctrine of collateral estoppel to a case where a convicted criminal defendant had sued his defense attorney for legal malpractice:

> Decisions addressing whether and under what circumstances a convict may sue his defense attorney for legal malpractice illustrate the difficulty the courts have encountered in resolving the issue in light of competing policy considerations. Numerous jurisdictions have held that a defendant who pleads guilty may not thereafter maintain such an action. In so holding, these decisions have generally applied collateral estoppel to preclude the action. For the most part, the doctrine has been applied in one or both of the following approaches toward barring the claim: (1) the plaintiff, who stands convicted, is precluded from re-litigating the issue of his admitted guilt in a collateral civil case and is thereby unable to establish his innocence, a prerequisite to proving one of the elements of the alleged negligence; and, (2) post conviction denial of relief based on ineffective assistance of counsel precludes a civil action for legal malpractice. The collateral estoppel effect of the previous decision in the ineffective assistance of counsel motion therefore precludes plaintiff from re-litigating the issue of defendant's negligence.

Accordingly, the Appeals Court adopted this general rule, and in applying it to the case *sub judice* (before the court), the Court held that since the issue of whether Spencer provided competent assistance to McNeeley during his representation of him on the murder charge had previously been determined adversely to McNeeley in the denial of his motion claiming ineffective assistance of counsel, McNeeley was barred by the doctrine of collateral estoppel from re-litigating that same issue in his subsequent legal malpractice civil action.

For the foregoing reasons, the order of the Johnson Circuit Court granting Spencer's motion for summary judgment was affirmed with all concurring.

Chapter 25. Stare decisis

Stare decisis ("starry dee-sye-sis") is also a term directly from the Latin. The *stare* part is the present active infinitive of the Latin verb *Sto, Stare, Steti, Status,* meaning *to stand.* The *decisis* component is from the Latin verb *Decido, Decidere, Decidi, Decisus* meaning simply *to decide,* so, "to stand by things decoded" would be a good translation.

The US court system has repeatedly stated that the common law is dynamic rather than static, and that it may be modified by judicial decision to meet the changing needs of society. However, it is recognized under the *doctrine of stare decisis* that once a point of law has been established, that point will stand in the court where it was made and all inferior courts of the system where it was made in all subsequent cases where the same legal issue is raised. Modification of the common law, you see, runs counter to the doctrine of *stare decisis. Stare decisis* as a doctrine of law is implemented through reliance on common-law precedent, precedent referring to a decided case that furnishes a basis for determining later cases involving similar facts or issues.

The doctrine of *stare decisis* permits society to presume that bedrock principles are founded in the law rather than in the whims and proclivities of individuals, thereby contributing to the integrity and validity of our constitutional system. While *stare decisis* is not an inexorable command to the judiciary, the careful observer will comprehend that any detours from the straight and narrow path in our judicial history have occurred for articulable reasons only when courts have felt obliged to bring judicial opinions into agreement with experience and with facts newly ascertained or changes in accepted public policy.

Imagine a situation where a disgruntled business owner of a small neighborhood grocery was being effectively evicted from his long established location by a landlord's overweening greed for increased rent. The business owner complained vociferously to his clientele with the result that one of his patrons wrote to the Letter-To-The-Editor column of the city newspaper excoriating the landlord.

The landlord, incensed at being publicly ridiculed in the local press, brought a lawsuit against the letter writer claiming defamation. The lower court granted summary judgment to the letter writer on the ground that the letter writer was protected by the free-speech guarantee of the first amendment to the United States Constitution. The landlord appealed to the state supreme court on a writ of error, claiming that the first-amendment protected opinions of the press but not those opinions of private persons displayed in the press.

On review, the Court determined that the opinions of individuals were just as sacrosanct when published as those of the press and that any departure from the settled law in the matter would invoke the *doctrine of stare decisis*, and that any departure from the *doctrine of stare decisis* demanded compelling justification for which the Court could find none. Judgment Affirmed!

Mary Louise Wakulich, Individually And As Special Administrator
of the Estate of Elizabeth Wakulich, Deceased, Appellant,
v. Dennis Mraz Et Al., Appellees
(Mraz won in lower court and is defending that decision on appeal).

Supreme Court Of Illinois
785 N.e.2d 843 (2003)
February 6, 2003

The State of Illinois has a three-court hierarchy as the system applies to the Superior-Court platform:

1) The Superior Court,
2) The Appeals Court and,
3) The Illinois Supreme Court where the final word reposes.

Legal Considerations

Governments / Stare decisis

The doctrine of *stare decisis* is a basic tenet of the Illinois legal system. Simply stated, *stare decisis* reflects the policy of the courts to stand by precedents and not to disturb settled points of law.

Civil Procedure / Pleading & Practice

The critical inquiry is whether the allegations of the complaint, when construed in a light most favorable to the plaintiff, are sufficient to state a cause of action upon which relief may be granted. In making this determination, all well-pleaded facts in the complaint must be taken as true (well-pleaded facts are facts pleaded with high specificity).

Torts / Alcohol Providers

Illinois has no common law cause of action for injuries arising out of the sale or gift of alcoholic beverages. The legislature has preempted the field of alcohol-related liability, and any change in the law governing alcohol-related liability should be made by the Illinois General Assembly, or not at all.

Torts / Alcohol Providers

In Illinois, the common law recognized no cause of action for injuries arising out of the sale or gift of alcoholic beverages. The legislature's adoption of the Dramshop Act, now codified at § 6-21 of the Illinois Liquor Control Act of 1934, created a limited and exclusive statutory cause of action by imposing a form of no-fault liability upon dramshops for selling or giving intoxicating liquors to persons who subsequently injure third parties. Through its passage and continual amendment of the Dramshop Act, the Illinois General Assembly has preempted the entire field of alcohol-related liability.

OPINION: In this appeal The Supreme Court of Illinois reviewed the dismissal of a complaint pursuant to section 2-615 of the Illinois Code of Civil Procedure (Code). Generally, the plaintiff alleged that defendants were negligent in providing an alcoholic beverage to plaintiff's minor daughter, and negligent in their performance of a voluntary undertaking to care for the minor after she became unconscious, and that such negligence was the immediate cause of the young person's death. In deciding whether the first claim was properly dismissed, as it was in the trial court, the Illinois Supreme Court had to consider whether the Court should revisit and overturn its decision in *Charles v. Seigfried*, 651 N.E.2d 154 (1995), and recognize a legal cause of action against adult social hosts for serving alcoholic beverages to minors who are subsequently injured. For the reasons discussed below, the Court adhered to its decision in *Charles* and declined to recognize any form of social-host liability. However, because the Court found that the plaintiff had adequately pled a negligence action based on a voluntary undertaking theory, this matter was remanded to the trial court for further proceedings on the plaintiff's complaint., i.e.: The early development of the law, and particularly of the forms of action of case and *assumpsit* led to a distinction as to tort liability (liability for personal injury) between misfeasance and non-feasance (*assumpsit*, in this case, is a Latin term meaning he undertook or attempted). A defendant who actually entered upon the performance of an undertaking became liable for harm to the plaintiff which resulted from the caregiver's negligent performance, whereas one who never commenced performance at all was not liable for his failure to help. (In other words, if you tried to help someone in need, and you botched the job, you were liable. If you did nothing, you were home free.)

Factual and Procedural Background

Following the death of her 16-year-old daughter Elizabeth Wakulich, plaintiff Mary Louise Wakulich, individually and as special administrator of Elizabeth's estate, brought an action in the circuit court of Cook County, Illinois, alleging claims under the Wrongful Death Act and the Survival Act. According to the 10-count Amended Complaint, during the evening of June 15, 1997, and continuing into the early morning hours of June 16, 1997, Elizabeth was at the home of defendants, Michael Mraz, his brother Brian Mraz, and their father Dennis Mraz. At that time, Michael was 21 years old, and Brian was 18 years old. Plaintiff alleged that Michael and Brian induced Elizabeth, "by offering monies, by goading and by applying great social pressure," to drink a quart bottle of Goldschlager, a "highly alcoholic and dangerous" beverage, and that Michael and Brian knew, or should have known, that Elizabeth, a minor, could not appreciate the dangers associated with the consumption of excessive amounts of alcoholic beverages.

According to the complaint, after consuming the entire bottle of Goldschlager, Elizabeth lost consciousness. Michael and Brian placed her in the family room of their home, where they observed her "vomiting profusely and making gurgling sounds." They later removed her vomit-saturated blouse and placed a pillow under her head to prevent aspiration of the fluid. Brian and Michael allegedly refused to drive Elizabeth home, did not contact her parents, did not seek medical attention, and "actually prevented other individuals at their home from calling 911 or seeking other medical intervention." Plaintiff further alleged in the complaint that, during the morning of June 16, 1997, Dennis "ordered" Michael and Brian to remove Elizabeth from their home, which they did. Elizabeth died later that day. The complaint indicates that Michael was subsequently convicted of contributing to the delinquency of a minor.

Plaintiff advanced two theories of recovery: (1) that Michael and Brian were negligent in providing alcohol to Elizabeth and inducing her to drink to excess, and, (2) that Michael, Brian and Dennis were negligent in failing to act reasonably to protect Elizabeth after voluntarily undertaking to care for her after she lost consciousness.

Defendants moved to dismiss the complaint pursuant to section 2-615 of the Illinois Code for failure to state a legal cause of action. Defendants principally argued that under this court's decision in *Charles*, (i.e., *Charles v. Seigfried*, 651 N.E.2d 154 (1995), there is no common-law social-host liability in Illinois. The trial court dismissed the complaint with prejudice. Plaintiff appealed. (When an action is dismissed with prejudice, the court will not allow the matter to be reentered in the trial court except on remand from a higher court.)

The Appeals Court reversed the dismissal of those counts of the complaint directed against Michael and Brian (Dennis Mraz's sons) based on their alleged negligent performance of a *voluntary undertaking* but affirmed the dismissal of the balance of the complaint, (the wrongful death complaint, etc.), and remanded the matter to the trial court for further proceedings. The Illinois Supreme Court allowed plaintiff's petition for leave to appeal and allowed the Illinois Trial Lawyers Association to file an *amicus curiae* brief in support of plaintiff. (*Amicus curiae* means friend of the court. In this instance the Illinois Trial Lawyers Association filed a brief supporting the plaintiff's wrongful death cause of action).* Subsequently, the Supreme Court affirmed the judgment of the appellate court.

ANALYSIS

I

A motion to dismiss under section 2-615 of the Illinois Code of Civil Procedure challenges only the legal sufficiency of the complaint. The Supreme Court reviews a section 2-615 motion to dismiss order de-novo (de-novo review is review rendered without deference to the lower-court decision. It is as if no decision had been previously reached: from anew, in other words. there are two types of review of lower-court decisions conducted by a higher court: deferential review and de-novo review). The critical inquiry was whether the allegations of the complaint, when construed in a light most favorable to the plaintiff, were sufficient to state a cause of action upon which relief could be granted. In making this determination, all well-pleaded facts in the complaint must be taken as true. (A well-pleaded fact is a fact that is stated with high specificity, particularity.)

Preliminarily, the Court noted that the plaintiff had not challenged the appellate court's affirmance of the dismissal of counts directed against Dennis Mraz, the father and that that issue was therefore moot. Accordingly, the Court considered only the viability of plaintiff's claims against Michael and Brian. (The author thinks Wakulich probably dropped her claim against Dennis Mraz, the father, because Illinois, unlike most states, has no law that prohibits an individual from plying a minor with alcohol. The author thinks the Wakulich lawyer thought he had a better chance of winning damages against the Mraz brothers because they attempted (assumpsit) to sober up the Wakulich girl and failed tragically.)

II

The Supreme Court considered first those counts which alleged that Michael and Brian were negligent in providing an alcoholic beverage to Elizabeth Wakulich and inducing her to consume a dangerous amount. Defendants contended that these counts were properly dismissed based on the Court's decision in *Charles v. Seigfried*, 651 N.E.2d 154 (1995).

In *Charles*, decided just two years prior to the events giving rise to the Wakulich litigation, the Supreme Court addressed whether it should recognize a cause of action against social hosts for serving alcoholic beverages to minors who are subsequently injured. The factual backdrop against which the Court decided this issue involved two different social gatherings at which minors were served alcoholic beverages, became intoxicated, and were involved in motor vehicle accidents. In the first case, Lynn Sue Charles, who was 16 years of age at the time, became intoxicated at the defendant's home. She left the party by driving her own automobile and was later involved in a fatal collision. In the second case, 15-year-old Paula Bzdek became intoxicated at the defendants' home, and left the party with an 18-year-old friend, who was also intoxicated. The 18-year-old friend lost control of his vehicle, crashing into oncoming traffic. Bzdek, who was a passenger in the vehicle, suffered permanent injuries. In each case, a complaint was filed premised on theories of social host liability. In each case, the trial court dismissed the complaint, the plaintiff appealed, and the appellate court reversed the dismissal. *Charles v. Seigfried*, 623 N.E.2d 1021 (1993); *Bzdek v. Townsley*, 634 N.E.2d 389 (1994).

In the *Charles* litigation, the appellate court recognized a cause of action against a social host who knowingly serves alcoholic beverages to a minor at the social host's residence, permits the minor to become intoxicated, and allows the minor to leave in a motor vehicle. In the Bzdek litigation, the appellate court recognized a similar cause of action against social hosts who knowingly serve intoxicants to persons under the legal drinking age of 21. In a consolidated appeal, the Supreme Court reversed both decisions. Relying on over a century of precedent, the Court held that "Illinois has no common law cause of action for injuries arising out of the sale or gift of alcoholic beverages; the Court held that the legislature has preempted the field of alcohol-related liability, and that any change in the law governing alcohol-related liability should be made by the General Assembly, or not at all." The Court thus declined to adopt any form of social host liability.

In the incident case, plaintiff requested that the Court reconsider and overrule *Charles* and recognize a common-law negligence action against adult social hosts, i.e., persons 18 years of age and older who knowingly serve alcohol to a minor. Based on the doctrine of *stare decisis*, the Supreme Court denied plaintiff Wakulich's request and adhered to its decision in *Charles*.

The doctrine of *stare decisis* is a basic tenet of our legal system. Simply stated, *stare decisis* reflects the policy of the courts "to stand by precedents and not to disturb settled points of law," *Zimmerman v. Village of Skokie*, 697 N.E.2d 699 (1998). In other words, "a question once deliberately examined and decided should be considered as settled and closed to further argument." *Prall v. Burckhartt*, 132 N.E. 280 (1921). The doctrine of *stare decisis* "promotes the evenhanded, predictable, and consistent development of legal principles, fosters reliance on judicial decisions, and contributes to the actual and perceived integrity of the judicial process." *Payne v. Tennessee*, 501 U.S. 808, 827, (United States Supreme Court). *Stare decisis* is "indispensable to the due administration of justice." Although the doctrine of *stare decisis* does not constitute an "inexorable command," the Court determined that it would depart from the doctrine only upon a showing of "good cause." Plaintiff in the instant case had failed to make a showing of good cause. Indeed, the grounds advanced by plaintiff for the adoption of social-host liability were identical to the grounds the Court considered and rejected in *Charles*.

Plaintiff argued that the Court should follow the "national trend" recognizing a cause of action against adult social hosts who provide alcohol to minors. The Court expressly rejected this argument in *Charles*, concluding that its decision should be "grounded upon the law of Illinois rather than upon contradictory trends elsewhere." As explained in *Charles*, Illinois common law recognizes no cause of action for injuries arising out of the sale or gift of alcoholic beverages. The legislature's adoption of the Dramshop Act created a limited and exclusive statutory cause of action by imposing a form of no-fault liability upon dramshops for selling or giving intoxicating liquors to persons who subsequently injure third parties. Through its passage and continual amendment of the Dramshop Act, the General Assembly has preempted the entire field of alcohol-related liability. (The Illinois Dramshop Act criminalizes providing alcohol to parties who injure third parties as a Class A misdemeanor, imposing a slap-on-the-wrist fine).

Plaintiff further contended that "public policy" dictates that the Court should recognize social host liability for providing alcohol to minors. In *Charles*, however, the Court observed that the "primary expression of Illinois public and social policy should emanate from the legislature."

The Supreme Court held that it was ill-equipped to fashion a law on the subject that would best serve the people of Illinois. The Court can consider only one case at a time and is constrained by the facts before it. If the Court were to undertake to change the rules concerning alcohol-related liability, the law would be in a confused, disorderly state for many years while the trial courts attempted to predict how the Supreme Court would eventually resolve these questions. (This is probably not a valid argument because many other states similarly situated as Illinois have developed considerable precedent that could be relied upon by the courts of Illinois to smooth the transition). The Court held, therefore, that judicial restraint in this area was appropriate and that any decision to expand civil liability of social hosts should be made by the legislature. The Court did not view the failed attempts on the part of the legislature as inaction. Rather, it viewed such attempts as evidence that the legislature continues to debate and consider the merits and contours of any form of social-host liability.

Thus far, the General Assembly has determined that civil liability for alcohol-related injuries is limited to two groups of defendants: (1) dramshop owners, and (2) persons 21 years of age or older who pay for a hotel or motel room knowing that the room will be used by underage persons for the unlawful consumption of alcohol. The liability of these defendants is limited and extends only to third parties, and not to the intoxicated person. The General Assembly has otherwise elected to treat the possession and consumption of alcohol by persons under the legal drinking age as a criminal matter; making it a Class A misdemeanor for licensees and other persons to sell, give or deliver alcoholic liquor to any person under the age of 21; making it a Class A misdemeanor for any person under the age of 21 to use false identification to procure alcoholic liquor or to have any alcoholic liquor in his or her possession on any street, highway or public place; making it a Class A misdemeanor for any parent or guardian to permit his or her residence to be used by an invitee of the parent's child or the guardian's ward, if the invitee is under the age of 21, in a manner that would violate the statutory prohibitions on the sale and possession of alcohol; making it a Class A misdemeanor for any person knowingly to permit a gathering at his or her home where that person knows that an individual under the age of 21 is in possession of or is consuming any alcoholic beverage and further knows that the underage individual leaves in an intoxicated condition; making it a Class A misdemeanor for any person to rent a hotel or motel room for the purpose of or with the knowledge that such room will be used for the consumption of alcohol by persons under the age of 21 years; making it a Class A misdemeanor for persons under 21 years of age to purchase, accept as a gift, possess or consume alcoholic liquor; making it a Class A misdemeanor for any person under the age of 21 years to represent that he is 21 years of age or over for the purpose of buying, accepting or receiving alcoholic liquor from a licensee.

In sum, plaintiff did not provide any principled basis for the Court to revisit its decision in *Charles* and depart from the doctrine of *stare decisis*. Plaintiff could not identify any compelling change in circumstance since the Court's decision was entered in *Charles* and has simply reargued points already considered and rejected in *Charles*. Accordingly, the Supreme Court adhered to its decision in Charles: apart from the limited civil liability provided in the Dramshop Act, there exists no social-host liability in Illinois.

CONCLUSION

For the reasons discussed above, the Court affirmed the judgment of the appellate court.